"*Moment in the Word* devotiona[...] depending on how God wanted to [...] faith. They have reminded me c[...] cautioned me to wait patiently. Th[...] most of all, they have pointed me to a big God who is not only greater than the devil and the world but also greater than my sin." **Chris Bekermeier,** Vice President, Marketing, PacMoore Products

"Ron's devotions are challenging, inspirational and encouraging. Perfect for busy people on the go." **Paul Jones**, MBA, Orlando, FL

"We have been reading these email devotionals for many years! We often share them with others. They are not like many other devotionals. They speak to real and deeply spiritual and emotional pain and need. They point to God's Word, His promises, His love for us and His presence in our lives." **Mary Kortenhoeven Van Dahm**

"Oh, such a blessing for all of us. I start my day by reading *Moment in the Word* and have for many years. So often it is just what I needed to hear. I have shared the message with many people. Your gift has touched my heart and I thank God for you." **Arlene Kaatz**

"I look forward to these posts on a daily basis. They inspire, encourage and comfort me. Excited to hear about the devotional!" **Janice Snapper**

"I do really love the background story following the main text. *Moment in the Word* has been a big source of blessing to me and my church group." **Edet Nduoyo**, Accountant, Financial Standards and Information, London, UK

"I would imagine you will receive many emails your e-votionals have been used by the Holy One to cause great events to break throughs; days I wondered if I could go on and helped loved ones of mine as I shared these morsels of grace and truth with others. Thank you for investing in God's creation to enlighten, help us persevere and take a moment out of our day to meditate on the life-giving Word of God. May God bless you." **Donna Holbrook**, Human Resources Assistant, Goodwill Industries of Tulsa, Inc

"Over the years I've truly appreciated the *Moment in the Word* daily devotionals. They've proven to be quite inspirational, excellent teaching aids and reminders of how great our God is. The messages usually speak to me each day I read them and have many times proven to be an answer or confirmation of prayer. The ministry you have here is commendable, and I encourage you to keep sending the devotionals...they have a significant impact. Blessings." **Ayinde R**.

"I have been enjoying *Moment in the Word* every day for quite a few years. In fact, more than enjoying; there have been times when the words that come out of my laptop screen have been words directly from the Holy Spirit and words directed most purposefully at me! Such has been their power and appropriateness in my life at certain times. I love the way these daily comments are written in everyday English, are not 'religious' and are written with a kind of honesty—as Ron Ovitt knows life and its complexities. Some Christian writings are just too couched in "Christian" talk and don't seem in touch with real life in the real world!" **Chris Voysey**, Cape Town, South Africa

"A *Moment in the Word* creates a lifetime in love." **Peter Hunsinger**, CMO Partner, Everyone's Earth, Ossining, NY

"For two years now, I have posted your daily devotions on Facebook. I always get lots of feedback telling me how awesome reading them means to their lives. I think it has changed lives all over Evansville. Keep up the amazing gift God has given you." **Jenny Hagan**

"I read your devotional every day before I start my day and it fills my heart. I forward some messages that I feel will touch a person in particular and get a heartfelt thank you. Thanks again for being a big part of my life." **Alexandra Paz,** Surgical Coordinator, Texas Retina Associates

"So many times, I have opened *Moment in the Word* and it was just the encouragement or conviction that I needed for that day. It is always biblical and balanced. I can trust that it is God's way of speaking to me at the right time." **Dana McCain**, Team Expansion

"Congratulations on finally publishing your devotional book! Your daily online devotions are a positive and enriching part of my faith journey. I so enjoy your honesty and personal accounts. Your devotionals have been, and continue to be, a bright and uplifting part of my day. Thank you for your powerful messages!" **Sheila H**.; Ada, OH

"My husband and I have thoroughly enjoyed your daily devotionals. Each and every day, we can depend on a God-inspired Word to encourage us on our Christian journey. Your devotions are biblically sound, very inspiring and empowering. We thank God for using you to bless the masses." **Rev. Blake & Melecia Scott**, Solid Foundation Marriage Ministry

"Thank you very much for your daily verse, which is a true blessing to me and my friends. Your daily verse has made me stronger and stronger in my faith, and to trust in God's Word." **Veronica Josef,** Florida

"Your daily devotions are always exactly what I need to hear at God's perfect time. You are an amazing steward of God's Word and He uses you to bless many. Thank you for finally bringing all these amazing devotions together!" **Michelle Kirk**, MSW, Orland Park, IL

"I'd highly encourage you to consider Ron Ovitt's Daily Devotional book! I've started my day with Ron's insight for a number of years and they continue to draw me closer the Lord, inform and challenge me. I often e-mail various messages to friends and family, as the content is so broad that it's bound to touch multiple people in their daily walk with God." **Kevin T.**

"*Moment in the Word* has changed the course of my day dramatically. It is always what I need to hear to start my day and gives me my personal challenge to walk in the word and with the Lord. I appreciate how the Holy Spirit directs every word spoken in truth. Praise God!" **Marianne D.**, Westmont, IL

"I have been so blessed by the *Empower* devotions you have shared. I have passed them on to others many times, to help someone have a more blessed day. I'm a retired RN, and I think your sharing creates a more positive attitude for each day, as well as drawing me closer to our Lord. They have become a staple I count on each day! I will look forward to getting the book of devotions!" **Laurie Klarman**, Lafayette, IN

"I am 81. Thank you for the Word enjoyed each day, which I look forward to immensely." **Amy Smith-Leeds**, Yorkshire, UK

"I have certainly been encouraged, enlightened and enriched by these early morning moments. Every morning I look forward to opening up my iPad to read your empowering *Moment in the Word*. May the Lord continue to inspire you with this inspirational outreach that will encourage many saints." **Dr. Leonard,** Vicksburg, MS

"Thank you so much for your encouraging *Moment in the Word* daily e-votionals. They so often speak exactly into the context of what's happening day by day, and are a testimony to God's living Word." **Jeremy Ford**, Pontefract, West Yorkshire, UK

"I include *Moment in the Word* as a part of my daily morning prayer time. God has used this ministry to speak directly to my needs many, many times. I know that it is created by writers who are led by the Spirit! I look forward to reading and worshipping with you in the days, weeks and months to come." **Jack James**, Lavaca, Arkansas

"I look so forward to my emailed word daily. It's always the scripture I need for the day. So grateful Ron is tuned to the Holy Spirit. God's continued blessings and favor upon *Moment in The Word*...so grateful to be connected!" **Shandra T.**

"Countless times, this was exactly what I needed. God spoke to me and answered prayer through this devotional; a perfect scripture at the perfect time. A great way to start the day with a positive, fresh outlook on life. God is good!" **Joel A.**, Palos Heights, IL

MOMENT
in the Word

Gilgal Press
12540 S. 68th Ct.
Palos Heights, IL 60463 708-601-0113

www.EmpowerMinistry.com

Acknowledgements

Nothing is done in a vacuum. There are many influences that lead a person to write a book. This devotional book started decades ago when I was the Director of Youth for Christ in Lima, Ohio, where I was offered a daily and weekly radio program by Ron Migell at WTGN to read Bible verses and give short devotionals. My thanks to Keith Curtis, the morning show host, and my twin brother Rod Ovitt, the evening show host who encouraged and trained me.

Hershel Jones, the father of one of the young people I had in Youth for Christ, owned an advertising agency and suggested that my devotionals be shared through a syndicated radio network. That initial idea—sharing my devotionals to a wider audience—planted a seed in my heart. Years later, that idea and dream inspired me to distribute devotionals online. While serving at Calvary Church in Orland Park, Illinois, thousands of people signed up to receive my e-votions five days a week. Three hundred and sixty-five of them were selected for this year-long devotional book.

I am grateful for the constant support of my wife, Janine. She has been an invaluable listener and helped me with this book by proofreading and editing.

I thank the board members of Empower Ministry—Mary and George Van Dahm, Howard Hoekstra, and Janine Ovitt—for helping make this book become a reality. To all the donors to Empower Ministry, this book would not be produced without your financial help.

Barbara Dega helped with the original layout and inspired me to continue with this project. Thanks to Pastor Howard Hoekstra, my Pastor at Calvary and a dear friend and co-minister. His encouragement and prayers have meant so much to me.

Many thanks to my twin brother Rod Ovitt for his editing and encouragement in this project. A special thanks to his wife Carolyn Ovitt for the final layout and cover art. She is truly gifted and has been an invaluable help in coordinating book branding and graphics for our book publishing.

My various forms of writing come out of my journey with the Lord and all those who I have lived and worked with. I especially want to thank my wife and three sons who shaped me during my adulthood and supported me during some of life's severe struggles. What I have learned about life from my children and grandchildren has continually inspired my writing.

Finally, all my praise goes to the Lord Jesus Christ and I pray that this book will bring Him honor and praise.

Introduction

I have always been interested in the "Aha!" You know—when a thought really hits home, as though it's speaking directly into your heart. At that moment, the thought moves from mere information to personal reality. It moves from extrinsic to intrinsic; from theoretical to personal truth; what may have been abstract becomes actual. God speaks to us in these numinous ways, and I've collected mine for a number of years.

Thousands of people read them online five days a week. Over the years, I've had many requests to provide devotionals in a digital and printed book format for personal use and gift-giving. I consider it a privilege to share some of my personal favorites with you in this daily devotional, Moment in the Word.

I trust that God will meet you in the "aha" like He has met me. I trust that He will inspire you, give you hope and fill your heart with love as you spend a moment in His Word.

Ron Ovitt
Executive Director, Empower Ministry

January

February

March

April

May

June

July

August

September

October

November

December

A Confident Heart

TODAY'S VERSE "My heart is confident in you, O God; my heart is confident. No wonder I can sing your praises! Wake up, my heart! Wake up, O lyre and harp! I will wake the dawn with my song. I will thank you, Lord, among all the people. I will sing your praises among the nations. For your unfailing love is as high as the heavens. Your faithfulness reaches to the clouds" (Psalm 57:7-10).

TODAY'S THOUGHT The scriptures say that David was a man after God's own heart, and how evident that is in today's passage. David had confidence in God. When I read, "My heart is confident in you, O God," I knew immediately that this was something I wanted. But what is confidence in God? What exactly does that mean? What does it feel like? What can I imagine doing if my heart felt that way? Is this something I can experience? I must conclude, "Why not?" Why can't my heart be confident in God? Surely, He is the same God. Surely, He loves me and is my Savior. As I read the passage again, I began to know what David felt like. I wanted to sing. I wanted to say with David, "Wake up, my heart! I will wake the dawn with my song. I will thank you, Lord, among all the people. I will sing your praises among the nations. For your unfailing love is as high as the heavens. Your faithfulness reaches to the clouds." What about you? Where is your confidence? Where is your hope? Where is your joy? Stop today and meditate on His love for you. Stop and consider that the Almighty God cares for you! He loves you! He created you for a purpose. Right now, stop and wake up your heart. Breathe in a deep breath. Breathe in all the love God has for you; all the care for and focus on you; and all the confidence that comes from the reality of His presence. Today, be confident in God's love and presence in your life, and then rejoice with David by saying, "My heart is confident in you, Oh God; my heart is confident."

TODAY'S PRAYER Father, I thank You that my heart can be confident in You. I can be confident in Your love for me; in Your power to protect me, and in Your wisdom to guide me. Thank You, Lord, for all that You do and all that You are. I praise You today from a confident heart. Amen.

Be Holy

TODAY'S VERSE "So think clearly and exercise self-control. Look forward to the gracious salvation that will come to you when Jesus Christ is revealed to the world. So you must live as God's obedient children. Don't slip back into your old ways of living to satisfy your own desires. You didn't know any better then. But now you must be holy in everything you do, just as God who chose you is holy. For the Scriptures say, 'You must be holy because I am holy'" (I Peter 1:13-16).

TODAY'S THOUGHT Holiness is a difficult subject to grasp. The Pharisees felt they knew what it was but fell short of what Christ came to teach. They thought they were holy by obeying the Old Testament and the hundreds of rules they had created. Instead, Christ came to earth to die, so we could substitute his death for our sins. This is salvation. Once we accept the gift of salvation, we become holy in the sight of God; born again as His children. As children, we are motivated to live in accordance with our Father's wishes. We live to please Him who gave Himself for us. Peter says we should live as obedient children. Leanne Payne in her book *Listening Prayer* writes, "Only in union with Him, listening to Him and carrying out His orders, are we holy. Those who treasure holiness and produce its fruit are the poor in spirit and the humble of the earth. They are fond of the Jesus Prayer. In one way or another, they pray it over and over: 'Lord Jesus Christ, Son of God, have mercy on me, a sinner.' They are quick to acknowledge their pride and lack of humility, repenting of it daily. Holiness is both a quality we are given and a way in which to live. It is the way of remaining in Christ, of walking in the presence of God." Peter tells us to think clearly and exercise self-control like obedient children, not slipping back into our old ways. This comes from a relationship with God through scriptures, meditation, prayer, and fellowship. Pray and ask God to reveal to you how you can live your life more holy today.

TODAY'S PRAYER Father, thank You for Your provision of salvation. I accept this gift and desire to live more for You. I desire to be holy and pray for wisdom and strength to be what You want me to be. In Jesus' name. Amen.

How Should We Live?

TODAY'S VERSE "And we are instructed to turn from godless living and sinful pleasures. We should live in this evil world with wisdom, righteousness, and devotion to God, while we look forward with hope to that wonderful day when the glory of our great God and Savior, Jesus Christ, will be revealed. He gave his life to free us from every kind of sin, to cleanse us, and to make us his very own people, totally committed to doing good deeds" (Titus 2:11-14).

TODAY'S THOUGHT Sometimes we lose focus. It is easy to become distracted and forget what life is really about. We get our priorities mixed up. However, in today's passage, Paul makes it quite simple. He instructs us to "turn from living out godless and sinful pleasures." Paul calls them *pleasures,* so it can be a difficult choice to turn away. However, he reminds us that they are godless and sinful pleasures, so the end never justifies the means. Instead, we're to live in this world with hope, wisdom, righteous living and a devotion to God. But how can we do this? How can we possibly resist godless and sinful pleasures and live with hope, wisdom, righteous living and devotion to God? There's only one way. Paul ends this passage with the answer. He writes, "Christ Himself gave His life to free us from every kind of sin, to cleanse us, and to make us his very own people, totally committed to doing good deeds." What glorious provision! What a mighty plan! Today, let this be your reality. Let this thought permeate everything you do: God loves you so much that He sent His son Jesus Christ to die on the cross and resurrect from the dead. Therefore, you can be free from every kind of sin, totally cleansed and committed to doing good deeds.

TODAY'S PRAYER Father, thank You for the hope, wisdom, and righteousness that You give me. Thank You for freeing me from every kind of sin and totally cleansing me. Help me today to turn from godless and sinful pleasures and devote myself to You and the good deeds You created me for. In Jesus' name. Amen.

Thinking of Me

TODAY'S VERSE "How precious are your thoughts about me, O God. They cannot be numbered! I can't even count them; they outnumber the grains of sand! And when I wake up, you are still with me" (Psalm 139:17-18).

TODAY'S THOUGHT What did you start your morning thinking about? Do you know what God thought about? He thought about you! How great is that? The God of the universe is thinking about you. Not only thinking, but *constantly* thinking about you. In this verse, David is saying that God's thoughts toward him are precious and there are so many that he can't even count them! What implications should this have on your day? Should knowing that God is conscious of you and that He dearly loves you make a difference? Should it change the way you think? What about the way we feel? Should it affect the plans that we make? We're not talking about religion—we're talking about God who wants a relationship with you; a vital, living, breathing kind of relationship. He's thinking about you. Now, why don't you do the same? Spend some time today and the next few days thinking about Him. Read His Word, meditate in His presence and talk to Him. When you do, it will reinforce how precious His thoughts are about you.

TODAY'S PRAYER Father, I thank You that You are always thinking about me. Thank You for loving me. I confess that I don't spend enough time thinking about You. I want to change that. Help me carve out the time I need to spend with You. Guide me in my meditation and prayers. Please help me know You better. Amen.

An Offering

TODAY'S VERSE "I will sacrifice a voluntary offering to you; I will praise your name, O LORD, for it is good" (Psalm 54:6).

"And so, dear brothers and sisters, I plead with you to give your bodies to God because of all he has done for you. Let them be a living and holy sacrifice—the kind he will find acceptable. This is truly the way to worship him" (Romans 12:1).

TODAY'S THOUGHT When is a sacrifice, not a sacrifice? When it's an offering. Is there anything that would really be considered a sacrifice when it pertains to someone you truly love? Did a father who laid down his life protecting his family make a sacrifice? No. Wouldn't he joyfully lay down his life, so his family could live? A mother willingly gives up her own chance at possessions so that her children may have good things. It's an honor, a true offering. She joyfully gives up her own pleasure for her children. Likewise, when we truly understand the unlimited love that God has for us, when we taste of the inexhaustible grace and mercy He extends toward us repeatedly, how can surrendering ourselves to Him be a sacrifice? Rather, it is an offering—something we gladly give. This is what David meant when he wrote, "I will sacrifice a voluntary *offering* to you; I will praise your name, O LORD, for it is good." Likewise, Paul pleads with us to give our lives as a sacrificial offering to our Lord God Almighty. Know that today, as you live for Him in a holy manner, your very act of living for Him is an offering pleasing to Him. You are gladly making an offering to God because of all He means to you. This is the true way to worship Him.

TODAY'S PRAYER Father, thank You for all that You are and have done for me. Thank You for Your love, mercy, and grace that You have freely extended to me. I count it an honor to be loved by You and gladly submit to You as Lord. I come now and offer my life this day and every day to You. Amen.

Rest

TODAY'S VERSE "My soul finds rest in God alone; my salvation comes from him" (Psalm 62:1).

"Come to me, all you who are weary and burdened, and I will give you rest" (Matthew 11:28).

TODAY'S THOUGHT Have you had something that was irreplaceable—something that was so good that nothing could ever take its place? David felt that way about God. When his soul was weary, David came to God alone. Nothing else could fill the void that he felt. We could search the world over to find something that will satisfy the yearning in our soul, but nothing will meet our need the way a relationship with God through Christ will. Jesus said, "Come to me, all you who are weary and burdened, and I will give you rest." Are you looking for something to fill the hole in your heart? Are you restless, confused, troubled or weary? Come to God today. He will fill your heart with love, purpose, and meaning. He will give you rest for your soul.

TODAY'S PRAYER Father, I am so glad that I can come to You for all my needs. You know my heart. You know how weary I get at times. You know how heavy my life can be. I come to you today, dear Father, and ask You to give me rest. Amen.

Living a Godly Life

TODAY'S VERSE "I have been sent to proclaim faith to those God has chosen and to teach them to know the truth that shows them how to live godly lives" (Titus 1:1).

"By his divine power, God has given us everything we need for living a godly life...he has given us great and precious promises. These are the promises that enable you to share his divine nature and escape the world's corruption caused by human desires" (II Peter 1:3-4).

TODAY'S THOUGHT In his book *Good to Great*, Jim Collins shares some of the traits that great companies have. One such characteristic was the pursuit of BHAGs. B.H.A.G. is an acronym for "Big Hairy Audacious Goals." As Christians, we are given a BHAG that separates us from others that merely exist in this world. The good-to-great BHAG that God assigns us is to be like Him. We are to live a godly life. This seems like an impossibility until we read what Paul and Peter instructed the church. Paul shares that he was sent to teach the truth that shows us how to live a godly life, and that is what he did. Paul fills his epistles with this amazing truth. Peter tells us that God, by His divine power, has given us everything we need for living a godly life. Part of this everything is the precious promises that God gives us, enabling us to share His divine nature. Today, you can begin a quest to recognize and understand all the truth and promises that God has for you in His word. As you do, His divine power will enable you to live like Him, resulting in a godlier life.

TODAY'S PRAYER Father, thank You for Your promises that are in Your Holy Word. Help me to know and understand them. Help me to apply Your truth to my life so that I may live a godly life. Amen.

Thriving in the House of God

TODAY'S VERSE "But I am like an olive tree, thriving in the house of God. I will always trust in God's unfailing love. I will praise you forever, O God, for what you have done. I will trust in your good name in the presence of your faithful people" (Psalm 52:8-9).

TODAY'S THOUGHT Not all growing environments are the same. Amount of sunlight, average temperatures, availability of water and soil composition can have a dramatic effect on the development of a plant. Accordingly, David used the illustration of an olive tree growing in the house of God. Within a Godly environment, David is saying the olive tree, which is symbolic of you and me, thrives. This is not just existing but living life to the fullest. What David is saying is that when we live in the presence of God, we do more than just grow spiritually, we thrive. The result of such thriving is praise and an abiding trust in Him. So, what can you do to create an environment that makes you conscious of the presence of God in your life? What can you do to make your spiritual life thrive? You can start as David did, by praising God and always trusting in His unfailing love.

TODAY'S PRAYER Lord, I come to praise You today for Your unfailing love. I trust Your leadership to guide me and help me grow in Your presence. I desire to be like the olive tree that thrives in Your house. Amen.

Quench Your Thirst

TODAY'S VERSE "Is anyone thirsty? Come and drink— even if you have no money! Come, take your choice of wine or milk— it's all free! Why spend your money on food that does not give you strength? Why pay for food that does you no good? Listen to me, and you will eat what is good. You will enjoy the finest food. Come to me with your ears wide open. Listen, and you will find life. I will make an everlasting covenant with you. I will give you all the unfailing love I promised to David" (Isaiah 55:1-3).

TODAY'S THOUGHT There is a thirst deep down inside of each of us. Each one of us has had droughts in our life that have left our soul parched and wanting. Our personal defects, upbringings, and life situations have failed to satisfy our dehydrated soul. So, we look for an oasis. We search for streams in the desert. We look but fail to find what we thirst for. Why? Because we go everywhere to quench our thirst, instead of the one who can satisfy. The Prophet cried out to Israel, "Is anyone thirsty? Come and drink—even if you have no money! Come, take your choice of wine or milk— it's all free!" But they refused to come to God for life. God offered them unfailing love, but they rejected Him. Jesus, hundreds of years later, spoke to a woman at a well about living water. She came looking to fill her bucket, but He offered to fill her soul. Jesus said, "If you knew the generosity of God and who I am, you would be asking me for a drink, and I would give you fresh, living water." That day, she opened her heart and accepted God's living water. What about you? Is your soul thirsty? Have you been drinking from other sources, only to be left wanting? Come today to Christ. Come to Him and share your needs. Talk to Him, pour out your heart, bare your soul to Him and He will quench your deepest thirst. He is the living water and desires to give you life. Hear God call out to you today, "Come and drink, I will give you fresh living water."

TODAY'S PRAYER Father, I thirst. My soul is parched. I need Your living water. I come now, mouth wide open, ready to drink. Please refresh my soul with Your word. Quench my thirst with Your Holy Spirit. Give me Your living water and I will be satisfied. In Jesus' name. Amen.

Stand Up, Stand Firm

TODAY'S VERSE "So, my dear brothers and sisters, be strong and immovable. Always work enthusiastically for the Lord, for you know that nothing you do for the Lord is ever useless" (I Corinthians 15:58).

"Do not let your hearts be troubled. Trust in God; trust also in me" (John 14:1, *New International Version*).

TODAY'S THOUGHT In life, we will have trials. We will have struggles. To grow is to stretch ourselves. With this comes a certain amount of risk. So, we step out in faith; and even then, we can have times of fear, doubt, and anxiety. Many times, we avoid conflict, hide from our struggles or simply try to escape pain through various ways. We can simply try and ignore our pressures, but sooner or later avoidance won't work anymore. We must face the situation we find ourselves in. The good news is that God is faithful. He knows our struggles, He knows our limitations. Through Paul the Apostle, God encourages us to stand firm and to let nothing move us. We can do this because of the love and power of God. Even Jesus knew that in this life we would have tribulation, so He encourages us not to let our hearts be troubled. Why? Because we believe in God. It is not just what we believe, it is who we believe in! God is almighty. He is all loving. And God is for us. He loves us. He is our strength. So today, put all your trust in God. Stand firm, exercise your faith and give all your struggles, trials and temptations to Him.

TODAY'S PRAYER Father, You know all about my situation. You know my worries, fears and anxious thoughts. Help me stand firm. Help my heart not to be troubled. I do believe in You, dear God. I come now and trust You with all my life. Amen.

Forgive Me, Lord

TODAY'S VERSE "And you have brought this upon yourselves by rebelling against the LORD your God, even though he was leading you on the way!" (Jeremiah 2:17, *New International Version*).

"For I know my transgressions, and my sin is always before me. Against you, you only, have I sinned and done what is evil in your sight so that you are proved right when you speak and justified when you judge" (Psalm 51:3-4, *New International Version*).

TODAY'S THOUGHT There comes a time when we need to agree with God and own up to our sinfulness. We can try to skirt around the issue, blame others or make excuses, but at the end of the day, it is our sins that have separated us and God. Jeremiah tried to tell the Israelites this. They had wandered far from God by making unholy alliances with other nations and worshipping their Idols. God brought ruin to Israel, and Jeremiah let them know that they brought the persecution on themselves. King David had his own sins to deal with, and God sent him the Prophet Nathan to show him the error of his ways. David repented and agreed with God about the evil that he did. David, however, did not let everything end there. David knew God and that he could count on His compassion. That is why the rest of the passage is such an encouragement. In Psalm 51: 1-2, David cries out to God, "Have mercy on me, O God, according to your unfailing love; according to your great compassion blot out my transgressions. Wash away all my iniquity and cleanse me from my sin." He ends in verse seventeen, writing, "The sacrifice you desire is a broken spirit. You will not reject a broken and repentant heart, O God." Make this your heart's theme today. Is there something between you and God? If so, come to God with a broken and repentant heart. Confess your sins to Him and He will blot them out of existence.

TODAY'S PRAYER Father, I confess that I have often wandered far from You. I come to You today and ask You to have mercy on me according to Your unfailing love. According to Your great compassion, forgive me and cleanse me from all my sins. In Jesus' name, I pray. Amen.

Who Have You Been With?

TODAY'S VERSE "When they saw the courage of Peter and John and realized that they were unschooled, ordinary men, they were astonished and they took note that these men had been with Jesus" (Acts 4:13, *New International Version*).

TODAY'S THOUGHT Have you ever noticed how deeply influenced we can be by those that we spend time with? Reading books by the same author will deeply influence you to their way of thinking. People who have been married for a long time become more and more alike. A student becomes much like their favorite teacher, and a disciple of martial arts much like their sensei. Today's verse tells us that those that were arresting Peter and John were astonished at how much influence Jesus had on these men. How about you? Can your family tell who you have been spending time with? Who do those at your work believe you are inspired by? Today, start to build a deeper relationship with Christ. Spend time with Jesus and let Him influence your mind and behavior. Let Christ teach you, guide you and direct your path. When you do, others will be astonished and be able to tell you have been with Jesus.

TODAY'S PRAYER Lord, I want to spend time with You. I want my life to be permeated with You so that others may recognize it and desire the same thing for their life. Teach me, guide me, mold me, I pray. In Jesus' name. Amen.

God's Glorious Grace

TODAY'S VERSE "So God can point to us in all future ages as examples of the incredible wealth of his grace and kindness toward us, as shown in all he has done for us who are united with Christ Jesus. God saved you by his grace when you believed. And you can't take credit for this; it is a gift from God" (Ephesians 2:7-8).

TODAY'S THOUGHT Have you awakened to the fact that you are special to God? Has your soul been stirred by the realization that God has decided to love you no matter what you have done? Does it matter to you that God has chosen you to be His child? If not, perhaps you do not really understand the concept of "grace." Grace is a word that Paul elevated to a whole new level of meaning. We find it throughout his writings. In today's verse, Paul is saying that God has lavished on you an incredible wealth of grace and kindness. The word *grace* Paul is referring to means "unmerited divine favor, approval, mercy, pardon, and forgiveness." The grace you receive from God is unmerited because nothing you have done, or ever could do, would merit the kind of love and forgiveness God has for you. This grace is also divine. It is divine because it is from God Himself. God Himself has chosen to extend His mercy, forgiveness, pardon, and approval to you. Finally, God's grace to you is a gift. There is nothing you could ever do that would allow you to take the credit for the amazing love and forgiveness God has for you. It is a gift from God Himself. Have you ever accepted His gift of grace? If not, you can accept this gift of forgiveness and eternal life today. Confess your need to God and then simply thank Him for His death on the cross for the payment of your sins. Thank Him for the amazing love He has for you. Thank Him for your total forgiveness and the promise of an eternal home with Him forever. Thank Him for His amazing grace.

TODAY'S PRAYER Father, I thank You for the grace You have extended to me. I accept the mercy, forgiveness and love Your grace has provided for me today. I praise You with all my heart. In Jesus' name. Amen.

Give What You Have

TODAY'S VERSE "Peter said, 'I don't have any silver or gold for you. But I'll give you what I have. In the name of Jesus Christ the Nazarene, get up and walk!'" (Acts 3:6).

TODAY'S THOUGHT A crippled man was sitting in the temple gate and was asking for money. When the Apostles Peter and John came by, the man asked them for money. Instead of giving the man money, Peter was moved by God to pronounce a healing for the man. He said, "I don't have any silver or gold for you. But I'll give you what I have. In the name of Jesus Christ the Nazarene, get up and walk!" I believe that God has called you and me to respond to those in need in a similar way. We are to give to those in need what we have. What was it that Peter had? First, we see that Peter had obedience to the prompting of the Holy Spirit. It was God who orchestrated the healing. He nudged Peter to do this act of kindness, and Peter obeyed. Second, we see that Peter had faith. Pronouncing the command of "get up and walk" was an act of faith. Peter trusted God to do what He had told him to do. Third, we see that Peter had authority. Peter commanded the man to be healed because Christ gave him the authority to act on His behalf. Today, you may be challenged to help others. If you are like Peter and your pockets are empty, do not despair. Give them what you do have. Give them love, hope, kindness, mercy, grace, and life. Command a blessing upon them in the name of Jesus. You are an ambassador of Christ; go forward in obedience, faith, and authority.

TODAY'S PRAYER Father, I want to be used by You to help others. Please guide me by Your Holy Spirit. Show me what You want me to do and then help me be obedient and have the faith to act in the authority. In Jesus' name. Amen.

January 15
Boast About This

TODAY'S VERSE "This is what the LORD says: "Let not the wise man boast of his wisdom or the strong man boast of his strength or the rich man boast of his riches, but let him who boasts boast about this: that he understands and knows me, that I am the LORD, who exercises kindness, justice, and righteousness on earth, for in these I delight," declares the LORD" (Jeremiah 9:23-24, *New International Version*).

TODAY'S THOUGHT As children, we have been taught not to be proud. That should be replaced with an earnest, heartfelt joy, welling up inside that expresses its appreciation for what we have. What of expressing our sincere appreciation and wonder at something so extraordinary, so surreal, that it defies us to keep our silence? There is such a boasting. It is a deep, holy appreciation for what God has done for us. The Lord told Jeremiah to tell the people not to boast in their human strength or in materialism, for they are nothing—they pale in comparison to what God has for us. If we are going to boast in anything, God says we should boast about: "Let him who boasts boast about this: that he understands and knows me, that I am the LORD, who exercises kindness, justice, and righteousness." How can we hold such a truth inside? How can we stop from sharing with others the tremendous privilege of knowing the Lord God of the Universe? That this same God has given us the privilege to call Him, "Lord of our life"? This same God, who exercises kindness, justice, and righteousness, calls us His children, and therefore we affectionately call Him Father. Today, rejoice in the fact that our Almighty God loves you. Go boast in this and as you tell others, assure them that He loves them too!

TODAY'S PRAYER Father, thank you that I can boast about the fact that You love me and that I know You. Thank You so much. Help me really understand the unbelievable privilege that is mine, so that I boast about Your amazing love to others and they will desire the same for themselves. Amen.

Real Hope

TODAY'S VERSE "Then he said, "Don't be afraid, Daniel. Since the first day you began to pray for understanding and to humble yourself before your God, your request has been heard in heaven. I have come in answer to your prayer. But for twenty-one days the spirit prince of the kingdom of Persia blocked my way. Then Michael, one of the archangels, came to help me, and I left him there with the spirit prince of the kingdom of Persia" (Daniel 10: 12-13).

TODAY'S THOUGHT I love this passage because of the hope it gives. Hope because God hears the cry of our heart. The angel assured Daniel, "Do not be afraid, Daniel. Since the first day that you set your mind to gain understanding and to humble yourself before your God, your words were heard, and I have come in response to them." What a precious reality painted by the angel. Since the very first time Daniel set his mind in the direction of God, the Lord was aware and heard his prayers. He does the same with us. Hope because God works on our behalf, even if we don't understand His timing. Daniel was fasting and praying that God would rescue him quickly. No doubt, he wondered what God was doing. However, the angel's delay did not limit God's benevolence. God was in control, and all worked for good. Perhaps my brother, Rod Ovitt, says it best in his commentary on this passage. He writes, "To me, this doesn't diminish my faith or cause me to doubt God's power and might. It just broadens the mystery! There is so much that we don't understand and so much going on in the cosmos that we must simply trust God and know that He will see us through to the end." God will see you through! Do not become weary and don't give up. Maintain a steady hope in God; He is aware of your prayers.

TODAY'S PRAYER Father, it is so hard to wait. I cry out to You and sometimes it seems that there is no answer. My heart despairs and is tempted to grow bitter. Forgive me, Lord. Help me to understand what You showed Daniel. You are conscious of my situation and Your solutions are always reliable. Thank You, Father, that You hear my prayers and I can trust You with the distribution of Your answers. Amen.

That People Would Know God

TODAY'S VERSE "O LORD, God of Abraham, Isaac, and Israel, let it be known today that you are God in Israel and that I am your servant and have done all these things at your command. Answer me, O LORD, answer me, so these people will know that you, O LORD, are God and that you are turning their hearts back again" (I Kings 18:36-37, *New International Version*).

TODAY'S THOUGHT Elijah challenged 450 Baal priests to a contest. Elijah and the priests would each put up an altar, complete with an offering. This was a test to prove the real god. Who would it be, Baal or Jehovah? Elijah was confident that it would be Jehovah because he was doing what Jehovah commanded him to do. Today, our faith in God is on trial more than ever before. God has given us commands, too. Not a command to call fire down from Heaven, but to live our Christian life out in front of the world. Why should we love others? Why should we care? Why should we live a life exhibiting the fruit of the Holy Spirit? Because, like Elijah, we are servants of the Most High and we are to do what He has commanded us to. God's great compassion is exhibited through our lives. As we love others in the name of Christ, others will notice. How can we do anything else? We who were snatched from our sinfulness, brokenness, and alienation from God, how could we not love others and pray for them to know God in the same way we do? Elijah cried out to God and said, "Answer me, O LORD, answer me, so these people will know that you, O LORD, are God and that you are turning their hearts back again." Do our hearts weep over those that do not know him? Do we live our life so that others recognize the Savior's influence? Oh, that God's holy fire would fall from the sky today through our acts of love and kindness. Might God receive the glory, and might people turn to Him.

TODAY'S PRAYER Father, like Elijah, I come to the altar of sacrifice. Please use me today to love, to sacrifice, and care for those in need. Might others see my life today and come to know You, the true and living God. Amen.

Speak, Lord

TODAY'S VERSE "'So Eli told Samuel. "Go and lie down, and if he calls you, say, 'Speak, LORD, for your servant is listening." So Samuel went and lay down in his place" (I Samuel 3:9, *New International Version*).

TODAY'S THOUGHT Have you ever put yourself in Samuel's position? Have you been at a place where you really desire to hear a word from God? God loves you and wants to communicate with you. He speaks through His word, the Bible. He also speaks to your heart through the Holy Spirit. Dallas Willard, in his book *Hearing God*, concludes, "Direction will always be made available to the mature disciple if without it serious harm would befall people concerned in the matter or the cause of Christ. If I am right, the obedient, listening heart, mature in the things of God, will in such a case find the voice plain and the message clear, as with the experiences of the friends of God recorded in the Bible. This is a claim that must be tested by experience, and anyone willing to meet the conditions and learn from failures as well as successes can put it to the test." Today, open your heart to hearing from God. Commit yourself to spend time with God in Bible reading, meditation, and prayer. Build a deep and trusting relationship with Him and ask Him to share His heart with you. Say with Samuel, "'Speak, Lord, for your servant is listening." When you come to God in this way, He will answer.

TODAY'S PRAYER Lord, I give my heart to You and desire to know You better. I desire to hear from You. I long to discern Your direction in my life. I come and say with Samuel, "Speak Lord, for your servant is listening." Amen.

His Perfect Peace

TODAY'S VERSE "You will keep in perfect peace all who trust in you, all whose thoughts are fixed on you!" (Isaiah 26:3).

TODAY'S THOUGHT What do you think about? Where do you fix your thoughts? God expects us to consider what we think and judge it according to His word. Trouble comes into our lives and we begin to fear. When it does, we have a choice to make. Will we remain in fear? Will we let it escalate into panic? Or will we obey today's verse and trust in God, fixing our thoughts on Him? When we do, He promises us peace. Not just any peace, His perfect peace. It is the same way with anger, jealousy, doubt and a hundred other thoughts that come into our lives every day. Today, when negative thoughts come to your mind, begin a new habit. Trade them in for peace. How? By giving the thoughts to God and then choosing to trust in Him by fixing your thoughts on His love for you.

TODAY'S PRAYER Father, help me trade my negative thinking for Your perfect peace. Today, help me to fix all my thoughts on You. Amen.

Consider the Poor

TODAY'S VERSE "Command them to do good, to be rich in good deeds, and to be generous and willing to share" (I Timothy 6:18).

"Oh, the joys of those who are kind to the poor!" (Psalm 41:1).

TODAY'S THOUGHT God created you for a great purpose. He created you to be His ambassador of love! All around us are people in need. No one is immune from heartache, illness or crisis. But there is a group of people close to the heart of God that He keeps reminding us of—the poor. It is so easy to forget them, yet He doesn't forget. And if we are going to be His disciples and do His business, then we must take seriously God's cry for us to help the poor and needy. Paul tells Timothy to command those with the means to do good. He wants us to be "rich" in good deeds and to be generous. God has called His children to be kind and compassionate to those in need, and when we are, David reminds us that there is great joy to those who are kind to the poor! And it is true, there is great joy. Today, ask God to help you find ways to help those that are less fortunate.

TODAY'S PRAYER Father, I confess that I get so wrapped up in my own life that I haven't taken the time I should take to consider the poor and needy. I worry about my own needs and do not feel the compassion I should for those in need. Please forgive me. Help me today to find something I can do. Guide me to someone who I can help. I want to be generous and willing to share with others in the way You have been so generous and loving to me. Amen.

The Lord Almighty

TODAY'S VERSE "The LORD Almighty is with us; the God of Jacob is our fortress" (Psalm 46:7, *New International Version*).

TODAY'S THOUGHT It is amazing to see the difference one sentence can make. Especially when it carries such an important message. But if this verse is such a revelation, why do most of walk around discouraged, overwhelmed and stressed out with life's issues? What does it take to make a sentence go from the head to the heart? How can focusing on the reality of Almighty God in our life make a difference? How would waking up tomorrow morning, conscious of what David is expressing in this verse, change our plans or behavior? What would you do differently knowing that the Lord Almighty is right there with you? The reality is that God is with us. He is our fortress, He is Almighty. Might this truth sink in and cause us to live accordingly.

TODAY'S PRAYER Father, make me aware of Your presence. Help me to see You in all Your power and glory. Help me trust You for everything I do this day. In Jesus' name. Amen.

Not Ashamed

TODAY'S VERSE "Do your best to present yourself to God as one approved, a workman who does not need to be ashamed and who correctly handles the word of truth" (II Timothy 2:15).

TODAY'S THOUGHT We have choices to make every day. Today, we can choose to live for God or to live for ourselves. Even if we choose to live for God, we will still have to make that choice each and every time we come to a decision that could potentially take us away from living the way He wants us to. Will we do the right thing or not? That is why Paul says to "do our best" at living out our Christian life. It is not easy to resist temptations, go the extra mile, love the unlovely, or put others before ourselves; yet this is the life God has called us to. He has called us to be a good worker who will not be ashamed when examined, one that will be approved of. A worker who knows God's word and can apply it correctly to their actions. Thankfully, we don't have to live the way God wants us to in our own power. We have the Holy Spirit to guide and empower us. Today, call upon the Holy Spirit to fill you, guide you and help you to "do your best to present yourself to God as one approved."

TODAY'S PRAYER Father, help me live for You as a workman who isn't ashamed. Fill me with Your Holy Spirit and empower me to honor You in everything I do today. Amen.

The Pits

TODAY'S VERSE "I waited patiently for the LORD to help me, and he turned to me and heard my cry. He lifted me out of the pit of despair, out of the mud and the mire. He set my feet on solid ground and steadied me as I walked along. He has given me a new song to sing, a hymn of praise to our God. Many will see what he has done and be amazed. They will put their trust in the LORD" (Psalm 40:1-3).

TODAY'S THOUGHT Have you found yourself in the pit? Does it seem like there is no way out? The walls are high and slippery, every time you try to escape you slip back down? David knew exactly how you feel. There are many pits in life we can fall into. Emotional pits of bitterness, depression, or fear. Financial pits of debt or inadequate income. Relational pits of alienation, fighting or loneliness. Career pits of unemployment or underemployment. The good news is that God knows about our situation. He is able to help us. As David waited patiently for God, God heard his cry. God lifted him out of the pit of despair and put him on solid ground. He can do the same for you. Cry out to God today. Tell Him about your situation. Share with Him how you feel. As you do, you will find God lifting you out of the pit you are in. He will put you on solid ground. He will give you a new song to sing. Best of all, as God works in your life, many will see what is happening and put their trust in God the same way you do. Give God your situation and begin to trust Him for deliverance today.

TODAY'S PRAYER Father, You know the pit I am in. I admit my participation in this and repent of any of my doing that has kept me here. I ask You, Father to lift me out of this. I will wait patiently for You, dear God, and trust You for Your deliverance. In Jesus' name. Amen.

Grace, Mercy, and Peace

TODAY'S VERSE "May God the Father and Christ Jesus our Lord give you grace, mercy, and peace" (II Timothy 1:2).

TODAY'S THOUGHT Could Paul possibly fit any more into one sentence? I don't think there is a time I read this salutation that I don't sense a deep stirring in my soul. It stops me dead in my tracks. I don't need to go any further. It is all here. What else could we possibly need in life? Grace. God's love, attention, and salvation, given to you freely, just because He wants to. Mercy. God's forgiveness of your sins and provision for your life when there is no way in this world you deserve it. Peace. A peace with God and from God, deep in your heart, passing all your understanding. What a privilege, what a blessing, what an unbelievable gift from God. Will you receive it today? Will you agree with Paul? Will you request what God is freely giving, what Christ has so graciously provided? Today, may God the Father and Christ Jesus our Lord give you grace, mercy, and peace.

TODAY'S PRAYER Father, I come now to receive what You so freely offer. I ask to be filled with your grace, mercy, and peace. Make me so conscious of these gifts that my heart overflows with praise and thanksgiving and my life reflects the joy of this reality. In Jesus' name. Amen.

My Generation

TODAY'S VERSE "So each generation should set its hope anew on God, not forgetting his glorious miracles and obeying his commands" (Psalm 78:7).

TODAY'S THOUGHT Some things are meant to pass on. Hope in God is one of them. We look back at the early church and say, "If only God would do His miraculous deeds today." Why won't He? Isn't He the same yesterday, today and tomorrow? Aren't we called to live by faith in the same way that Paul taught the early church? All the promises of God's provision are as true today as they were centuries ago. Jesus said that we would be commissioned by Him in the power of the Holy Spirit to do even greater things than He did! This is our generation. It is time for our hope to be realized. May we not forget His miracles and obey Him fully, expecting God to do great and mighty things, even today.

TODAY'S PRAYER Lord, I am thankful to be living in such a time as this. You are alive and mighty. You are loving and compassionate. I hear of all Your miracles in time past and say, "This is my generation and I put my hope in you. Work through me in all Your power as You have in the past." Amen.

Share the Good News

TODAY'S VERSE "I have told all your people about your justice. I have not been afraid to speak out, as you, O LORD, well know. I have not kept the good news of your justice hidden in my heart; I have talked about your faithfulness and saving power. I have told everyone in the great assembly of your unfailing love and faithfulness" (Psalm 40:9-10).

TODAY'S THOUGHT People are dying for the lack of a Savior! All around us are people with deep needs that God can help them with. We need to be a witness to the love of God and share with them the good news that He loves them. As we experience our relationship with God and learn to understand the love He has for us, the more we will be able to share this love with others. This is what David did. As he experienced God's unfailing love and faithfulness, he told others about it. He didn't hide it in his heart. Paul asks, "How can people believe in Christ if they have never heard of Him? And how can they hear about Him unless someone tells them?" Today, let God lead you. Ask Him to bring you into a situation where you can share with others how God has been faithful in your life. Share how you have experienced the love that God has for you or how He has provided for you in some way. Offer to pray for them so they, too, can experience the love and power of God. Remember, you're not doing this alone. God will use the Holy Spirit to prepare the way and open the door for you to share.

TODAY'S PRAYER Father, thank you for what you have done in my life. Please open the door for me to share this with others. Prepare their hearts. Give me wisdom to know what to say and the courage to say it. As I speak of your love and mighty power and all that You are doing in my life, might Your Holy Spirit help them to receive the truth for themselves. In Jesus' name. Amen.

Fear Not

TODAY'S VERSE   "When Pharaoh finally let the people go, God did not lead them along the main road that runs through Philistine territory, even though that was the shortest route to the Promised Land. God said, 'If the people are faced with a battle, they might change their minds and return to Egypt'" (Exodus 13:17).

TODAY'S THOUGHT   We live in two worlds. The spiritual world is real, and we are at war—not only for our own spiritual life but for the salvation of the world. In battle, there's plenty of opportunity for fear. God knew if the Israelites saw battle too early in their commitment, they would be tempted to run and return to Egypt. Paul also knew our temptation and encourages us to live like citizens of Heaven, standing together in one Spirit and purpose, fighting together for the faith! In his book *When Heaven Invades Earth*, Bill Johnson writes, "When we refuse to fear, the enemy becomes terrified. A confident heart is a sure sign of his ultimate destruction and our present victory! Do not fear - ever. Return to the promises of God, spend time with people of faith, and encourage one another with the testimonies of the Lord. Praise God for who God is until fear no longer knocks at the door. This is not an option, for fear actually invites the enemy to come to kill, steal and destroy." James tells us to resist the Devil—his lies and fear tactics—and he'll flee from us. More importantly, James gives us the real spiritual secret to overcoming fear. He tells us to run to God, and God Himself will come close to us. Today, resist fear and submit yourself to God. Ask Him to use you, this day, for His purposes. Ask Him to give you all the courage and strength you need to do His will.

TODAY'S PRAYER   Father, You know that this is another day and I need Your strength. I want to do Your will in my life today and I pray that You will help me resist Satan and his lies. Help me to renounce all fear and to run to You. I come now, Lord, running to Your loving and strong arms, thanking You that You will draw close to me. I go forward now in Your strength and power to do what You would have me do today. In Jesus' name. Amen.

Trust, Delight, and Commit

TODAY'S VERSE "Trust in the Lord and do good. Then you will live safely in the land and prosper. Take delight in the Lord and he will give you your heart's desires. Commit everything you do to the Lord. Trust him, and he will help you" (Psalm 37:3-5).

TODAY'S THOUGHT Attitude is everything. How we react to situations makes all the difference in the world. David knew this, and God shared with him the secret to spiritual success. First, when circumstances arise, we are to trust in the Lord. We need to move ahead in faith. But even going forward in faith, if we want to experience joy in the journey, we need to take the time to delight in God. Getting to know Him, building a relationship and learning to really enjoy living for God will keep us through the difficult times. Secondly, we need to come to God with total commitment. How many times do we start out with trust and delight in God, but when things go sour, or when there seems to be no relief in sight, we give up? Committing everything to God means we trust Him for the long run. Today, we can start our journey with the attitude that David had. Today, we can bring everything to God and trust, delight and commit.

TODAY'S PRAYER

Father, help me with my attitude. I come to You today and trust You with my life. Help me know You and delight in You. Lord, I commit everything I am and have to You and thank You that You will indeed help me. In Jesus' name. Amen.

Contentment

TODAY'S VERSE "Yet true godliness with contentment is itself great wealth. After all, we brought nothing with us when we came into the world, and we can't take anything with us when we leave it. So if we have enough food and clothing, let us be content" (I Timothy 6: 6-8).

TODAY'S THOUGHT What if the world really believed today's passage? Would corruption flourish? How about envy, jealousy, bribery? If contentment was our goal instead of wealth, fame or one-upmanship, how much better would the world be? How better would our life be? But why would the world do this if the church isn't? When is the last time you heard a sermon on contentment? Instead, how many times do we think a person who is successful in business should be our spiritual leader? A person in a lesser station in life could be very devout in their faith, yet never be considered an eligible leader. This is simply wrong. Paul is teaching us true Kingdom standards. He is saying that being godly and having contentment is true wealth in Kingdom currency. If we have our basic needs met, we should be satisfied, and devote our time to spiritual pursuits. In today's world, most of us have an opportunity to make a good living. Some will make an extraordinary amount of money and have what the world calls success, but all of us can have contentment. All of us can be rich in the kingdom of God. Today, let's find it in our hearts to be thankful and pray that God would teach us more about contentment.

TODAY'S PRAYER Dear Father, I have so much to be thankful for, yet I wrestle with being content. Help me understand Your values. Help me to strive for godliness. Teach me about true contentment, so I may have life's true wealth. Amen.

Idolatry

TODAY'S VERSE "'Has anyone ever heard of anything as strange as this? Has any nation ever traded its gods for new ones, even though they are not gods at all? Yet my people have exchanged their glorious God for worthless idols! The heavens are shocked at such a thing and shrink back in horror and dismay,' says the LORD" (Jeremiah 2:11-12).

TODAY'S THOUGHT This passage shows the real heart of God and how He desires us to know and love Him. You may ask, "But how am I guilty of giving up God for idols?" Perhaps it makes more sense if we exchange the word "idol" and read it as, "traded their God for television." Perhaps career, wealth, or busyness would be better word substitutes? God desires us to know Him, to love Him, to worship and serve Him, and yet as humans, we find ourselves so distracted, so fickle in our commitment to Him. Look over the last month. How would heaven react to the preference you have given God? Today, give up whatever has stolen your heart, your time, and your dedication to God and come back to Him. Worship Him as the true and living God.

TODAY'S PRAYER Father, I have let other things crowd You out of my everyday experience. I have been guilty of idolatry by not making You first in my life. Today, I choose to reignite my love for You. I declare that You are Almighty God and give You my allegiance. In Jesus' name, I pray. Amen.

You Choose

TODAY'S VERSE   "Today I have given you the choice between life and death, between blessings and curses. Now I call on heaven and earth to witness the choice you make. Oh, that you would choose life so that you and your descendants might live" (Deuteronomy 30:19).

"But if you refuse to serve the Lord, then choose today whom you will serve" (Joshua 24:15).

TODAY'S THOUGHT   Our life is full of choices. Every day we make dozens of them. What are we going to eat? What responses are we going to give to the many questions we are asked? How are we going to respond to the various circumstances we find ourselves in? However, some of the choices we make are serious, very serious. They are between life and death. Some choices are about our physical life, but many choices are of a more spiritual nature. Moses tells us that we have a choice between life and death, blessings, and curses. God then pleads with us through Moses, saying, "Oh, that you would choose life so that you and your descendants might live!" How serious is that? It is enough to cause you to freeze from making any choice, but that won't help. You see in spiritual issues, sometimes not choosing is really a negative choice. Joshua helps us with our everyday choices by forcing us to consider the primary decision. If we make the primary choice, many of the others will come much easier. Joshua asks us to choose who will be the Lord of our life, or in other words, who are we going to serve? If not God, then choose something--but something you will choose. Out this choice will come a host of other choices. Today, choose life. Choose to follow God and His word. Surrender your will and commit your way to Him and He will direct your choices.

TODAY'S PRAYER   Father, I come to You today and choose to follow You. I need Your help in every choice I make. I want to choose life in all that I do. Please guide me and direct my choices. In Jesus' name, I pray. Amen.

February 1
The Fruit of the Spirit

TODAY'S VERSE "But the Holy Spirit produces this kind of fruit in our lives: love, joy, peace, patience, kindness, goodness, faithfulness, gentleness, and self-control" (Galatians 5:22-23).

TODAY'S THOUGHT When I think of our human propensity for anger, confusion, impatience, harshness, lack of control and impulsiveness, I am amazed at God's solution. Our humanness, a result of man's fallen condition, has been trumped by God's Holy Spirit. What a plan. God gives us a body in which we house our personality with enough room for His Holy Spirit. When we do this, the Holy Spirit will produce in us new attitudes, motivations, and behaviors. Paul calls it fruit. What a great analogy - the Holy Spirit alive in us, growing into a beautiful fruit tree. The fruit that the Holy Spirit produces is love, joy, peace, patience, kindness, goodness, faithfulness, gentleness, and self-control. You don't have to make an apple tree produce apples. When watered, nourished and receiving adequate sunlight, an apple tree produces beautiful, luscious apples. Likewise, you don't have to manufacture the fruit of the Spirit; rather, you begin reading and meditating on His Holy word and spending time in a relationship with God through confession and prayer--the Holy Spirit will generate the results. Begin today to nourish your spiritual life and let the Holy Spirit produce its fruit.

TODAY'S PRAYER Dear Father, I desire the fruit of the Holy Spirit to be evident in my life. Help me to read and meditate on Your word. Help me to relate to You in prayer and confession. Help me, Holy Spirit, live the life You want me to. Produce Your fruit in my life, even today. Amen.

Seek Him

TODAY'S VERSE   "My son, if you accept my words and store up my commands within you, turning your ear to wisdom and applying your heart to understanding, and if you call out for insight and cry aloud for understanding, and if you look for it as for silver and search for it as for hidden treasure, then you will understand the fear of the LORD and find the knowledge of God" (Proverbs 2:1-5).

TODAY'S THOUGHT   There is a mystery to knowing God. His love draws us to Him. God has made it abundantly clear that "whosoever will" may come to Him; but this is the beginning, not the end. If we are to follow Him, be His disciple and take knowing Him seriously, then He demands preeminence in our life. Solomon knew this. He prayed for Godly wisdom. He sought it more than anything else God could offer him, and God gave it to him. He writes that it's the same for us. We must *want* to know God more than anything else. We need to "call out for insight and cry aloud for understanding." God assures us that knowing Him will come when we look for Him like we would look for silver. We must search for God as we would search for hidden treasure. Jeremiah says it another way. He says that we will find God when we seek Him with all our heart. How much have you wanted to know God? What treasure are you seeking? What has your heart sought after? If God is going to be a serious part of your life, if you are going to live in His wisdom, then you must make knowing Him a priority. God didn't say we had to be smart, wise, rich, talented or gifted to know Him. The only requirement is desire. Turn your desire toward God. When you do, He promises, "I will be found by you."

TODAY'S PRAYER   Father, I admit I have let my desire wander. I have sought for fools' gold. I have put other priorities ahead of knowing You. I come today and seek You with all my heart. Father, I yearn for Your wisdom. I desire to have understanding. I want to know You more than anything else. Teach me, guide me, lead me. I pray this in the precious name of Jesus. Amen.

Joint-Heir with Christ

TODAY'S VERSE "And since we are his children, we are his heirs. In fact, together with Christ, we are heirs of God's glory. - And having chosen them, he called them to come to him. And having called them, he gave them right standing with himself. And having given them right standing, he gave them his glory. What shall we say about such wonderful things as these? If God is for us, who can ever be against us?" (Romans 8:17, 30-31).

TODAY'S THOUGHT I don't think we really understand who we are in Christ. If we did, the Church would be a more powerful force in the world. Instead, we go around blinded to our true inheritance. We are like a child who, separated at birth from its Father the King, grows up never realizing the birthright that was theirs. They never accept the reality that they are the child of a King. In his book *When Heaven Invades Earth*, Bill Johnson drives this point home. He writes, "At what point do we start thinking of our worth through His eyes? If it is true that the value of something is measured by what someone else will pay, then we need to rethink our worth. Jesus paid the ultimate price to make it possible for us to have a change in our identity. Doesn't it honor Him more when His children no longer see themselves only as sinners saved by grace, but now heirs of God?" Today, let that fact sink in. You are God's child. You are a co-heir with Christ in our Heavenly Kingdom. If God is for you, what in this world could possibly be significant enough to be against you?

TODAY'S PRAYER Father, I have judged myself by so many false standards. I have seen myself with blurry vision. I have looked in a stained mirror, never seeing what You see. Today, help me believe. Help me really understand that I am Your child, a joint-heir with Christ. Amen.

After God's Own Heart

TODAY'S VERSE "The one thing I ask of the LORD, the thing I seek most, is to live in the house of the LORD all the days of my life, delighting in the LORD's perfections and meditating in his Temple. - My heart has heard you say, 'Come and talk with me.' And my heart responds, 'LORD, I am coming'" (Psalm 27:4, 8).

"But God removed Saul and replaced him with David, a man about whom God said, 'I have found David son of Jesse, a man after my own heart. He will do everything I want him to do'" (Acts 13:22).

TODAY'S THOUGHT David was a shepherd boy who knew and loved God. Because of David's heart toward God, God called David to be king of all Israel. And a great king he was. But more than a king, David remained a man that sought after the heart of God. I can imagine David in his palace, a long way from the cold nights in the fields with the sheep, wishing he was back in the fields with the stars in the sky, playing his harp and worshiping God. How his heart cried out, "I want to live in the house of the Lord, delighting in Him!" And that is what he did. In fact, his heart did become a house of God. From his heart, he wrote the Psalm. What an offering of worship and praise to God. God would invite us to do the same. What is your heart? Is it a home for God? Is it a Temple of praise and thanksgiving? If not, it can be. Like David, God comes to you and says, "Come and talk with me." When He does, respond like David and say, "Lord, I am coming." Today, you can begin to be a person after God's own heart.

TODAY'S PRAYER Father, You have bid me come to You. I am coming even now. Like David, I want to be a person after Your own heart. I come today and ask You to take my heart and make it Your home. I want to know You, love You, worship You and live for You this very day. In Jesus' name. Amen.

Don't Forget

TODAY'S VERSE "'If only the LORD had killed us back in Egypt,' they moaned. 'There we sat around pots filled with meat and ate all the bread we wanted. But now you have brought us into this wilderness to starve us all to death'" (Exodus 16:3).

TODAY'S THOUGHT One month after the Lord had delivered them from the hand of Pharaoh, the Children of Israel found themselves in a desert. Did they remember the mighty miracles that God used to deliver them from slavery? Did they remember the dry ground they walked on that was once again covered by the Red Sea? No, they forgot and complained to Moses that they would have been better off back in Egypt! What is it about the human nature that causes us to forget good things so quickly? Charles Spurgeon said it this way: "I don't know which to marvel more at—God's faithfulness or man's forgetfulness." Today's verse tells us to be careful and watch ourselves closely so that we don't forget what God has done. Why is this so important? Because remembering is key to our survival. God teaches us life lessons that are needed later in our life, but our propensity is to forget. The lesson for the Israelites would be, "In the desert, don't forget what you learned at the Red Sea." What about you? Do you remember how faithful God has been to you in the past? Do you remember the life lessons you have learned and apply them to the rest of your life? Or do you forget? Today, stop and remember all that God has done for you. Remember His faithfulness. Remember His provision. Remember His presence in times past, and go forward in the reality that God is the same yesterday, today and forever.

TODAY'S PRAYER Father, forgive me for my forgetfulness. You have been so faithful, and yet when there is a threat of something bad, I assume You are not there. I forget how faithful You have been and act as if You did not care. Lord, help me remember all that You have promised. Help me remember all that You have done. Might I share with others how faithful You have been as I put my faith in You for my future. Amen.

Wholehearted Devotion

TODAY'S VERSE "Acknowledge the God of your father, and serve him with wholehearted devotion and with a willing mind, for the LORD searches every heart and understands every motive behind the thoughts. If you seek him, he will be found by you" (1 Chronicles 28:9).

"And if you search for him with all your heart and soul, you will find him" (Deuteronomy 4:29).

TODAY'S THOUGHT Have you ever felt like the famous U2 song, "And I still haven't found what I'm looking for"? Is it possible that you have been looking in the wrong places? What are you seeking after? What is it that your heart desires? What does your soul seek? If it is fulfillment, if it is significance and meaning, then come to God and you will find what your soul thirsts for. Today's verse promises that if you seek God with all your heart and soul, He will be found. It is when you acknowledge that He is the God of your life and you serve Him with your whole heart that you will be able to find Him ever near. Today, seek Him. Open your heart and ask God to reveal Himself to you. Come to Jesus, admit your need, accept His gift of salvation and you will find His love to be more than enough, more than you will ever need.

TODAY'S PRAYER Father, I admit how easy it is to take my eyes off You. How easy to focus on temporal, earthly matters and miss what really counts. You are what my heart has been searching for. You are all that I really need, and I come now seeking You with my whole heart. Guide me and lead me to a deeper understanding of Your love and grace. In Jesus' name. Amen.

Keep It Simple

TODAY'S VERSE   "Your heavenly Father already knows all your needs. Seek the Kingdom of God above all else, and live righteously, and he will give you everything you need" (Matthew 6:32-33).

TODAY'S THOUGHT   We can really complicate life, can't we? There are so many situations that keep us crazy with demands. There are so many things that we think we must do. We have lost all sense of simplicity. Jesus comes along and would say to us, "Stop the insanity! Stop filling your life with false needs and let Me fulfill your real need." You see, Jesus knows the "one thing." He knows what is really important and offers it to all His followers. He said, "Seek the Kingdom of God above all else, and live righteously, and he will give you everything you need." The real secret to this life is found in the next. If we want success in this life, then we need to live in His Kingdom instead of our own. We need to live in this world with heaven's priority. God really does love you. Trust Him, live for Him and He promises that He will give you everything you need.

TODAY'S PRAYER   Father, You know my name. You know who I am. You also know my needs. Thank You, Father, that You promised that if I seek your Kingdom above everything else, You will give me everything I need. So, I come to you now, Father, and ask that You would help me live for You. I entrust my needs to You. In Jesus' name. Amen.

I Cannot See

TODAY'S VERSE "Then Jesus told him, 'Because you have seen me, you have believed; blessed are those who have not seen and yet have believed'" (John 20:29).

"But he said to me, 'My grace is sufficient for you, for my power is made perfect in weakness'" (II Corinthians 12:9).

TODAY'S THOUGHT Sometimes we just have to step out in faith. Sight is not an option. We can't see a way out. We don't know which way to go. Everything is cloudy. We are so tired, so weary, so confused, and we have nowhere to go. But then grace appears. Not just any grace, God's *sufficient* grace. Grace to help you trust Him. Grace to give you courage. Grace to give you hope. Grace to give you wisdom. Grace to help you hold on when you think your strength is gone. Grace to go to bed and get up to face another day. Grace to let God be God. Jesus said you will be blessed if you believe when you have not seen a reason. So, get up, lift your hands, and give to Jesus whatever it is that you cannot see. He promises that His grace is sufficient for you.

TODAY'S PRAYER Father, I come to You in my weakness. I cannot see. I have no answers. All I have is Your grace and You promised that it will be sufficient. You promised that if I believe when I cannot see, I will be blessed. So, I bow to You. I place my heart at your feet. You are my Lord and I will follow You. Amen.

Your God Is Too Small

TODAY'S VERSE "May you have the power to understand, as all God's people should, how wide, how long, how high, and how deep his love is. May you experience the love of Christ, though it is too great to understand fully. Then you will be made complete with all the fullness of life and power that comes from God" (Ephesians 3:18-19).

TODAY'S THOUGHT How big is your God? In 1952, J.B. Phillips wrote a book called *Your God Is Too Small*. It shook the Christian world. His theory was that many believers had misconceptions about God that were no more than superimposed human characteristics. To some, it seemed that God was a Santa Claus, a stern father, an impersonal clockmaker or a killjoy. His book begged the question: How big is the God we visualized as we worship? In today's scripture, Paul knows that we cannot begin to understand how magnificent God really is by ourselves; so, he prays that we may have power from God to really understand how wide, long, high and deep His love is. How can we begin to know how vast God is? How do we keep from making God too small? Paul shares the secret. He writes, "May you experience the love of Christ, though it is too great to understand fully. Then you will be made complete with all the fullness of life and power that comes from God." Ask God to help you experience His love today. To really know it, feel it, sense it and see it. Ask Him to reveal Himself to you right now, in ways you have never experienced Him before. If you do, what does God promise? He promises, "Then you will be made complete with all the fullness of life and power that comes from God."

TODAY'S PRAYER Father. Can it be true? Can I really experience Your love today? Can I begin to know how deep, high, long and wide it really is? Pour into my heart a sense of Your presence. Help me imagine who You really are. Forgive me for making You so small. Enlarge my vision today, I pray. Amen.

Real Trust

TODAY'S VERSE "But blessed are those who trust in the Lord and have made the Lord their hope and confidence" (Jeremiah 17:7).

TODAY'S THOUGHT It is one thing to say we trust someone, it is another to put confidence in them. A famous tightrope walker was going to cross Niagara Falls with a person in a wheelbarrow. He asked the crowd watching how many thought he could make it to the other side with someone in the wheelbarrow. Most in the crowd raised their hand. Then he asked for volunteers to sit in the wheelbarrow. No one volunteered. How many times has God said to us, "How many believe I can supply all your needs? How many believe that I love you and will help you overcome your struggles?" We quickly raise our hand and say, "Yes, Lord, I believe." But when struggles come, when doubt raises its head, when God brings the wheelbarrow and tells us to jump in, we slither to the back of the crowd. True trust, true faith, is acted out in hope and confidence. Might you go forth this day trusting in God. Might you have all the faith you need to sit in the wheelbarrow. If anyone can get you to the other side, it is God your Father.

TODAY'S PRAYER Father, help me put my faith in You. Help me trust You, really trust You. Help me have real confidence in Your resurrection power and hope in Your undying love for me. Amen.

Lead Me

TODAY'S VERSE "Trust in the LORD with all your heart, And lean not on your own understanding; In all your ways acknowledge Him, and He shall direct your paths" (Proverbs 3:5-6).

TODAY'S THOUGHT When I was trained in wilderness school, the goal was to teach us to be a good guide. They took us on courses and training where our lives were literally in the hands of the person leading us. The training guide knew where we were and how to get us where we were going. They knew the terrain and how to survive any and every condition. A wilderness is a wild and unpredictable environment, and a good guide will get you through it. We need a guide to get us through the mountains and valleys of this life. We need a guide to lead us through the difficult times when we seem lost and all is hopeless. Solomon said to "Trust in the Lord with all our heart" and He will direct our path. More specifically, Jesus promised that He will give us the Holy Spirit to be our guide. God, through the Holy Spirit, will lead us into all truth. And in the wilderness, the truth is King! There is no room for error; you need the truth to guide you every step of the way. So, where are you today? Where are you going? How will you get there? You need the Holy Spirit to be your guide. The Book of Proverbs warns us not to lean on our own understanding but to acknowledge our need for God. Come to God today and ask Him to lead you. Surrender to His guidance and let Him direct your paths. Might the verse of an old Sunday School song be your prayer today, "My God knows the way through the wilderness, all I have to do is follow."

TODAY'S PRAYER Lord, You know how I need You to direct my path today. I can't do it by myself. I surrender to You and ask that You would lead me through the power of Your Holy Spirit. Guide me, direct me, lead me this day. Amen.

Rest for the Weary

TODAY'S VERSE "Come to me, all you who are weary and burdened, and I will give you rest. Take my yoke upon you and learn from me, for I am gentle and humble in heart, and you will find rest for your souls. For my yoke is easy and my burden is light" (Matthew 11:28-30).

TODAY'S THOUGHT It is easy to get weary. There are so many demands on your life. You live at such a fast pace, burning the candle at both ends. The result is that you end up tired much of the time. Where do you turn? Where do you turn for relief, comfort, and escape from all the pressure? If not careful, you can find yourself a victim to addictions, unhealthy relationships or negative emotions. But Jesus has a better way. He said, "Come to me, all you who are weary and burdened, and I will give you rest." More than that, Jesus invites you to learn from Him. His teaching is easy, and His burden is light. So today, turn to Jesus. Bring your weary soul to Him. Give Him your circumstances and your emotions. Surrender yourself to His care. He promises that you will find rest for your soul.

TODAY'S PRAYER Father, You know my condition. I am weary and in need of renewal. I am so glad that You have invited me to come to You for rest. I know that You are gentle and humble in heart and will give me rest for my soul. So, I come to You even now, Jesus. I put my soul into Your capable hands. Help me and heal me even now. I pray this in Jesus' name. Amen.

His Word

TODAY'S VERSE "All Scripture is inspired by God and is useful to teach us what is true and to make us realize what is wrong in our lives. It corrects us when we are wrong and teaches us to do what is right. God uses it to prepare and equip his people to do every good work" (II Timothy 3:16-17).

TODAY'S THOUGHT How often do we pray for direction? How many times do we just long to hear God's voice? How many times a week do we cry out for wisdom? The good news is that God has created a way to speak to us, give us wisdom and guide us. It is through His written word, the Bible. Paul was telling Timothy how important the Bible was. He shared that the Bible is inspired by God for teaching us, convicting us, correcting us and equipping us for His service. There is no other source that God uses to communicate to us more effectively. Through the power and guidance of the Holy Spirit, God is able to speak to us in a personal and intimate way. It is easy to get busy and a day goes by, then two—soon a week, then a month. Before you know it, you are not spending any time getting to know God or His word. We were not meant to live life without the word of God. It is like going through life with a hole in your heart. Instead, let God fill the emptiness. Get a Bible today and put it near your favorite chair. And then each day, start spending a few minutes letting God teach you. He will. He longs to fellowship with you and teach you His word, but you have to make the first move. Why not start today?

TODAY'S PRAYER Dear God, thank You for the Bible. I know that it was written to give me wisdom and guidance. Help me to read it, learn it and use it in my everyday experience. Teach me, Father, to love Your word, that I might live for You. Amen.

Your Heart's Desire

TODAY'S VERSE "May he grant your heart's desires and make all your plans succeed" (Psalm 20:4).

TODAY'S THOUGHT At first glance, this verse sounds like it came straight from a fortune cookie factory. You read it and think, "Did I see this on a success motivation poster?" But then, if you take the time to remember that this is God's Word and start to meditate on this phrase, you will find that it is full of deep meaning. First, I stop to think about the responsibility this verse puts on me as a person who dreams and has desires. When is the last time I desired a God-sized desire? What have I desired that would be worthy of God's consideration, let alone His blessing? What do I want to see happen that would possibly be aligned with the will of God? More than desire, what have I spent time on and planned for the Kingdom of God? What success am I asking for that would be worthy of God's favor? Finally, who will get the glory if our desires came true and our plans succeeded? God put you and me here to live for Him. He wants us to use our heart to desire great and mighty things for Him. We are His ambassadors, and He chooses to live His will through our lives. Let us plan and desire with all our hearts to do great and mighty things for His glory.

TODAY'S PRAYER Father, birth in my heart a desire to do Your will with my life. Give me a dream. Give me a passion. And then Father, help these desires, passions, and dreams turn into a plan. Might the plan become a reality through Your mighty power and for Your glory and honor. In Jesus' name. Amen.

Boast About God's Love

TODAY'S VERSE "This is what the LORD says: 'Don't let the wise boast in their wisdom, or the powerful boast in their power, or the rich boast in their riches. But those who wish to boast should boast in this alone: that they truly know me and understand that I am the LORD who demonstrates unfailing love and who brings justice and righteousness to the earth'" (Jeremiah 9:23-24).

TODAY'S THOUGHT "Blessed are the meek, for they shall inherit the earth." This is one of the beatitudes that Jesus taught us. God puts a premium on humility. This runs counter to worldly wisdom. In modern society, there is a premium put on self-reliance. Kudos are given to the person who is a success. With success comes bragging rights. We live for that elusive fifteen minutes of fame. Why? Because we want recognition. We want to feel important and appreciated. So, we boast. But God offers a better way. He says not to boast of our wisdom, power or riches—instead, we are to boast in the fact that we know Him and understand Him as the Lord. What makes this so ironic is that the very thing that we are looking for, love and acceptance, is found in Jesus Christ. We get to boast in the fact that God loves us with unfailing love. We don't have to earn it. We don't have to perform to certain expectations. He loves us unconditionally. So today, rejoice in all that He has done for you. Bless Him for His love for you. Boast in the fact that God is a gracious and loving God.

TODAY'S PRAYER Father, forgive me for bragging about my own abilities. Forgive me for putting such a high importance on my own possessions and accomplishments. Instead, I praise You, Dear Lord, for Your unfailing love for me. In Jesus' name. Amen.

Give Him Your Future

TODAY'S VERSE   "But I am trusting you, O LORD, saying, 'You are my God!' My future is in your hands" (Psalm 31:14-15).

TODAY'S THOUGHT   How much of our present is influenced by the fear of our future? What will people think of us? What will people say? Have you ever stopped to realize how many times a day you say, "What if?" Now, it is not bad to stop and consider consequences. Jesus Himself said if we were going to war, we would need to first consider the size of the enemy's army to see if we could win. Strategy is good, but not to the point that it takes the place of trusting God in everything we do. David told God, "I am trusting You, O Lord." He then followed it with a strong affirmation of God's love and power. He wrote, "My future is in your hands." How about you? Where is your trust today? Do you say you trust God, but spend time worrying about your future as if God did not exist? If so, surrender to God today. Make Him the Lord of your today and tomorrow. Like David, put your future in God's hands. It's the best place to put it.

TODAY'S PRAYER   Father, I thank You that I can come to You with my future. Please guide me, comfort me and direct my every step. I renounce fear and pray that Your Holy Spirit will help me live this day with faith, hope, and love. Amen.

Taste the Lord

TODAY'S VERSE "Taste and see that the LORD is good; blessed is the man who takes refuge in him" (Psalm 34:8).

TODAY'S THOUGHT Have you ever stopped to think of how many different ways you can experience the Lord? Worship is multi-dimensional. With the use of our mind, God has allowed us the capacity to really know Him and love Him. Certainly, we can read His word. God does speak to us through the scriptures. What He has written connects with us in a personal way. We can sense His presence. He is the God of all comfort, and the Holy Spirit bears witness with our spirit that He is God. We can hear His voice. Whether it is a still soft voice deep in our soul or, as some have heard, an audible voice, God speaks to us. We can see His glory. Even though a beautiful sunset or a significant moment, we can often see evidence of God. We can also use our inner mind and see Him with the eyes of our heart. When Jesus healed people, many others would come up to Him and touch Him. Have you ever reached out to Him, lifted your hands and experienced a moment as if you touched Him? We can sense that God is weighty, that He has substance. David said that we can taste and see that the Lord is good. When we commune with God, we can know that He is real. God wants us to know Him--really know Him--in many different and personal ways. Today, determine to start spending time with God in silence and worship Him with the different senses. Love Him, worship Him, and experience Him today. Oh, that you would taste of the Lord and know that He is good.

TODAY'S PRAYER Father, I give myself to You. I want to know You in all of Your fullness. Help me worship You in new and fresh ways. Enlarge my capacity to know You, that I might love You more and more. Amen.

Fear Not

TODAY'S VERSE "I prayed to the LORD, and he answered me. He freed me from all my fears. Those who look to him for help will be radiant with joy; no shadow of shame will darken their faces. In my desperation, I prayed, and the LORD listened; he saved me from all my troubles. For the angel of the LORD is a guard; he surrounds and defends all who fear him" (Psalm 34:4-7).

TODAY'S THOUGHT How many times a day do you fear something? You get called into the office and you are sure you are going to get fired. Your child is late, and your mind goes crazy with thoughts of what might have happened. Your spouse is in "that" mood again and you know it is going to get ugly. The credit card bills came in the mail and you don't know how you are going to pay them. You found a lump and you are waiting for the report from the doctor's office. Fear can be healthy, as in, "Don't step in front of traffic." But fear can also be false, an exaggeration or a lie. It started with Adam and Eve, and it is the same today; most of our spiritual struggles center around a fear-based lie. Most spiritual battles are a struggle between the truth or a lie. Which will we believe? Lie or truth? Our fear or God? David knew the answer. He prayed to God, and God answered him and freed him from all his fears. The Lord listened and saved David from his troubles, and He will save you, as well. What is it today that you fear? What is holding you back? What lie has you bound? What keeps you from being still and knowing God? Today, renounce your fear. Bring it to God. Present it to Him. Choose to believe the truth about God and your circumstance, and He will free you.

TODAY'S PRAYER Father, You know my fears. I bring them to You. Help me, protect me, free me from this bondage of lies. Thank You that You have not given me a spirit of fear. I choose to believe the truth and live by faith in You. Amen.

February 19
Lead My Heart

TODAY'S VERSE "May the Lord lead your hearts into a full understanding and expression of the love of God and the patient endurance that comes from Christ" (II Thessalonians 3:5).

TODAY'S THOUGHT It will take a lifetime to fully mature in Christ. Although our salvation is immediate, maturing in Christ is a process. But we don't see it that way. We want instant spirituality--and here is the real twist: we want it without the spiritual discipline of prayer, meditation, and scripture reading. Nor do we want to be busy with ministry. Instead, we have our life to lead, with all its important tasks and duties. Is it a wonder that we don't know what Jesus is talking about when He says that He has come to give us an abundant life? Paul prays that the Lord would lead our hearts to a full understanding of who He is. An understanding that comes when we experience God expressing His love towards us. It is personal and real. The result of God leading us into that personal understanding of His love is the hope, faith, trust and confidence that produces patient endurance. What a gift--and it is yours for the asking. Might your prayer be today, "Lord, lead my heart."

TODAY'S PRAYER Father, please lead my heart to a full personal understanding of Your love. Help me today to be purposeful in knowing You and living for You in all I do. In Jesus' name. Amen.

Confess to God

TODAY'S VERSE "When I refused to confess my sin, my body wasted away, and I groaned all day long. Day and night your hand of discipline was heavy on me. My strength evaporated like water in the summer heat. Finally, I confessed all my sins to you and stopped trying to hide my guilt. I said to myself, 'I will confess my rebellion to the LORD.' And you forgave me! All my guilt is gone" (Psalm 32:3-5).

TODAY'S THOUGHT David paints an accurate picture of someone who is under the hand of conviction. He wrote about the physical effect that guilt played on his body. But David did not allow it to stay that way. Instead, he confessed all his sins to God and experienced what John was talking about in I John 1:8-9, "If we claim we have no sin, we are only fooling ourselves and not living in the truth. But if we confess our sins to him, he is faithful and just to forgive us our sins and to cleanse us from all wickedness." The result of David's confession was the joy of knowing that all his guilt was gone. How about you? Are you burdened with some nagging issue that you need to talk to God about? Have you been consumed with bitterness, anger, fear or worry, and God is saying that you need to repent of it? Is the guilt of being separated from God affecting your thinking, behavior, and health? If so, repent. Confess to God and ask Him to cleanse you and set you free. He will forgive you. He will restore your body, mind, and soul.

TODAY'S PRAYER Father, you know how I can let things build up. Instead of dealing with issues in the way I should, I let them build up until they are sins festering in my soul and body. Show me today where I need to confess. Point out areas in my life that need forgiveness. Help me to live the life of freedom that You desire for me. Help me break free from this bondage of guilt. In Jesus' name, I pray. Amen.

Quench the Thirst of Your Soul

TODAY'S VERSE "Jesus replied, 'Anyone who drinks this water will soon become thirsty again. But those who drink the water I give will never be thirsty again. It becomes a fresh, bubbling spring within them, giving them eternal life.' - The woman left her water jar beside the well and ran back to the village, telling everyone, 'Come and see a man who told me everything I ever did! Could he possibly be the Messiah?' So the people came streaming from the village to see him" (John 4:13-14, 28-29).

TODAY'S THOUGHT What a beautiful picture God is painting for us. Here is a woman who is coming to the well for water during the heat of the day. She must have been an outcast, for why else come alone in the heat? Why not come early in the cool of the morning with the other women? Regardless, she comes for water for her physical thirst and Jesus offers her water for her soul. Jesus touches her heart so she leaves the water at the well and runs and tells everyone in the village about Him. She had found what her soul really thirsted for. How about you? What do you need? Is it to be heard and understood? Is it to be affirmed or blessed? Do you want to be loved? Do you need to be forgiven? Perhaps you long to be included or to be chosen? Perhaps it is just to be safe? Whatever the longing of your heart, Jesus has the living water that can quench your thirst. His love for you is the living water you have been looking for. Come to Him today. Drink of His love, forgiveness, understanding, affirmation, and blessing. When you do, you too will be telling everyone, "Come and see this Jesus who knows me and quenches the thirst of my soul."

TODAY'S PRAYER Lord, You know the longings of my heart. You know my needs, my fears, and my desires. I come to You today to be filled. Fill me with Your living water. Holy Spirit, come and quench the desires of my heart. In Jesus' name. Amen.

Unworldly Peace

TODAY'S VERSE "I am leaving you with a gift—peace of mind and heart. And the peace I give is a gift the world cannot give. So, don't be troubled or afraid" (John 14:27).

TODAY'S THOUGHT Have you ever had a crisis of faith? A time when you were so filled with grief, sorrow, and anger that you didn't know where God was? It's then that I need to remind myself of the context of today's verse. Read the whole chapter and you will see that Jesus had just introduced an entire "other" reality. It was a cosmic introduction to the blending of this world and the next. Jesus was getting ready to go back to His father. He was about ready to face an unbearable death and spiritual suffering we cannot imagine. In a matter of moments, He, too, would say, "Father, why have you forsaken me?" And yet, with deep empathy, Jesus tells us in the first verse of this chapter not to be troubled because He was about to prepare another reality for us. It was obvious that His disciples did not understand, so He tells them that He will give us the Holy Spirit to comfort us and help us in this world until we reach the next. And then, Jesus shared today's verse, "I am leaving you with a gift—peace of mind and heart. And the peace I give is a gift the world cannot give. So, don't be troubled or afraid." He was right. The world cannot give us peace during our dark nights of the soul. Neither can religion. Only in blending this world and the next can we even begin to make any sense of our suffering here. Only in a larger reality can we find any peace in this dimension. Jesus came so we could live in both. I pray that today, you will have a glimpse of this world in light of the next life, and see that Jesus is the Lord of both. May that reality begin a process of peace even in your darkest hour.

TODAY'S PRAYER Dear Jesus, there are times when I ask, "Where is the peace in the darkest nights of the soul? Where is the comfort in such unbearable pain?" And yet, today, I see that You, who suffered such pain and anguish, have taken the harsh realities of this world and blended them with the next life. Please help my heart live in both realities. Help me begin to experience the peace that You are talking about. Amen.

February 23
Our Chief Purpose

TODAY'S VERSE "Honor the LORD for his glory and strength. Honor the LORD for the glory of his name. Worship the LORD in the splendor of his holiness" (Psalm 29:1-2).

TODAY'S THOUGHT What do you think is the most significant purpose God has for us on this earth? You could certainly build a case for loving others. The Apostle John told us that God is love, so loving others is most certainly on God's agenda. Evangelism must be a priority. Jesus left us with the great commission to go and make disciples of all nations. Personal worship is another purpose God has created us for. God longs for our adoration. He is worthy of all our praise and worship. What a privilege it is to bow down before the Almighty Creator of the Universe and know that He cares deeply about our worship. David said to "Honor the Lord" and "To worship Him in the splendor of His holiness." It is nearly impossible to fathom what it is like to be before God in all His splendor and majesty, but that is what we are invited to do. Take the mountaintops, the streams, sunsets, ocean views, canyons, and any other majestic visuals images that you have been privileged to see, and let it equal one drop of water. Now put that drop in the ocean, and you will begin to see how our paltry earthly images compare to His splendor. So today, no matter where you are, stop and participate in one of the most sacred and special purposes of our human experience. Right this moment, praise Him for who He is. Thank Him for all He has done. Worship Him in all His glory. He has invited you to come and adore Him. Don't take His invitation for granted. It is a rare gift from God Himself. Worship Him with all your heart, soul and mind.

TODAY'S PRAYER Father, I come right now to worship You. Thank You for Your love for me. I bow before You this moment and adore You for all Your goodness. You are the true and living Almighty God and I praise You for all You have done for me. Thank You for making me Your child through the death of Your Son, Jesus, on the cross for me. I love and worship You in Jesus' name. Amen.

Worthy of His Calling

TODAY'S VERSE "With this in mind, we constantly pray for you, that our God may count you worthy of his calling, and that by his power he may fulfill every good purpose of yours and every act prompted by your faith. We pray this so that the name of our Lord Jesus may be glorified in you, and you in him, according to the grace of our God and the Lord Jesus Christ" (II Thessalonians 1:11-12).

TODAY'S THOUGHT Did anyone ever ask you, "What do you want to be when you grow up?" Or have you ever taken a test to help you determine your passions and purpose in life? You could spend your whole life trying to find your purpose, that perfect job or the fulfillment of your childhood dream, and never come close to what Paul was praying for the Christians in Thessalonica. What a magnificent prayer. The good news is that you can pray the same thing for yourself. He has called you to serve Him and you can pray with Paul, "that by His power He may fulfill every good purpose of yours and every act prompted by your faith." Can you imagine that? You see, this is God's true desire for you, to use His power to help you fulfill every good purpose of yours. The result is that the name of our Lord Jesus will be glorified in your life! So, what good purpose do you have today? What act prompted by your faith will you engage in today? Might He empower you by His grace to do all that He has called you to this day so that He Himself will be glorified.

TODAY'S PRAYER Father, I thank You that You can fulfill every good purpose of mine and every act prompted by my faith! What an exciting thought. Please help me understand what this really means in my life. Help me not to waste this precious life You have given me. Might I live it today for Your glory. Amen.

Clothe Me with Joy

TODAY'S VERSE "You have turned my mourning into joyful dancing. You have taken away my clothes of mourning and clothed me with joy, that I might sing praises to you and not be silent. O LORD my God, I will give you thanks forever!" (Psalm 30:11-12).

TODAY'S THOUGHT We go through seasons. Good times, bad times, times of sorrow and times of joy. I went through a season of depression, and this passage from Psalm brought me comfort many times. I identified with David when he wrote in this same passage, "I cried out to you, O LORD. I begged the Lord for mercy." I knew that God knew what I was going through, so I claimed that He would turn my mourning into joyful dancing. I took solace when David wrote, "Weeping may last through the night, but joy comes in the morning." Through time, prayer, and counseling, the Lord did bring me to the other side. What are you mourning? What has broken your heart? What has you depressed or distraught? Bring it to Him today. I would not trifle with your sorrow. I would not minimize your pain. I only come today to offer you hope. Only God can turn your mourning into dancing. That may seem so far from where you are right now, but it is not too far for God. The light slowly penetrates the back of a dark cave. The sound of laughter at camp seems so faint when you are on the back side of the forest. But know this, there is light for you. There will be joy for you in the morning. I pray that God's grace will fill you with this truth and complete a healing process in you.

TODAY'S PRAYER Dear Father, I don't even know how to pray for my sorrow. I don't know how to release the deep pain I feel. I come today crying out for your mercy. I thank You that weeping may last through the night, but joy will come in the morning. Holy Spirit, I give You my heart— mend it, bring it back to life with Your breath of love. Please begin a process in me to turn my mourning into dancing. Amen.

Live for Him

TODAY'S VERSE May he give you the power to accomplish all the good things your faith prompts you to do. Then the name of our Lord Jesus will be honored because of the way you live, and you will be honored along with him. This is all made possible because of the grace of our God and Lord, Jesus Christ" (II Thessalonians 1:11-12).

TODAY'S THOUGHT Who are we that the Almighty God of the universe would allow us to serve Him? Yet, that is what God has done. He specifically created us to love Him, worship Him and serve Him. But what is so amazing is that He did not create us like robots and program us to serve Him or beat us down and force us to live for Him. No, He has drawn us toward Him by His grace. Grace, that mixture of His love, mercy, compassion, forgiveness, concern, and favor, all rolled into one. It is His grace toward us that encourages our faith and compels us to live for Him. God pours His love into our heart and then empowers us to do whatever our heart desires. What has your faith in God prompted you to do for Him lately? If the answer is vague, it is not too late. God has grace enough to forgive you. He has grace enough to encourage you. He has grace enough to empower you. Come to God today, and may your faith prompt you to accomplish good things for Him.

TODAY'S PRAYER Thank You, Lord, for Your grace in my life. I pray that You will prompt me to do great things for You and then give me the power to do them. Father, might You be honored today in the way I live for You. Amen.

February 27
The Gift

TODAY'S VERSE "I will ask the Father, and he will give you another counselor, who will never leave you. He is the Holy Spirit, who leads into all truth" (John 14:16).

TODAY'S THOUGHT Can you imagine someone knocking on your door and giving you a check for a hundred million dollars? Think of all you could do with that. How tragic would it be if you thanked the person, closed the door and put the check on your dresser top and never used it? Never helped anyone, never bettered your own situation. Instead, you live a meager existence, paycheck to paycheck, and die a pauper. We would shake our heads and mutter, "What a shame to waste such a resource." And yet, what must God the Father think of what we have done with the precious gift of His Holy Spirit? Jesus asked the Father to give us a counselor who will never leave us and lead us into all truth, and He has. You and I, when we became a child of God, received His Holy Spirit into our lives and yet we barely know this third part of the Trinity. When have we ever asked the Holy Spirit to fill us, guide us, or lead us to the truth? We have been given spiritual gifts, but do we know what they are or how they work? How much time have we spent contemplating how to cultivate the "fruit of the Spirit" in our life? God has indwelled us with the person of the Holy Spirit. Might we seek to understand more about this treasure that God has given us.

TODAY'S PRAYER Father, thank You for the gift of the Holy Spirit. Forgive me for not knowing more about Him. Forgive me for not living in His power. Oh, Holy Spirit, I ask that You make me conscious of Your presence in my life. Teach me, guide me, fill me and lead me into all truth. I give You control of my life and pray that You would produce Your fruit in my life and activate the spiritual gifts that You have given me. I pray this in Jesus' name. Amen.

Cry for Mercy

TODAY'S VERSE "Listen to my prayer for mercy as I cry out to you for help, as I lift my hands toward your holy sanctuary." – "Praise the LORD! For he has heard my cry for mercy. The LORD is my strength and shield. I trust him with all my heart. He helps me, and my heart is filled with joy. I burst out in songs of thanksgiving" (Psalm 28:2, 7-8).

TODAY'S THOUGHT David knew what it was like to be tormented. He knew the pain that comes with great need. He experienced difficulties that had no escape, except by the mercy of an Almighty God. So, David came to God and he cried out for mercy and help. That was the beginning of today's passage. Verses later, David is praising God. God had heard his cry. As David faced his situation, we see that God became his strength and protection. David trusted God with all his heart. The result was a deep spiritual joy. God did not take David out of his situation. David still faced his problems, but instead of doing it on his own, God provided David with strength. God protected David like a shield. Do you have a story similar to David's? Are there times when you need to cry out to God for His mercy? Rest assured, He hears you. You, too, can end up praising God for He promises that He will be your strength. He will be your shield. You can trust Him with your situation. When you do, you too will experience the deep joy that can only come from Him.

TODAY'S PRAYER Father, I come to You today asking for Your mercy in my life. I thank You for hearing my cry and offering to be my strength and shield. I accept this promise and put my all my trust in You. Thank You that I will not be disappointed. Fill my heart with a deep joy today so that I too will burst out with thanksgiving. In Jesus' name, I pray. Amen.

You Are His Masterpiece

TODAY'S VERSE "For we are God's masterpiece. He has created us anew in Christ Jesus, so we can do the good things he planned for us long ago" (Ephesians 2:10).

TODAY'S THOUGHT For every truth, there is a lie waiting to deceive us. Why is it so much easier to believe a lie? Why can doubt have so much impact on belief? A million people can believe the truth, and yet one dissenter will get the nation's attention. It is that way in the spiritual realm. Paul writes that we are significant. Specifically, "we are God's masterpiece created to do the good things he planned for us to do" and what do we believe? Be honest--don't we often believe we are no good, inferior, damaged goods and even hopeless? Where did that come from? It didn't come from God! If we want to change what we believe, we must renounce the lies. Do it today. Lift up your heart and say it out loud, "I renounce the lie that I am no good, inferior, damaged goods or hopeless." My friend, it is time to believe the truth about yourself. You are significant. You are a masterpiece made by God Himself. He absolutely loves you and desires you to accept the love He has for you. Renounce the lies; today, choose to believe the truth.

TODAY'S PRAYER Dear Father, my Father. I confess I have believed lies about myself. I renounce these negative thoughts and feelings and command their power over me to be broken in the precious name of Jesus Christ! I choose to accept the truth, that You personally created me as a masterpiece to do the good things You have sent me here for. Thank You, Dear Father, for giving me significance. Amen.

Wait on the Lord

TODAY'S VERSE "Wait patiently for the LORD. Be brave and courageous. Yes, wait patiently for the LORD" (Psalm 27:14).

"But they that wait upon the LORD shall renew their strength; they shall mount up with wings as eagles; they shall run, and not be weary; and they shall walk, and not faint" (Isaiah 40:31).

TODAY'S THOUGHT It is no surprise that the word *wait* has only four letters. Doesn't it often seem like a curse word? We would rather hear God say, "Yes, that is a great idea!" or "Certainly, anything else I can get you?" We want instant gratification. We want what we want, with little consideration for any other variables and become impatient if we do not get it. Or what about the times when we have waited and waited. We pray, seek God's face, and still, there is no answer. The last thing we want to be told at a time like that is to wait. Yet David and Isaiah both insist that part of our spiritual journey is learning to wait. David knew firsthand how hard it was to wait on God. He was named king by God but had to run and sleep in caves, running from the armies of Saul. David was brave and courageous over and over again and waited on God to work things out. He encourages us to do the same. Isaiah inspires us to wait on God. He shares how, in time, we will renew our strength, we will eventually run and not be weary, we will walk and not faint. What a picture. Life is hard; we have struggles on all sides. It may seem like God doesn't care, perhaps not even there ... but be encouraged today. You are not alone! God knows your situation. Pray, trust, hope and wait. God will renew your strength.

TODAY'S PRAYER Father, waiting is so hard sometimes. I confess I get so impatient. Forgive me and help me to focus on Your love and to put my trust in You. Help me to wait patiently and not to worry. Lord, I claim the promise that You will renew my strength as I wait on You. Amen.

Show Me the Right Path

TODAY'S VERSE "Show me the right path, O LORD; point out the road for me to follow. Lead me by your truth and teach me, for you are the God who saves me. All day long I put my hope in you. Remember, O LORD, your compassion and unfailing love" (Psalm 25:4-6).

TODAY'S THOUGHT Life is a journey. We are not settlers in this world. Heaven is our final destination. Instead, we are called to go through life as an ambassador of heaven, a soldier in God's army, a sojourner commanded to give away God's peace and love--and the journey can get messy. That's why it is so important to learn to navigate, to solve problems and to discern what to do next. David is crying out that God would direct his path. But notice that it is a special kind of leading. He said, "Lead me by your truth and teach me." Jesus said that truth would set us free. So much of our hardships, misdirection and hurts in this life are due to deception and denial. We need to pray that God would show us the truth and then teach us through each experience. This is how we derive our faith and hope in Him. They are learned behaviors that God imparts as we are led by His Spirit in each situation we find ourselves in. Life is a process. We succeed and make progress by learning. David learned to put his hope in God and trusted that God's compassion and love would not fail. That is what we need to do. May God lead you by His truth today and point out the road for you to follow. May He teach you more about the depths of His compassion and unfailing love.

TODAY'S PRAYER Father, I need Your guidance today. Show me what road to follow. Guide me by Your truth and teach me to trust You. I put my hope in You and Your compassionate, unfailing love. Amen.

As Far as the East Is from the West

TODAY'S VERSE "I am dying from grief; my years are shortened by sadness. Sin has drained my strength; I am wasting away from within" (Psalm 31:10).

"For as high as the heavens are above the earth, so great is his love for those who fear him; as far as the east is from the west, so far has he removed our transgressions from us. As a father has compassion on his children, so the LORD has compassion on those who fear him" (Psalm 103:11-13).

TODAY'S THOUGHT Guilt is an insidious emotion. The Psalmist knew this first hand. His sin had caused him much grief. It affected him emotionally and physically. Our misbehavior, our rebellion toward God, does the same to us today. Hundreds of studies have linked toxic emotions to physical disease. But it doesn't have to be that way. God has provided a way for us to have freedom from guilt. It is through the forgiveness offered by the death of His son, our Lord Jesus Christ. The Apostle John wrote, "If anyone does sin, we have an advocate who pleads our case before the Father. He is Jesus Christ, the one who is truly righteous. He Himself is the sacrifice that atones for our sins and not only our sins but the sins of all the world." Do you know this same Jesus as your personal Savior? Have you accepted His death on the cross as the penalty for your misdeeds? If so, you can say with the Psalmist that as high as the heavens are above the earth, so your personal history, with all its pain and regret, is removed from God's sight. They are as far as the east is from the west.

TODAY'S PRAYER Father, thank You for the death and resurrection of Jesus Christ for my sins. Thank You that when I confess and renounce any wrongdoing, that You are swift to forgive and cleanse me. I thank You for Your unconditional love that takes all my guilt and casts it into the deep sea. I praise You for Your unbelievable grace You give to me. In Jesus' name. Amen.

I Will Be with You

TODAY'S VERSE "When you pass through the waters, I will be with you; and when you pass through the rivers, they will not sweep over you. When you walk through the fire, you will not be burned; the flames will not set you ablaze" (Isaiah 43:2).

"And be sure of this: I am with you always, even to the end of the age" (Matthew 28:20).

TODAY'S THOUGHT The difference between Christianity the religion and Christianity the lifestyle is the personal application of biblical truth. We take His word personally. When God says, "I will be with you," it is not a religious phrase, it is a reality that brings us comfort, strength, and hope. When there was a famine in the land, God told Isaac to stay in the land, for "I will be with you." When Jacob was in danger, God told him to return to his homeland and said, "I will be with you." When God commissioned Moses to lead His people out of Egypt, Moses shared how he felt that he was incompetent. God said to do it anyway because "I will be with you." When God asked Joshua to take over for Moses and lead the people into the Promised Land, He told Joshua, "As I was with Moses, so I will be with you." God asked Gideon to lead His people into battle and Gideon was afraid and asked God, "How can I rescue Israel?" God said, "I will be with you." When Jesus was leaving earth to return to God's right hand and commissioned the Church to make disciples, He promised, "I will be with you always." Life has its trials. God has commissioned you and me to serve Him. The tasks may be difficult. We may face trials, temptations, and struggles, but take comfort in this, even today, God is with you. He will never, never, never leave you or forsake you.

TODAY'S PRAYER Father, thank You for Your ever-abiding presence. Thank You for the comfort I find in the fact that You are with me. Today, make me keenly aware that nothing can separate me from You. Help my heart be filled with faith in the reality that You will never leave me or forsake me. In Jesus' name. Amen.

Walk the Talk

TODAY'S VERSE "If someone has enough money to live well and sees a brother or sister in need but shows no compassion—how can God's love be in that person? Dear children, let's not merely say that we love each other; let us show the truth by our actions" (I John 3:17-18).

"A new command I give you: Love one another. As I have loved you, so you must love one another" (John 13:34).

TODAY'S THOUGHT It is harder to "walk our talk" than to "talk our walk." We can say all we want about how loving we are, but the real proof is in our actions. If God's love is a motivating force in our lives, then helping others is going to be a natural byproduct. Christians have lost much of their witness because we have not helped the poor and needy to the best of our ability. Sure, our budgets are tight, but look at what we spend our money on. Expensive cars, homes, furnishings, hobbies, entertainment, and food all take their toll on our annual budget. Downsizing will allow us to have discretionary income that we can help others with. We are God's ambassadors. If we are going to represent Him in this world, then we need to be able to be compassionate toward those that He brings across our path. John says it best, "Let's not merely say that we love each other; let us show the truth by our actions." Ask God to bring someone across your path today that you can help.

TODAY'S PRAYER Father, You have blessed me with so much. Help me to be wise with the resources You have given me, so I can have compassion toward those that You bring across my path. Even today, Lord, show me someone that I can be compassionate toward. Might there be no doubt that Your love dwells in me. Amen.

The Father Loves Us

TODAY'S VERSE "See how very much our Father loves us, for he calls us his children, and that is what we are!" (I John 3:1).

TODAY'S THOUGHT I don't know how John could have contained himself when He wrote this verse. It has to be one of the most celebratory verses in the entire Bible. John understood the significance of being a child of God and implores us to understand it, too. With the excitement of a child on Christmas morning, John exclaims, "See how much our father loves us!" Can you see it? There are four points to notice. First, "How very much." God's love for us is unfathomable. John wants us to see and examine the concept that God loves us very much, and to really believe it. Second, is the phrase, "Our." John is getting personal. He isn't talking about a God beyond our grasp, an impersonal Deity. Rather, John is saying that this is our Father, which leads to the third point: God is our *Father*. Not a dysfunctional or absentee parent. He is our loving, faithful and trustworthy Father. Finally, John shares with us that this Father, who calls us His children, also "loves" us very much. Knowing this should change everything. When you love someone and know that they love you, you trust them. You want to be with them. You want to share in their life. I pray that we will grasp with the Apostle John, how wonderful it is to know that the Father loves us. Rest assured, we have been called *children of God*, and this is what we are!

TODAY'S PRAYER Dear Father, thank You for loving us and making us Your children. What a privilege to know You. What a joy to be Your child. By Your love, fill my heart and guide my thoughts today. In Jesus' name. Amen.

Bless Me, Lord

TODAY'S VERSE "Tell Aaron and his sons to bless the people of Israel with this special blessing: 'May the LORD bless you and protect you. May the LORD smile on you and be gracious to you. May the LORD show you his favor and give you his peace.' Whenever Aaron and his sons bless the people of Israel in my name, I myself will bless them" (Numbers 6:22-27).

TODAY'S THOUGHT You probably recognize these verses as a doxology that is given at the end of a worship service. It was really given to Moses by God Himself, so he could bless the children of Israel. I pray that you have the assurance that God will bless you and protect you. May you sense the smile of God deep in your heart and experience His graciousness to you. May the very favor of God Almighty fill you with strength. May knowing how He loves you and wants to bless you give you all the peace you will need to get you through this day. Know this—God Himself loves you so much and is the one who will bless you this day!

TODAY'S PRAYER Father, who am I that You would bless me? And yet, You have said that it is your desire to do so. So, Lord, bless me today. Bless me till my heart overflows with the realization that I am Yours and You are mine! Thank You, dear Father. Amen.

Faith, Love, and Hope

TODAY'S VERSE We always thank God for all of you, mentioning you in our prayers. We continually remember before our God and Father your work produced by faith, your labor prompted by love, and your endurance inspired by hope in our Lord Jesus Christ. And so, you became a model to all the believers in Macedonia and Achaia. The Lord's message rang out from you not only in Macedonia and Achaia—your faith in God has become known everywhere" (I Thessalonians 1:2-3, 7-8).

TODAY'S THOUGHT Christianity is more than a belief system; it's a tour of duty. When we became a Christian, we enlisted in the service of Jesus Christ. There is a spiritual battle in the world. Poverty, injustice, abuse, and hatred are all part of the human suffering going on around us. Depression, divorce, drug abuse, and psychosomatic disease are all part of the world we live in, and God has created us to be His ambassadors of love. You and I have a purpose beyond mere existence. We are disciples of Jesus Christ. No one knew this better than the church in Thessalonica. Paul was blown away by their seriousness and dedication. He thanked God for their faith, love, and hope, and committed himself to pray for them. But it wasn't what we would consider faith, love, and hope. Listen to what Paul wrote. He said, "Your work produced by faith, your labor prompted by love, and your endurance inspired by hope." When is the last time we did something because of faith in a mighty working God? When did we labor in love? When have we had to endure hanging on to nothing else but hope? That's what it is to serve Jesus. You take the responsibility seriously. You involve yourself in the life of others. You step out, way over your head, and know that only faith in God can get results. You take on situations that try your love beyond reason. It is very hard work. And when nothing seems to be going right, God comes through and you are inspired to get up and do it all again because there is hope. We live in a hurting world. We have the answer. May we follow the example of the Thessalonians.

TODAY'S PRAYER Lord, give me faith to live for You today. Help me love the way You want me to. Fill my heart with hope so it spills over onto everyone I meet. Lead me on, Dear Jesus. Amen.

Lay Your Burden Down

TODAY'S VERSE "Then Jesus said, 'Come to me, all of you who are weary and carry heavy burdens, and I will give you rest'" (Matthew 11:28).

TODAY'S THOUGHT Some days are harder than others. There are so many things that can get us down. Long hours at work, difficult relationships, financial difficulties, medical conditions, emotional stress and family responsibilities are just a few of the pressures that can weigh on us. Jesus knew the human condition. All around Him, He witnessed human suffering. He worked tirelessly to help those who were sick and oppressed. More importantly, He left behind a system to replace His efforts and to expand His influence. He gave us the Church, sent the Holy Spirit and took His rightful place at the right hand of the Father. The church works on His behalf to help and heal us, the Holy Spirit indwells us in order to guide and comfort us, and Jesus Himself intercedes for us with the Father. So, when Jesus said, "Come to me, all of you who are weary and carry heavy burdens, and I will give you rest," He meant it. What burden do you have? What is weighing you down? Bring it to Jesus. He will comfort you, He will guide you, He will give you rest.

TODAY'S PRAYER Lord, I bring to You my burdens. You know my situation. I cannot make it without You. Comfort my heart today. Guide me. Give me strength. Help me carry on. I give You my burdens; please give me Your rest. Amen.

Loved by God

TODAY'S VERSE "And I am convinced that nothing can ever separate us from God's love. Neither death nor life, neither angels nor demons, neither our fears for today nor our worries about tomorrow—not even the powers of hell can separate us from God's love. No power in the sky above or in the earth below—indeed, nothing in all creation will ever be able to separate us from the love of God that is revealed in Christ Jesus our Lord" (Romans 8:38-39).

TODAY'S THOUGHT Christ died on the cross to pay the penalty for your alienation from God. When you came to God and repented of your rebellion to Him and accepted His gift of eternal life, you became His child. You were what Jesus called, *born again*! This started you on a brand-new life as a Christian, with a fresh relationship with God Almighty. As God's child, the Bible is clear on the fact that you are loved by Him. This is the cornerstone of our Christian experience. Paul states it very clearly. He was emphatic that nothing can ever separate you from God's love. In his book *Abba's Child*, Brennan Manning writes, "God created us for union with Himself: This is the original purpose of our lives. And God is defined as love (I John 4:16). Living in the awareness that we are beloved is the axis around which the Christian life revolves. Being the beloved is our identity, the core of our existence. It is not merely a lofty thought, an inspiring idea, or one name among many. It is the name by which God knows us and the way He relates to us." If you believe nothing else today, believe this: God loves you! If you experience nothing else today, experience this: God loves you! If you let nothing else today bring you joy deep into your soul, get joy from this: God loves you! Nothing, nothing, nothing will ever be able to separate you from the love that God has for you!

TODAY'S PRAYER Father, I thank You for Your love. And I thank You that You promised that nothing will ever separate me from Your love. I accept Your love today and pray that I would live from a heart of gratitude and joy that I am Your beloved. Amen.

March 12
Delight and Desire

TODAY'S VERSE "May he grant your heart's desires and make all your plans succeed" (Psalm 20:4).

"Delight yourself in the LORD and he will give you the desires of your heart" (Psalm 37:4).

TODAY'S THOUGHT God cares about our plans and desires. He cares about our dreams and aspirations. David knew this and prayed that God would grant our heart's desires and make all our plans succeed. But he also knew that we are fickle, immature and many times unspiritual. Can you imagine God granting every selfish and immature desire we have had? Can you imagine, if God allowed our envy, jealousy, and lustful desires to come true? What about vengeance; isn't that a desire of the heart? That is why in Psalm 37:4, we read the "rest of the story." David says that our first goal should be to delight ourselves in the Lord, then we will get the desires of our hearts. I heard one preacher say it this way: "Love God, and do as you please." What he was saying was, if we truly love God, then our desires will line up with His. So today, start to delight in God. Really delight in Him. Love Him, get to know Him, worship Him. Start to delight in what He thinks and desires for your life. If you do, you will align your desires with His. When this happens, you can pray with David, "May He grant my heart's desires and make all my plans succeed."

TODAY'S PRAYER Lord, help me delight in You today. Might You be my source of joy, passion, and purpose. Help my plans and desires line up with Your goals for my life. I commit my life to You and trust You to guide me day by day. In Jesus' name. Amen.

A Relationship with God

TODAY'S VERSE "Then King David went in and sat before the LORD and prayed, 'Who am I, O LORD God, and what is my family, that you have brought me this far?'" (I Chronicles 17:16).

TODAY'S THOUGHT There is more to prayer than simply asking God for something. God desires a relationship with us. It is said of David that he was a man "after God's own heart." He had a relationship with God unlike any other. Today's verse is proof. "Then King David went in and sat before the Lord." Think about it. This was Almighty Jehovah. Only the priests were allowed into the Holy Place before the Lord. They were to purify themselves, make a sacrifice, and go in and stand in reverence before the Lord of Hosts. Here is David. Does he purify himself? No, he had pure motives. Did he bring a sacrifice? No, he had a humble and contrite heart. Did he stand before the Lord? No, notice he, "went in and sat before the Lord!" How great is that? This is what Christ came for. His death was the payment for our sins, so we could come before God and pray. But notice how David prayed. Did he ask for something? No, he started to relate to God. He shared his heart. He asked God a question. What a model for us to follow. You can come to God today and sit before Him. You can simply tell Him what is on your heart. Tell Him how you feel. Ask Him questions. Praise Him for His goodness in your life. Spend time with Him, letting Him penetrate your heart with His love. Then love Him back. Today, work on your relationship with God. When you do, praying will take on a whole new meaning.

TODAY'S PRAYER Father, help me to sense Your presence. Help me see You, hear You, feel You. More than anything else in the world, I want a relationship with You that is real and vibrant. Lord, let it start right now. I pray this in the name of Jesus Christ. Amen.

Right on the Inside

TODAY'S VERSE "May the words of my mouth and the meditation of my heart be pleasing to you, O LORD, my rock and my redeemer" (Psalm 19:14).

TODAY'S THOUGHT It is so easy to fall into a habit of deceit. It is easy to say what people want to hear. We use half-truths, never saying what is really on our mind. It is easy to "promise" with all sincerity and yet never take the steps necessary to follow-through. We cover one missed deadline with another. We say, "Tomorrow," but tomorrow never comes. I find this happens the most when I am trying to be a people-pleaser and the words coming out of my mouth don't match the thoughts going on in my heart. If we are going to be honest with others; if we are going to do what we say; if we are going to stop covering one lie with another, then we must change the way we think. We will have to ask God to take over our mind, emotions, and will. He will have to be the master of all we think and do. The great news is we can start today. Today we can come to God and start to meditate on what He wants us to do. We can bring Him all our emotions and thoughts. We can be honest with Him and then let Him be honest with us. As we do, He will begin to affect our behavior. Today, ask God to invade your mind and guide your meditation. Pray with David, "May the words of my mouth and the meditation of my heart be pleasing to you, O LORD, my rock and my redeemer."

TODAY'S PRAYER Father, You know what goes on in my mind. You know my meditations, thoughts, and emotions. You know how far off base I can get. You know how I can become so unspiritual in my thought life. Help me, Lord! Correct my thinking. Help me Lord be the person You want on the inside. I pray today that the words of my mouth and the meditation of my heart will be pleasing to You. Amen.

March 15

What Do You Treasure?

TODAY'S VERSE "Some nations boast of their chariots and horses, but we boast in the name of the LORD our God" (Psalm 20:7).

"But store up for yourselves treasures in heaven, where moth and rust do not destroy, and where thieves do not break in and steal. For where your treasure is, there your heart will be also" (Matthew 6:20-21).

TODAY'S THOUGHT It is easy to get our priorities mixed up. It seems that people are judged by the money they earn and the things they acquire. Even criminals are honored if they have the "rich and famous" lifestyle. Fame and fortune are the goals that we aspire to. The issue isn't whether "riches" are good or bad. The issue is that there is something more important than our materialism. There is a spiritual reality that we need to be concerned about. Jesus told us to store "spiritual" treasures in heaven. David said not to boast of our earthy positions and pleasures but to "boast in the Lord." Why is this important? Because what we treasure is a reflection of what we are inside. If we treasure God, it is because He has the affection of our heart. If we boast in the Lord, it is because we are pleased with our relationship with Him. Do we want to have a deeper, more satisfying relationship with God? Seek Him like we would gold. Go after Him like a lost treasure. Make Him the most valuable part of our lives, and our hearts will follow.

TODAY'S PRAYER Father, I want to treasure You more than gold. I want to love You more than my possessions. Help me to know You. Help me to experience Your love. Help me love You more and more until I understand the valuable treasure Your love really is. Amen.

How Deep Is His Love?

TODAY'S VERSE "And may you have the power to understand, as all God's people should, how wide, how long, how high, and how deep his love is. May you experience the love of Christ, though it is too great to understand fully" (Ephesians 3:18-19).

TODAY'S THOUGHT Unconditional love. What a thought; better yet, when we realize it, what a reality! God loves us with no strings attached. But do we really believe that? Brennan Manning, in his book *Abba's Child*, challenges whether we do or not. He writes, "It is one thing to feel loved by God when our life is together, and all our support systems are in place. But what happens when life falls through the cracks? What happens when we sin and fail, when our dreams shatter, when our investments crash, when we are regarded with suspicion? What happens when we come face-to-face with the human condition?" If we are honest with ourselves, we would probably begin to doubt whether God could love us. Why is that? Could it be that we want something to do with our own salvation? Is it the cross plus our worthiness? Is it His death plus all the good things we have done? We need to pray what Paul prayed, that we would have the power to understand how much He really loves us. Manning wrote it this way: "Whether you understand it or not, God loves you, is present in you, lives in you, dwells in you, calls you, saves you and offers you an understanding and compassion which are like nothing you have ever found in a book or heard in a sermon." May you really begin to believe and experience this reality.

TODAY'S PRAYER Father, thank you for the fact that you love me unconditionally. Please give me the power to fully understand how deep Your love really is and the fact that it is a gift, not something I have to earn. Thank you for such an amazing truth. In Jesus' name. Amen.

Living with Purpose

TODAY'S VERSE "I am your brother Joseph, the one you sold into Egypt! And now, do not be distressed and do not be angry with yourselves for selling me here, because it was to save lives that God sent me ahead of you. But God sent me ahead of you to preserve for you a remnant on earth and to save your lives by a great deliverance. So then, it was not you who sent me here, but God" (Genesis 45:4-8).

TODAY'S THOUGHT Joseph had a dream, in which his family was bowing down to him. His family felt it was a vision of grandeur and were appalled at his seeming arrogance. Because of the dream and the way his father favored him, his brothers sold him to slave traders. For years, Joseph worked as a slave and even went to prison. But no matter what, everywhere he went, he believed God had a purpose for him. This deep belief carried him through each day. He was a faithful worker and eventually, God led Joseph to become a great leader in Egypt. Warned of a famine, he stored up grain so when others were starving, Egypt was able to survive. Hearing that there was grain in Egypt, his brothers went to buy some. It was here that they were reunited with Joseph. When Joseph revealed himself, they were horrified. Joseph shared with them the key to his success, to his survival and to his extraordinary life. He believed that God was in charge and had a purpose for him. He said, "I am your brother Joseph, the one you sold into Egypt! And now, do not be distressed and do not be angry with yourselves for selling me here, because it was to save lives that God sent me ahead of you." Victor Frankl, in his book *Man's Search for Meaning,* shared about the ability of some people to survive the concentration camps of Nazi Germany when others did not. He concluded that those that seemed to have a purpose, a calling, a dream about their life had the will to live that helped them survive such severe atrocities. What about you? Come to God. He knows you. He loves you. He has a purpose for your life. Live for Him today.

TODAY'S PRAYER Father, I thank You that You have a divine purpose in my life. Help me trust You and live for you today. Amen.

Amazing Grace

TODAY'S VERSE "Each time he said, 'My grace is all you need. My power works best in weakness.' So now I am glad to boast about my weaknesses so that the power of Christ can work through me" (2 Corinthians 12:9).

TODAY'S THOUGHT There are so many variables in life. It is good to have dreams, to make plans and to choose paths; however, you and I know that things don't always go the way we plan. Troubles happen. So, what do we do when things seem to get all messed up? We've asked for wisdom, for guidance, but now it calls for something more. It calls for grace. According to Merriam-Webster, grace means "unmerited divine assistance." This was given to us when we asked Him to forgive us. It was totally unmerited. There was nothing we could do to deserve it. So, in today's verse, Paul is saying that God wants us to live life in the same way we received His forgiveness; that is, to live by relying on His unmerited divine assistance. Paul did. When nothing was going right, Paul kept asking God to move in certain directions. But God said, "No, you're going to have to trust me; but don't worry, my grace is going to get you through." This is what hope is about. This is what faith is based on. This is the reality of our walk with Christ, no matter what we go through, God promises that His grace is all we need! Today, admit to God your need for His grace in your life. Humble yourself before Him and acknowledge His desire to see you through this day.

TODAY'S PRAYER Father, I need You in my life today. I need Your divine assistance. I need Your amazing grace. I know that I do not deserve it. You have lavishly poured Your love into my life and I praise You. Thank You for all that You have done for me. Thank You that today, Your grace is all I need to get me through. In Jesus' name. Amen.

Never Forsaken

TODAY'S VERSE "Be strong and courageous. Do not be afraid or terrified because of them, for the LORD your God goes with you; he will never leave you nor forsake you" (Deuteronomy 31:6).

"Be content with what you have, because God has said, 'Never will I leave you; never will I forsake you'" (Hebrews 13:5).

TODAY'S THOUGHT One of the first things they teach you in marriage communication is to stay away from using emotionally fatalistic words like "never" or "always," as in, "You never help around here!" or "You always waste money." It's rare that human behavior is *always* or *never*. But what about God? The Bible makes it clear that His ways are not our ways. In Romans 3:4 it says, "Even if everyone else is a liar, God is true!" Now consider today's verse in light of the fact that God does not lie. Moses tells us to be strong and courageous and not afraid. The author of Hebrews insisted that we are to be content with what we have. Why all the optimism? Why the courage? Because God has said, "Never will I leave you; never will I forsake you." God, Himself has said to you and me, "Never." Never. NEVER! Let it sink in—He will never leave you or forsake you! Today, right now, let this fact change your day. Let it reshape your emotions. Let it precede all your decisions. He will never leave you or forsake you.

TODAY'S PRAYER Father, I wander through most days with so much doubt. Perhaps apathy is a better word. I live as if You half exist. I haven't taken most of Your promises seriously. I have not been content. Most the time, I am not strong or courageous. Forgive me for this. Instead, help me today really grasp what it means that You will never leave me or forsake me. In Jesus' name. Amen.

Light Your Corner of the World

TODAY'S VERSE "You are the light of the world. A city on a hill cannot be hidden" (Matthew 5:14).

TODAY'S THOUGHT I love synergy. That is the result of different entities working together to create a bigger response than they could by themselves. Have you ever been to a candlelight sing, when at the end of the service one candle is lit and one by one each candle in the auditorium sends forth its illumination? What a beautiful sight. How amazing that one little candle can be part of such brightness. This is the effect Jesus had in mind when He said that we were the "light of the world." He was leaving this world, and with the power of the Holy Spirit in each of our lives, we would each shine our own light. Together we would become the light of the world. In his book *Hearing God,* Dallas Willard writes, "Those who receive the grace of God's saving companionship in His word are by that very fact also fitted to show humankind how to live. Collectively the 'called out' people of God, the church is empowered to stand up for wandering humanity to see. When faced with starvation, crime, economic disasters, and difficulties, disease, loneliness, alienation and war, the church should be, because it alone could be, the certified authority on how to live to which the world looks for answers." We are called to be the light where we are. Today, come to Him, bring Him your candle; let Him light it for you and then light up your corner of the world. I'll light mine. If everyone reading this devotional would let Christ light their light, someone is bound to be affected. There are people all around us dying to come out of the darkness.

TODAY'S PRAYER Lord, speak to me, ignite my heart and then help me shine that light today. Help me share the light that I have with those hurting in utter darkness, so they too can live in the light of Your love and glory. Amen.

He Is Right Beside You

TODAY'S VERSE "I know the Lord is always with me. I will not be shaken, for he is right beside me" (Psalm 16:8).

TODAY'S THOUGHT As a child I was afraid of going down to the basement by myself. It was dark and creepy. Yet that is where my mom stored the canned vegetables. And every day after school, my mother would ask me to go and get a can and bring it upstairs. Once, after my brother turned off all the lights on me, I was really frightened. My father, who arrived home as I was expressing my panic and fear, asked what the trouble was. I explained to him my concern about the basement. He took me downstairs and had mom turn out the lights. I grabbed his hand, and after a few moments, I relaxed and realized he was holding mine. He walked with me through the basement, explaining to me that there was nothing to worry about. What a difference his presence made. What a relief to know that this giant of a man was beside me and that I had nothing to fear. David knew about darkness. He was a lonely shepherd, out many nights taking care of the sheep. But he knew the secret to overcoming the fear of the dark. He wrote, "I know the Lord is always with me. I will not be shaken, for he is right beside me." Today you can have that same assurance. Acknowledge His presence. Spend time with Him and allow Him to guide you throughout this day. He truly is right beside you.

TODAY'S PRAYER Father, I thank You that You are with me. Help me today to be keenly aware of Your presence. Guide me, direct me and make me conscious that you are always at my side. Amen.

Give God the Glory

TODAY'S VERSE "When you have eaten and are satisfied, praise the LORD your God for the good land he has given you. Be careful that you do not forget the LORD your God. Otherwise, when you eat and are satisfied, when you build fine houses and settle down, and when your herds and flocks grow large and your silver and gold increase and all you have is multiplied, then your heart will become proud and you will forget the LORD your God" (Deuteronomy 8:10-14).

TODAY'S THOUGHT God warns us to be careful, very careful, to not forget about Him when things go well. How could that happen, you ask? Moses tells us that when we feel satisfied and have good things, we can become proud. We may start to believe that it's our ability, skills, intelligence and savvy that has produced all that we have. We fail to give God glory, and soon our heart grows cold toward spiritual things. There is hope for the wounded heart to be healed, but what hope is there for the callous, dried-up heart? The only hope is to repent! Give God back His glory which you have stolen. Fall down before Him and praise Him for all that you have. Ask Him to renew your heart and open your eyes to His goodness. Give all that you have back to Him for His use. Make Him the Lord of your income and possessions. When you do, you will find that materialism will lose its hold on your heart and your soul will be free and alive with the love of God.

TODAY'S PRAYER Father, I rob You of Your glory when I think I've created my own income, that I'm the master of my own possessions and the sole reason for my own success. Forgive me when I forget that You are the Giver of all good things. I give you back all that I have. Be Lord of everything I am and own. Help me to live my life for You and to give You praise and glory for every blessing You give me. Amen.

Jealousy and Selfish Ambition

TODAY'S VERSE "If you are bitterly jealous and there is selfish ambition in your heart, don't cover up the truth with boasting and lying. For jealousy and selfishness are not God's kind of wisdom. Such things are earthly, unspiritual, and demonic. For wherever there is jealousy and selfish ambition, there you will find disorder and evil of every kind" (James 3:14-16).

TODAY'S THOUGHT There is a plague in our world. At its worst, it is the root of wars, poverty, hatred, and injustice. In our everyday life, it is what causes arguments, hurt feelings, disappointment, and ungodly behavior. James calls this plague "jealousy and selfish ambition." He goes further to call it, "unspiritual and demonic behavior" and assures us that wherever jealousy and selfish ambition exist, there is disorder and evil of every kind. Now, does this mean that it's wrong to have ambition? Is it wrong to desire goals? Is it wrong to have nice things? The answer to all three questions is, "No!" Where wrong comes in is when we live our lives independently of God. It's when we make our goals without considering the way He desires us to live that we are susceptible to major discontent. We listen to the world and start to desire fame and fortune. We create goals that we think will lead us to the place we need to be, and nothing had better get in our way! The cure for jealousy and selfish ambition is to develop a relationship with Christ. Talk to Him. Tell Him about your desires and dreams. Ask Him to show you how you should live. Ask Him to help you create goals that will honor Him. When you do, you can also leave the results to Him. You are already accepted by Him and loved unconditionally. When you really start to believe that, there will be no room in your heart for cheap imitations. There will be no reason for jealousy or selfish ambition.

TODAY'S PRAYER Father, forgive me for taking my eyes off you and setting up my own kingdom. I know that jealousy and selfish ambition have been prevalent in my life. I renounce these attitudes and ask that you would show me your will for my life. Help me be content and live a life that is pleasing to You. Amen.

Change Your Clothes

TODAY'S VERSE "Therefore, as God's chosen people, holy and dearly loved, clothe yourselves with compassion, kindness, humility, gentleness, and patience. Bear with each other and forgive whatever grievances you may have against one another. Forgive as the Lord forgave you. And over all these virtues put on love, which binds them all together in perfect unity" (Colossians 3:12-14).

TODAY'S THOUGHT I like to lay out my clothes the night before I have to get up and go to work. It is one less thing I need to think about when I get up. It allows me to be more objective and intentional, instead of rushing to decide what to wear. Paul shares that intentionally is also important in wearing the wardrobe that God has for us to wear. Paul uses the analogy of clothing because our behavior is something that people see. Just like a bad suit, we look bad in negative behavior. Instead, Paul admonishes us to clothe ourselves in love. He then says to accessorize love with compassion, kindness, humility, gentleness, patience, and forgiveness. What an ensemble. Can you imagine if we were intentional in putting on this behavior every day? What a difference it would make in our lives and the lives of those around us. Today, decide what you want to wear. It is your choice. God, through the power of the Holy Spirit, has custom-made an outfit just for you. The clothes fit perfectly and bring out your true self. Go ahead, find a quiet changing room, and go change. Clothe yourself today with love, compassion, kindness, humility, gentleness, patience and forgiveness.

TODAY'S PRAYER Father, I know I need to wear something different in my heart. I haven't been wearing the clothes You gave to me when I became a Christian. Help me today to change the clothes of my heart and put on love, compassion, kindness, humility, gentleness, patience and forgiveness. Amen.

First Love

TODAY'S VERSE "So then, just as you received Christ Jesus as Lord, continue to live in him, rooted and built up in him, strengthened in the faith as you were taught, and overflowing with thankfulness" (Colossians 2:6-7).

"I know your deeds, your hard work, and your perseverance…yet I hold this against you: You have forsaken your first love. Remember the height from which you have fallen! Repent and do the things you did at first" (Revelation 2:2, 4-5).

TODAY'S THOUGHT Remember when you first came to Christ? You were aware of your need. You were humbled by His love, appreciative of His sacrifice for you. You wanted to help everyone else know Him. What happened? How did we allow our intimate relationship with Christ become a ritual? When did we trade our freedom? When did we forsake our joy? Have we traded our relationship with Christ for a religion? Have we given up grace for rules and regulations? Have we traded the mission of the church for membership in a country club? Paul encouraged the church in Colossians to continue to live in Christ just like they did the first day they tasted of salvation. The first day the Spirit of God was born in their heart, the first time the tears from God's forgiveness stained their cheeks. John wrote to the church in Ephesus that even though they worked hard and persevered, they had lost their first love. He admonished them to repent and do the things that they did at first. Oh, that we would never forget the wonder that God loves us … or extinguish the joy of knowing that He has chosen us to be His children. Today, examine your heart. Do you feel far from God? Who moved? Go back to the place you met Christ. Rededicate your heart to Him. Just as you received Christ Jesus as Lord, continue to live in Him.

TODAY'S PRAYER Father, take me back to the time I first knew You. Renew the joy in my soul. Reignite the fire that burned in my heart. Help me to remember and to live this day in the fresh awareness of Your love and forgiveness. Amen.

Slow to Speak

TODAY'S VERSE "Who may worship in your sanctuary, Lord? Who may enter your presence on your holy hill? Those who lead blameless lives and do what is right, speaking the truth from sincere hearts. Those who refuse to gossip or harm their neighbors or speak evil of their friends" (Psalm 15:1-3).

"If you claim to be religious but don't control your tongue, you are fooling yourself, and your religion is worthless" (James 1:26).

TODAY'S THOUGHT The Lord puts a premium on what we say. James warns us, "The tongue also is a fire, a world of evil among the parts of the body. It corrupts the whole person, sets the whole course of his life on fire, and is itself set on fire by hell. All kinds of animals, birds, reptiles, and creatures of the sea are being tamed and have been tamed by man, but no man can tame the tongue. It is a restless evil, full of deadly poison." David makes a list of the qualities of a holy life and includes speaking the truth, refusing gossip, and not speaking evil of others. It is so easy to let what we say get out of hand. We say Jesus is the "Lord of our life." Jesus would ask, "Am I the Lord of your tongue?" Today, give God control of your words. Make a conscious effort to weigh what you say to honor Him. James said it best when he wrote, "Be quick to listen and slow to speak."

TODAY'S PRAYER Lord, I give You control of my tongue. Please help me guard my mouth today. Help me be quick to listen to others and slow to speak. Help me weigh carefully everything I say, that I may be a testimony of Your love and grace. In Jesus' name. Amen.

March 27
Today, You Can Rejoice

TODAY'S VERSE "This is the day the LORD has made; let us rejoice and be glad in it" (Psalm 118:24).

TODAY'S THOUGHT *Happiness is a Choice,* the title of a book that helped change my life. For me, the "aha" came when I realized that my worry, fear, and sadness was a habit. I knew that a habit could be broken and a new habit could take its place. So, it was very exciting to consider that happiness could be a habit, too. To help me start the day with the habit of *happiness*, I would get up and quote today's verse out loud, "This is the day the Lord has made; let us rejoice and be glad in it." That simple habit would allow me to focus and begin a string of thoughts that would lead to a more joyful outlook on life. It would allow me to energize my faith before negative and pessimistic thinking could take root in my morning. How about you? Is happiness the choice that you have made today? If not, it is not too late. Happiness, joy, peace, and faith can be yours today. God has provided it, you need to choose it. This is the day the Lord has made; go ahead, rejoice and be glad in it.

TODAY'S PRAYER Father, today I choose happiness, joy, and faith. Thank You that this is a day that You have made; please help me to rejoice today and be glad in it. Amen.

Love the Lord

TODAY'S VERSE "I love you, LORD; you are my strength. The LORD is my rock, my fortress, and my savior; my God is my rock, in whom I find protection. He is my shield, the power that saves me, and my place of safety" (Psalm 18:1-2).

TODAY'S THOUGHT As King of Israel, David knew conflict. He knew war. He knew what it was like to be outnumbered, to face armies that had superior weapons and others that had giants. David was no stranger to danger. But David also knew God. He trusted in God and depended on Him for his very survival. In this Psalm, David says that God is his strength, rock, fortress, savior, protection, shield, power that saves and place of safety. But even more than knowing God, David loved God. Look how he starts this meditation. "I love you, Lord." When is the last time you quieted your heart before God, rested in His arms and let Him know that you love Him? Now, you may be facing trials, conflicts, and horrific situations. If so, today you can cry out to God and He will indeed be your strength, rock, fortress, savior, protection, shield, power that saves and place of safety. But in the midst of all that is going on in your life, be sure to find time to do what David did. Tell God you love Him.

TODAY'S PRAYER Dear Father, I love You. I just want to stop everything now and say it again, "I love You, Lord." I commit my life to You today and thank You that You are indeed my strength, rock, fortress, savior, protection, shield, power that saves and place of safety. In Jesus' name. Amen.

Strength in Our Inner Being

TODAY'S VERSE "I pray that out of his glorious riches he may strengthen you with power through his Spirit in your inner being" (Ephesians 3:16).

TODAY'S THOUGHT We are complicated creatures. We think and communicate on many different levels. Our thinking is a combination of many drives, emotions, assumptions, beliefs, instincts, and memories, creating a labyrinth of inner voices. We can be talking to someone and at the same time have an inner dialog going on guiding our conversation. We are so much more than what comes out of our mouth. This is our inner being. Paul knew about this. He was a man who experienced the battles that war for who we are on the inside. This is why he prayed that God would strengthen us. He knew if you and I were to have any real spiritual life with God, we would need God's strength in the person of the Spirit to reside in us and to help us. Paul prayed that God would strengthen us with power through His Spirit in our inner being. Imagine, the God who created the divine order of the universe wants to do the same in our inner being. He wants to produce love, joy, peace, patience, kindness, goodness, faithfulness, gentleness, and self-control in our inner being so what goes on the inside of our mind is congruent to what goes on in our life. Today, make God the Lord of your inner being. Give Him all the inner turmoil, confusion, struggles, strife, fears, and pain and ask Him to take control and strengthen you with His power through His Holy Spirit.

TODAY'S PRAYER Lord, You know my inner being. You understand me better than I do. I need Your strength in my inner being to help me live the way You want me to. I pray that today, through Your power, You would produce Your spiritual fruit of love, joy, peace, patience, kindness, goodness, faithfulness, gentleness, and self-control in my inner being. In Jesus' name. Amen.

March 30
Get Comfort, Give Comfort

TODAY'S VERSE "Praise be to the God and Father of our Lord Jesus Christ, the Father of compassion and the God of all comfort, who comforts us in all our troubles, so that we can comfort those in any trouble with the comfort we ourselves have received from God" (II Corinthians 1:3-4).

TODAY'S THOUGHT It's important to not fall into the trap of thinking that we have to be perfect because when we feel pressured to be perfect, we can't admit our problems. When problems are not presented to God and each other, we can't be comforted. When we cry out to God in private desperation and see relief, we can't share our testimony because we'd have to admit to the problem in the first place. This also means that we can't comfort others! In his book *Abba's Child*, Brennan Manning shares the insight that Mike Yaconelli, author, and co-founder of Youth Specialties, had after he went on a spiritual retreat. Mike writes, "Finally, I accepted my brokenness. I never came to terms with that. I knew I was a sinner. I knew that I continually disappointed God, but I could never accept that part of me. It was a part of me that embarrassed me. I continually felt the need to apologize, to run from my weaknesses, to deny who I was and concentrate on what I should be. I was broken, yes, but I was continually trying never to be broken again—or at least to get to the place where I was very seldom broken. It became clear to me that I had totally misunderstood the Christian faith. I came to see that it was in my brokenness, in my powerlessness, in my weakness that Jesus was made strong. It was in the embracing of my brokenness that I could identify with other's brokenness." Might we learn the same lesson that Mike learned. Might we cry out to God and be comforted, and then invite others to experience the same kind of comfort we received. This is the true Christian experience.

TODAY'S PRAYER Lord, I admit that I have troubles. I bring them to You for comfort. Help me in return not to have false shame, but rather embrace my humanness and Your grace, and comfort others in the way You comfort me. Amen.

Unimaginable Reality

TODAY'S VERSE "Now to him who is able to do immeasurably more than all we ask or imagine, according to his power that is at work within us, to him be glory in the church and in Christ Jesus throughout all generations, forever and ever!" (Ephesians 3:20-21).

TODAY'S THOUGHT I love my imagination. At night, I would sit and make up stories for my boys. We would go away to faraway places, do things we could never do in this life, be with characters from another world. Every night was an adventure. But at the end of the day, it was just imagination. There was no reality. But what if? I have always been a dreamer. I see what others would consider impossibilities and start to wonder what it would be like if it came to pass? But all my dreams, visions and imaginations pale in comparison to what God has in store for you and me. In today's passage, Paul is giving glory to God. But not the God we normally think of. No, he is giving glory to a God "who is able to do immeasurably more than all we ask or imagine." What? More than I can imagine? No. Immeasurably more than I can imagine! I don't know where to begin. What could Paul be thinking of? I can't put my arms around it, but I know this. If you and I would start to believe that God *could*, and more importantly *wants* to, do a fraction of what we could imagine, let alone what we can't imagine, it would change our lives. Why not start today? Ask God for something unimaginable to pray for. Ask Him to give you a dream, a vision, and an unimaginable prayer for your life. He will fulfill it according to His power that is at work within you!

TODAY'S PRAYER Father, I don't know where to begin. You said You can do more than I can imagine according to Your power that is within me. So, Father, I ask You to show me what to pray. What unimaginable prayer do You want me to believe You for? Speak to my heart I pray. In the precious name of Jesus. Amen.

April 1
Love God

TODAY'S VERSE "After breakfast, Jesus asked Simon Peter, 'Simon son of John, do you love me more than these?'" (John 21:15).

"When he finally came to his senses, he said to himself, 'At home, even the hired servants have food enough to spare, and here I am dying of hunger! I will go home to my father and say, "Father, I have sinned against both heaven and you, and I am no longer worthy of being called your son. Please take me on as a hired servant'" (Luke 15:17-19).

TODAY'S THOUGHT It is so easy to love *what we can get* from God more than *God*. It is easier to love God when things are going according to our preconceived idea of a happy life than it is when things go crazy. Peter had denied Jesus and Jesus had died, so Peter did what he knew best—he went back to fishing. Jesus rose from the dead and met with the disciples and prepared them for their ministry. He came to Peter and asked him, "Do you love me?" Three times Jesus had to ask Peter in order to break down his facade and get him to commit. In his book *The Papa Prayer*, Larry Crabb points out that in the story of the Prodigal Son, the son decided to return home not because of his love for his father but because he wanted what his father could provide. The truth is, he knew that the hired servants lived better than he was living, and he came home to be provided for. He never once told the father that he loved him. What about us? Do we love God, or do we really love what He provides? As long as things are great, or at least status quo, God is deserving of our love. But what happens when things turn sour or there's conflict in our life? We're the first to doubt Him. Today, love God. Just love Him. Tell Him so. Love Him because He is! Love Him, not to get something, but just because you want to. This way you can say, "Yes" when He asks you, "Do you love me more than these?"

TODAY'S PRAYER Father, today, I just want to love You. I want to love You for who you are. Help me to examine my heart and repent of a consumer mentality that comes to You for what I can get. Forgive me for attaching strings to my love. Holy Spirit, guide me into a deeper love for the Triune God today. Amen.

April 2

The Father Prayer

TODAY'S VERSE "One day Jesus was praying in a certain place. When he finished, one of his disciples said to him, 'Lord, teach us to pray, just as John taught his disciples.' He said to them, 'When you pray, say: Father, hallowed be your name, your kingdom come'" (Luke 11:1-2).

TODAY'S THOUGHT There is much to learn about praying. It seems so easy when we hear, "Just talk to God." Then why don't we do it? Instead, we act as if we're calling in a take-out order at a restaurant. Nothing personal—just putting in our request. Or we leave messages on the heavenly answering machine because we don't expect God to "pick up." Where is the relationship? The disciples saw Jesus pray and they knew the impact it had on His ministry. They saw the relationship between Jesus and His Father. Can you imagine witnessing that? One of His disciples asked Jesus to show him how to pray. And what was the first thing Jesus modeled? He said, "Father." For Jesus, prayer was about His relationship with His Father. Larry Crabb, in his book *The Papa Prayer,* writes, "The chief purpose of prayer is to get to know God, to deepen our relationship with Him, to nourish the life of God He's already placed within us, and to do it all to satisfy His desire for a relationship with us." God wants a relationship with you! He created you for fellowship. Prayer is more than just a shopping list; more than simple confession and more than a one-way conversation. It's dialog; a relationship. It's you getting to know God and fellowshipping *with* Him, not *at* Him. Today, picture God *with* you while you pray. Talk to Him, share your thoughts and ask Him to share His thoughts with you. Be still, listen, share and fellowship *with* Him. As you do, He'll do with you what He did with the disciples. He will teach you to pray!

TODAY'S PRAYER Father, I come to You now and ask You to teach me to pray! I want a real relationship with You. I want to know You and fellowship with You. I want to know Your thoughts, Your desires, Your direction for my life. Help me today relate to You throughout the day so prayer becomes second nature to me. Thank You for Your love for me. I love You, Father. In Jesus name. Amen.

Remain in Him

TODAY'S VERSE "But if you remain in me and my words remain in you, you may ask for anything you want, and it will be granted! When you produce much fruit, you are my true disciples. This brings great glory to my Father" (John 15:7-8).

"But the Holy Spirit produces this kind of fruit in our lives: love, joy, peace, patience, kindness, goodness, faithfulness, gentleness, and self-control" (Galatians 5:22, 23).

TODAY'S THOUGHT How do we bring glory to God in our life? Jesus was clear. He said that we need to remain in Him and produce the kind of fruit that His disciple would. Paul later explains that the fruit that the Holy Spirit produces in our life is love, joy, peace, patience, kindness, goodness, faithfulness, gentleness, and self-control. So how do we remain in Jesus? Larry Crabb, in his book *Papa Prayer,* explains it this way: "To remain in Him means to live for the single purpose that ruled His life, with the same passion that kept Him on track. He loved His Father, He loved spending time with His Father in prayer, and He wanted nothing more than to let everyone see how wonderful His Father was, even if it cost Him His life. And that life, His life, is now in us. His passion and purpose are in our hearts." So, the secret to bringing glory to God is to create a strong relationship with God the Father. Everything else flows from that. Jesus only did what His Father told Him to do. Do we spend enough time with the Father to know what He wants? As we relate to Him in meditation and prayer, as we sit in His presence and let Him guide our life, we will see the fruit of love, joy, peace, patience, kindness, goodness, faithfulness, gentleness, and self-control more and more present in our life. This brings glory to God.

TODAY'S PRAYER Father, help me relate to You in a more personal way. I need Your help to do this. Help me draw near to You and listen. Help me desire You above all things. Teach me, guide me, reveal Yourself to me so that I may bear Your fruit in my life and that I may bring glory to You. Amen.

Be Still

TODAY'S VERSE "Be still, and know that I am God" (Psalm 46:10).

TODAY'S THOUGHT Have you ever noticed how we hate silence? I don't mean the momentary silence after you walk inside from loud street noise. I mean the "quiet yourself down and think" kind of silence. It is so hard to shut off the inward noise. We are obsessed with busyness. It's as if we are afraid to face who we really are and where we are in our journey. But we must face our loneliness. Leanne Payne makes this point in her book, *Listening Prayer*. She writes, "Our pastoral task is to help all needy individuals face their inner loneliness, and there begin to hear God and their own true self. Everyone one of us—not just those who are the most visibly wounded by the darkness in humanity and the world—has to face the inner loneliness and separation from God. We all need to begin the rigorous but sternly magnificent work of converting the 'desert of loneliness' within into the spaciously beautiful 'garden of solitude' where the true self comes forward and flourishes. This is the self-capable of friendship and Christian fellowship." As we face our life, we need to stop filling in the gaps with empty busyness. Instead, we need to consider who we are and all that God is. This will lead us on a beautiful journey of the soul. Why not start today? Throughout this day, stop and listen to your inner self, bring it to God and dialog with Him. May you begin to hear God and embrace your true self in Him.

TODAY'S PRAYER Lord, so many times during the day You cry out my name, but I am too busy *keeping busy* that I do not hear You. How many times, Lord, You have wanted me to turn to You in my loneliness, but I fill the void with noise. Lord, I am sorry. I want to hear You, I want to know You. Help me start today to convert my desert of loneliness into a garden of solitude. Amen.

Our True Role

TODAY'S VERSE "Is not this the kind of fasting I have chosen: to loose the chains of injustice and untie the cords of the yoke, to set the oppressed free and break every yoke? Is it not to share your food with the hungry and to provide the poor wanderer with shelter—when you see the naked, to clothe him" (Isaiah 58:6-7).

TODAY'S THOUGHT The children of Israel had forgotten that God had them here on this earth to be His representatives, to show people the way to God. They were to love people and share the importance of knowing Jehovah. Instead, that they thought that they somehow deserved the title of *Children of God*. They began to act as though they were gods unto themselves. When God favors us with a certain status or vocation, we can easily fall into the trap of thinking that we achieved it on our own merits. This leads to pride and arrogance and is exactly what God pointed out to the Israelites. They were fasting, and God was not listening to their pomp and circumstance. Instead, God wanted equality, justice, and love among all people. The prophet Isaiah asked the people, "What is it that God has required of each of us?" He answered with a sobering indictment, "Is not this the kind of fasting I have chosen: loose the chains of injustice and untie the cords of the yoke, to set the oppressed free and break every yoke? Is it not to share your food with the hungry and to provide the poor wanderer with shelter—when you see the naked, to clothe him." Today, let's do all we can to help those in need.

TODAY'S PRAYER Father, You take the plight of the poor seriously. You hate injustice and love mercy. Help me to love others the way You do. Help me live my life for the well-being of others in need. Show me how I can make a difference in the lives of others. Amen.

Calm the Inner Sea

TODAY'S VERSE "He got up, rebuked the wind and said to the waves, 'Quiet! Be still!' Then the wind died down and it was completely calm. He said to his disciples, 'Why are you so afraid? Do you still have no faith?' They were terrified and asked each other, 'Who is this? Even the wind and the waves obey him!'" (Mark 4:39-41).

TODAY'S THOUGHT I have never been on a stormy sea and can only imagine how fierce this storm must have been. Seasoned fishermen were exceedingly afraid. Now, it didn't help that they were going across the lake. The deep part of the lake in the center regions was referred to as the *abyss*. Many frightening fishermen stories were based on journeys into the abyss. Add to that the fact that they left in the evening, and it was dark! Finally, they were going to the "other side." Everyone knew what the other side was—it was where a horrific, demon-possessed person lived in the caves. Jesus, too, knew where they were going, and fell asleep in the back of the boat. The storm was fast, furious and fierce, and they cried out to Jesus. What they saw happen next was shocking to them, and they had seen healing miracles! Jesus stood and commanded the sea to be still. And it did! Now, I don't know about storms on the sea but I do know about storms in the sea of my mind. There is an abyss, there is an "other side," that frightens all of us. Dread, fear, worry, remorse, addictions, obsessive thinking; it seems that our ship is going to sink. When you feel all is lost, do what the disciples did—cry out to Jesus. Name your fear. Tell Him exactly what it is that you dread; be specific with your doubts. This same Jesus that said to the sea, "Be still" says to you, "I am leaving you with a gift—peace of mind and heart. And the peace I give is a gift the world cannot give. So, don't be troubled or afraid."

TODAY'S PRAYER Dear Jesus, You calmed the sea, please calm my troubled heart with the peace only You can give. I take the horrific storms of my life and submit them to Your command. You say, "Peace be still" so I choose not to be troubled or afraid. Amen.

Where Will You Spend Eternity?

TODAY'S VERSE "Don't let your hearts be troubled. Trust in God, and trust also in me. There is more than enough room in my Father's home. If this were not so, would I have told you that I am going to prepare a place for you? When everything is ready, I will come and get you, so that you will always be with me where I am. And you know the way to where I am going.' 'No, we don't know, Lord,' Thomas said. 'We have no idea where you are going, so how can we know the way?' Jesus told him, 'I am the way, the truth, and the life. No one can come to the Father except through me'" (John 14:1-7).

TODAY'S THOUGHT I officiated a funeral today. It was a beautiful, sunny day in San Diego, California. People were going to the ocean in droves. At the same time, thirty-five of us made our way to a little chapel near the beach. Judy, the deceased, loved California. The flowers, sun, beaches, and mountains all brought Judy much joy during her life. But the real passion of her heart was her relationship with Jesus Christ. Judy came to a place where she understood what Jesus meant when He said, "I am the way, the truth, and the life. No one can come to the Father except through me." Today, you can, as well. If you're not sure what will happen when you die, if you are not sure that your eternal home will be with Jesus in Heaven for all eternity, then settle it today. Receive Christ as your Lord and Savior. Receive His death on the cross as the payment for your sins and become a new person in Him. Your heart doesn't have to be troubled over your eternal destiny. Jesus has prepared a place for you.

TODAY'S PRAYER Dear Jesus, You said not to let my heart be troubled, but instead, to believe in You. You said that You have prepared a place for me. You said that You are the way, the truth, and the life. No one can come to the Father except through You. I come today, confessing that my attitudes and behavior have separated me from You. I ask Your forgiveness. Thank You that You died on the cross for my wrongdoing and I now receive Your gift of eternal life. Be the ruler of my life. In Jesus' name. Amen.

More Than Caring

TODAY'S VERSE "Suppose a brother or sister is without clothes and daily food. If one of you says to him, 'Go, I wish you well; keep warm and well fed,' but does nothing about his physical needs, what good is it?" (James 2:15-16).

TODAY'S THOUGHT It is so easy to get wrapped up in our own lives that we forget about those all around us who are in need. We can't save the whole world, so we don't try to save just one. "Someone else will help," we think as we walk away. But James says that we have to do more than just "care" about the poor, we need to help. In his book *Irresistible Revolution*, Shane Claiborne shares a survey he took of American Christians. He found that 80% believed that Jesus spent time with the poor. When asked if they spent any time with the poor, only 20% of the same group said, "yes." Shane concluded, "We can admire and worship Jesus without doing what He did. We can applaud what he preached and stood for without caring about the same things. We can adore his cross without taking up ours." James talks about our apathy toward the poor in this way: "But someone will say, 'You have faith; I have deeds.' Show me your faith without deeds, and I will show you my faith by what I do." It is not good enough to care about the poor. If we follow Christ, we need to do something.

TODAY'S PRAYER Father, there are so many people hurting and in desperate need. It is overwhelming. My heart aches but I don't know what to do. Please forgive me for my inactivity and help me today find something that I can do. Help me make a difference in someone's life, even if it is just a small difference. In Jesus' name. Amen.

Be Like Elijah

TODAY'S VERSE "Elijah was a man just like us. He prayed earnestly that it would not rain, and it did not rain on the land for three and a half years. Again, he prayed, and the heavens gave rain, and the earth produced its crops" (James 5:17-18).

TODAY'S COMMENT I love the way James starts this example of Elijah and his miraculous prayer life. He says, "Elijah was a man just like us." I'm sure that the image of Elijah that James had in his mind wasn't just the praying for rain to stop and start again; not just the fire coming from heaven to consume the altar; not just the flour and oil continuing to be supplied to the widow and her son; nor was it just the image of Elijah asking God to raise the widow's son from the dead. I am sure that James also remembered the fact that Elijah was afraid of Jezebel's threat to kill him and ran, fleeing for his life. He knew that Elijah became exhausted and sat down under a tree and prayed that he would die. James knew that Elijah was a person just like you and I. Elijah had emotions that could lead to despair. He had depression, doubt, and fear. Like us, Elijah exercised doubt and faith; fear and courage; advance and defeat. But he also saw God work through his life and prayers. God used Elijah, even with his imperfections. God can do the same for you and me. We don't have to be perfect. We don't have to pretend to be something we're not. We can be like Elijah—real with God about our deepest feelings and fears. God will meet us where we are and give us the strength to live for Him. Be real with God today.

TODAY'S PRAYER Father, thank You for the example of Elijah. What a wonderful testimony of Your grace. How You took this person, who could be so courageous one moment and so afraid the next and used him for Your glory. Father, use my life. I give it to You, in all its complexity and contradictions. Thank You that I do not have to be perfect, just available. Use me for Your glory, I pray. Amen.

The Real Deal

TODAY'S VERSE "My ears had heard of you but now my eyes have seen you" (Job 42:5).

TODAY'S THOUGHT It is so easy to walk in our Christian experience and really believe that we know God. We are like a baseball fanatic. You know the kind. He can tell you everything about a certain player. He can quote their batting average and the number of homers and lifetime RBIs. He knows where they played college ball, the names of his wife and children. He even has an autographed baseball. Yet he has never met the player. Never gone to his house, sat with him at dinner or even had a discussion. Everything he knows is from reading or listening to commentators. Now don't get me wrong, there is passion! He may even fight with you if you say something derogatory about the player. There is passion, but it is based on admiration, not friendship. Job came to a place where everything he thought he knew about God seemed empty and vain. And then He met God. Job knew all about God, He worshipped God, He even lived the way he thought God wanted him to; but when he saw God, it all changed. Knowing God in a personal and intimate way changes everything. And the beauty is that God created each of us with the ability to know Him. He has equipped us with the Holy Spirit, who is to teach us all things and bring us into intimate fellowship with God. But the choice is yours. You can choose to spend time with God and ask Him to reveal Himself to you, or you can continue to "know" about Him. Cry out to God today and ask Him to open your eyes like He opened Job's and you will be able to say, "My ears had heard of you but now my eyes have seen you."

TODAY'S PRAYER Father, sometimes I feel so phony inside. I talk about You, I read about You, I pray to You, but I don't seem to see You. Today, Lord, help me be conscious of Your presence. Father, speak to me. Help the eyes of my heart to see You. I want to know You in a deep and personal way. I pause now Lord, fill me with Your Holy Spirit, reveal Yourself to me. I will wait here till I sense Your love for me. (Wait) Thank You, Lord, for Your reality. I love You Lord with all my heart. In Jesus' name. Amen.

Prayer and Thanksgiving

TODAY'S VERSE "Do not be anxious about anything, but in everything, by prayer and petition, with thanksgiving, present your requests to God. And the peace of God, which transcends all understanding, will guard your hearts and your minds in Christ Jesus" (Philippians 4:6-7).

TODAY'S THOUGHT Prayer changes things. Karl Barth, a twentieth-century theologian, wrote, "He is not deaf, He listens; more than that, He acts. He does not act in the same way whether we pray or not. Prayer exerts an influence upon God's action, even upon His existence. That is what the word 'answer' means. The fact that God yields to man's petitions, changing His intentions in response to man's prayer, is not a sign of weakness. He Himself in the glory of His majesty and power has willed it." Paul knew this. That is why he tells us to stop being anxious. Instead, we are to pray, petitioning God, with thanksgiving in our heart. Why? Because we are coming to our Heavenly Father, who loves us, cares for us, is all-powerful and will work everything according to His will. We can trust God with the ultimate outcome, and in exchange, He gives us something greater than any answer we could ever ask for. He gives us a promise. A promise to guard our heart and mind with His own peace. Not just any peace, but a peace that transcends anything that we can imagine. What is bothering you? What is it you need? What is breaking your heart? Talk to God about it. Today, right now, bring your requests to God and let His peace guard your heart and mind.

TODAY'S PRAYER Father, You know my needs. You know my anxious thoughts. I bring my circumstances to You and ask for Your help with all my requests. Thank You, Lord, for hearing me. Thank You for caring. Thank You most of all for the peace that You bring to my heart and my mind. Amen.

April 12
Joy Is a Choice

TODAY'S VERSE "Whatever happens, my dear brothers and sisters, rejoice in the Lord" (Philippians 3:1).

TODAY'S THOUGHT I remember years ago reading a book that deeply touched me. It was called *Happiness is a Choice*. Often, we're tempted to think that joy is the result of our circumstances. However, the premise of *Happiness is a Choice* is that we don't have to be subject to all the variables around us. We can choose to be happy. We can choose joy. Webster defines joy as "the emotion evoked by well-being, success, or good fortune or by the prospect of possessing what one desires." As a Christian, we can agree with the first part. Our joy does come from a deep sense of well-being. However, unlike the rest of the definition, our joy is not dependent on success, good fortune or the prospect of possessions. Rather, our joy is an emotion that is evoked by a faith in a God that loves us. Nehemiah tells us that the joy that comes from God is a great source of strength. Paul takes the definition of our joy to a new level and says that no matter what happens, we should be joyful. In fact, he says we should *always* be full of joy in the Lord. He repeated it for emphasis when he wrote, "I say it again—rejoice." What are you facing today? What circumstances do you find yourself in? It doesn't matter, you can choose joy! If you are struggling and not sure how you can be joyful, ask God to supernaturally open your eyes to who He is and to give you a joyful heart. He will.

TODAY'S PRAYER Father, today I choose joy. Fill me from the top of my head to the depth of my soul with joy. Help me rejoice today dear God in who You are, and that I am Your child. Help me rejoice today, that all my sins are forgiven, that You know me personally and love me unconditionally. This is a fantastic reality and, today, Lord, I choose joy! Amen.

Help My Unbelief

TODAY'S VERSE "Against all hope, Abraham in hope believed. Abraham never wavered in believing God's promise. In fact, his faith grew stronger, and in this, he brought glory to God. He was fully convinced that God is able to do whatever he promises" (Romans 4:18, 20-21).

"The father instantly cried out, 'I do believe, but help me overcome my unbelief!'" (Mark 9:24).

TODAY'S THOUGHT Every day, you get a choice. Circumstances may change, but your choice never does. Will you choose to live with faith and hope today or not? You don't get much time to make up your mind. Fear comes knocking on your heart's door. It brings worry and doubts into your life—with self-pity, anger, and apathy right behind. Before you know it, you have wandered down the road with all those familiar companions that you have walked with so many times before. Faith and hope were never invited to come along. It would be like inviting light to join darkness. They can't coexist. Abraham was no different than you or me. He was human. He had emotions. He had struggles and disappointment. But he knew God and he chose, against all hope, to hope. He decided not to waiver in believing God, and the result was that his faith grew. As his faith grew, he became convinced the God was able to do whatever He promised. God can grow this same faith in you. You can respond today, the same way the father who wanted his boy healed by Jesus did. When Jesus told him, "Anything is possible if a person believes," the father said, "I do believe, but help me overcome my unbelief!'"

TODAY'S PRAYER Father, I want to believe with all my heart. I want to experience Your supernatural presence in my life. So, today I choose hope. Today, I choose to put my faith in You. I cry out from the depth of my being, "I do believe, help me overcome my unbelief!" Thank You that You will indeed help my faith get stronger. In Jesus' name, I pray. Amen.

Forget the Past

TODAY'S VERSE "I have not achieved it (perfection), but I focus on this one thing: Forgetting the past and looking forward to what lies ahead. I press on to reach the end of the race and receive the heavenly prize for which God, through Christ Jesus, is calling us" (Philippians 3:13-14).

TODAY'S THOUGHT Paul started the whole "No perfect people allowed" movement! He knew the pressure that Christians were getting from the religious people. Get circumcised, follow the commandments, obey the law. Paul knew that this was a trap. He knew that there were two kinds of people that miss God's standard of perfection. Those that say they do, and those that pretend they don't. Paul did not have to pretend to be perfect, he had a better way! He forgot his sin. Paul knew his struggle. He knew his shortcomings, but instead of putting on the pretense of perfection, he focused on one thing: "Forgetting the past and looking forward to what lies ahead." How about you? There comes a time when you have to make a choice. Are you going to let the past dictate your life or your future? Follow Paul's example: "I focus on this one thing: Forgetting the past and looking forward to what lies ahead. I press on to reach the end of the race and receive the heavenly prize for which God, through Christ Jesus, is calling us."

TODAY'S PRAYER Father, You know my past better than I do, and yet You are willing to forgive. Help me to do the same. Help me to forgive and forget the past and focus on what's ahead. Help me live in the present reality of Your love and forgiveness and then press on toward living my life for You. Amen.

Thinking Right

TODAY'S VERSE "We demolish arguments and every pretension that sets itself up against the knowledge of God, and we take captive every thought to make it obedient to Christ" (II Corinthians 10:5).

"Whatever is true, whatever is noble, whatever is right, whatever is pure, whatever is lovely, whatever is admirable—if anything is excellent or praiseworthy—think about such things" (Philippians 4:8).

TODAY'S THOUGHT You have heard the saying, "You are what you eat." I think in reality, we are more like what we *think*. Thoughts, whether conscious or on a more hidden level, affect the way we feel, perceive reality, act or react. Thoughts help create our moods, attitudes, and beliefs. Anger, jealousy, pride, envy, sadness, rebellion, and many other negative emotions or behaviors have their root in the way we think. That is why it is so important to be aware and take responsibility for our thoughts. Paul instructs us to consider our mind in the spiritual war we find ourselves in. We are to demolish any rouge thoughts that set itself up against Godly thinking. We are to take our thoughts captive and put it through a Godly filter, so it becomes the way He would have us think. Paul also gives us a list of the kinds of thoughts we should dwell on. We should dwell on thoughts that are noble, right, pure, lovely, admirable, excellent and praiseworthy. We have a choice—we can rule our thoughts, or we can let them rule us. Today, let Jesus be the Lord of your thought life. Let Him help you with the way you think.

TODAY'S PRAYER Father, I bring You my mind and my subconscious mind. Help me bring all my thoughts into the light of Your Holy Spirit. Today, dear Lord, help me dwell on thoughts that are noble, right, pure, lovely, admirable, excellent and praiseworthy. In Jesus' name. Amen.

Greatest Commandment

TODAY'S VERSE "'Teacher, which is the greatest commandment in the Law?' Jesus replied: 'Love the Lord your God with all your heart and with all your soul and with all your mind. This is the first and greatest commandment'" (Matthew 22:36-38).

TODAY'S THOUGHT It is so easy to stay busy. Family, work, church. Responsibilities, duties, ministry. Should, could, would. Everyday pressures mount up and we find ourselves running from one activity to another. Like a giant hamster wheel, we go and go and yet get nowhere. Jesus knew this, but not the Pharisees. All they knew was the law and all the activity it required. So, they asked Jesus which commandment He thought was the greatest. They weren't ready for how profound His answer would be. Jesus didn't say that the greatest commandment involved ministry, family or career. He didn't suggest tremendous feats or a myriad of activities. Instead, Jesus said, "'Love the Lord your God with all your heart and with all your soul and with all your mind." In her book *Listening Prayer*, Leanne Payne, writes, "Centering on the work of the Lord and the helping of others can cloud our first duty of loving, glorifying and enjoying God always. As Oswald Chambers says, 'The greatest competitor of devotion to Jesus is service for Him.' It is never 'do, do' with the Lord, but 'be, be' and He will 'do' through you.'" So today, let us be conscious of Him. Let us worship Him, love Him and spend time with Him. If we do, we will find that everything else will fall into place.

TODAY'S PRAYER Dear Lord, help me love You today with my whole heart, soul, and mind. Take my life; I give You complete control. I want to spend time with You, share my thoughts with You and hear from You today. Help me take charge of my schedule and all my busyness so that I can carve out the time I need to better worship You. Amen.

God's Plans for You

TODAY'S VERSE "For I know the plans I have for you," declares the LORD, "plans to prosper you and not to harm you, plans to give you hope and a future. Then you will call upon me and come and pray to me, and I will listen to you. You will seek me and find me when you seek me with all your heart" (Jeremiah 29:11-13).

"Faith is the confidence that what we hope for will actually happen; it gives us assurance about things we cannot see" (Hebrews 11:1).

TODAY'S THOUGHT Faith is such an important part of our spiritual walk. But faith in what? The author of Hebrews says that faith is "the confidence that what we HOPE for will happen." What do you hope for? Jeremiah shares three great truths that you can put your faith in. The first truth is that God has plans for you, plans to give you hope and a future. What a promise. Have you claimed it? The second truth that Jeremiah shares is that when you call upon God and pray that God will listen! What a truth, what a precious reality; God listens to you when you pray. The last truth is this: when you seek God with all your heart, He will be found! There are many goals and aspirations that you have had in life that, for one reason or another, ended up being an elusive dream, but not God. When you seek God with all your heart, He promises that you will find Him. Today, stop and consider that God has plans for your life. His plans are to give you a hope and a future.

TODAY'S PRAYER Father, I have come today seeking You with all my heart and know that You are listening to me. I am so glad that I have found You, the true and living God. I claim today the fact that You have plans for me. Plans with a hope and a future. Thank You, dear Father, that I can put my full confidence in that promise. In Jesus' name. Amen.

April 18
Be Strong in the Lord

TODAY'S VERSE "Finally, be strong in the Lord and in his mighty power" (Ephesians 6:10).

TODAY'S THOUGHT We need strength. Suffering from chronic pain. Struggling to pay the bills. Arguing with your teenage daughter or son. Feeling discouraged about your job. Rocking from a ruined relationship. All of us have a story. None of us goes unscathed. But we do not have to bear our sorrows alone and be afraid. We don't have to be helpless victims. Instead, Paul ends Ephesians with this word, "Finally, be strong." Be strong. The presence of a resilient attitude, a hopeful spirit, a resolve to never give up, to fight, to hang on. But how? How can we get the strength we need? Listen to how Paul finishes his verse. "Be strong in the LORD and in His mighty strength." What a difference a few words can make. We can be strong in His strength. It is a mighty strength. It is loving strength. It is *not* your strength, but God's. Like a child is carried in the strength of his father's arms, so let God carry your burden today. Today, be strong, but not in yourself. Be strong in the Lord and His mighty power!

TODAY'S PRAYER Father, You told me to be strong. You know I need to. But I confess, Lord, I have tried to be strong in my own power, not Yours. I need Your power. I need You. Please take my burdens. Help me today to be strong in You and Your mighty power. Amen.

April 19
Do We Live Like We Are Forgiven?

TODAY'S VERSE "Then Peter came to Jesus and asked, 'Lord, how many times shall I forgive my brother when he sins against me? Up to seven times?' Jesus answered, 'I tell you, not seven times, but seventy times seven'" (Matthew 18:21-22).

TODAY'S THOUGHT It is interesting that Peter was the one that came to Jesus and asked, "How many times should we forgive another person?" Peter thought he was generous and asked, "Seven times?" But the answer that Jesus gave Peter was based on grace and mercy, not on merit or our puny benevolence. Jesus said, "Seventy times seven." Peter learned to identify himself with Christ's answer. When the crowd came to crucify Jesus, Peter denied that he knew Jesus three times. When he realized the wrong he committed he went and "wept bitterly" over his sin. How awful Peter must have felt. When Jesus rose again, he went and found Peter. Jesus forgave Peter and told him three times to go and serve Him. And that's what Peter did. He did not go and become self-righteous. He did not go and think of himself as some sinless leader of the church. He did not set up a Country Club church for members in good standing. No, Peter never lost sight of the fact he was just a forgiven fisherman, saved by the grace of God. And other people recognized it, too. The book of Acts says, "When they saw the courage of Peter and John and realized that they were unschooled, ordinary men, they were astonished, and they took note that these men had been with Jesus." Peter and his followers carried a sign saying, "No perfect people allowed! We are just ordinary people forgiven of our sins." Shouldn't we do the same?

TODAY'S PRAYER Dear Jesus, thank You for all that You have forgiven in my life. Might I live filled with Your Holy Spirit, and in the fresh awareness that I am loved by You. Help me, in turn, to love and forgive others, so when they see me they will take note that I have been with You. Amen.

April 20
A Word of Encouragement

TODAY'S VERSE "The LORD your God is with you, he is mighty to save. He will take great delight in you, he will quiet you with his love, he will rejoice over you with singing" (Zephaniah 3:17).

TODAY'S THOUGHT Sometimes we are tempted to forget. Perhaps it is the darkness, life's circumstances with its mystery, that causes our lapse of memory. Could it be our haste, all the interruptions, deadlines and pressures of everyday life that crowds out our remembrance? Whatever the reason, today cast your eyes upon this treasure. Feast your senses on this thought: "The Lord, YOUR God, is with you!" Not only that, comfort yourself with the fact that "He is mighty to save you." But what should radiate joy deep in your heart right this moment is the fact that God takes great delight in you! If that is not enough, breathe in this truth: He will quiet you with His love. What peace He offers you this moment. And if you are quiet and use your imagination, you can picture in your mind this magnificent conclusion that Zephaniah offers, "God, our own Heavenly Father, is right this moment singing and rejoicing over you." Believe it, it is true.

TODAY'S PRAYER Oh, my dear Lord and Father. Who am I that You would rejoice over me with singing; that You take delight in me is so much to comprehend? But You have said it, and now I choose to believe it. Thank You, dear Father. Thank You for Your love for me. Help me live today in the reality of this truth. Amen.

God as My Friend

TODAY'S VERSE "Greater love has no one than this, that he lay down his life for his friends. You are my friends if you do what I command. I no longer call you servants, because a servant does not know his master's business. Instead, I have called you friends, for everything that I learned from my Father I have made known to you" (John 15:13-15).

TODAY'S THOUGHT It is an incredible concept that a God, who created all the expanse of space, designed the most complicated systems and is beyond time and space, would create us—not as some impersonal piece of matter, but as a friend. A friend! We are fortunate if we go through life with four or five good friends. Jesus called His disciples friends. Why? Because He spent time with them. He knew them. And He wants to do the same with us. If we're going to be a friend of God, then we must build a relationship. That doesn't happen by just going to church. We need to fellowship, worship and hear the Word of God. But even that is not enough. A relationship with God doesn't come by reciting creeds, as good as they are. It doesn't come by reading about God, although this certainly gives us context. It doesn't come by simply reading the Bible, although this is an indispensable part of relating to God. Friendship with God comes by spending time with Him. It comes through conversation with Him. It comes through an exchange of feelings, thoughts, concerns, and aspirations. Today, carve out some time to be alone with God. Share with Him, tell Him you want His friendship. Listen to Him, wait for Him and enjoy His presence. Start today, to spend time with God and build a friendship with Him.

TODAY'S PRAYER Father, I am known to You. We pass in life's circumstances, but I must admit, I don't know You very well. I know in my head that You love me, but I haven't sensed a friendship with You in my heart. I want to be Your friend. I want to know You in a much deeper and more personal way. Help me to that end. Guide me into a friendship with You, I pray. In Jesus' name. Amen.

Does It Get Any Better Than This?

TODAY'S VERSE "Let me hear of your unfailing love each morning, for I am trusting you. Show me where to walk, for I give myself to you. Teach me to do your will, for you are my God. May your gracious Spirit lead me forward on a firm footing" (Psalm 143:8,10).

TODAY'S THOUGHT There is something about an isolated sandy beach along the ocean. Sitting on the sand listening to the ocean waves hit the shore. Sun caressing your face. A gentle breeze awakening your skin. Birds chirping in the background. Does it get any better than this? Well, yes! David talks about a place that is much more satisfying. A place where the warmth of the sun pales in comparison. Where the sound of the ocean is replaced with the whisper of God. Where the gentle breeze is overshadowed by the mighty wind of the Holy Spirit. This place David is talking about is the very presence of God. He is talking about his time with God in the morning. "Let me hear of your unfailing love each morning," he writes. He shares about hearing God's voice, sensing His love, learning His will, trusting His Word and being led in which way to go. It really doesn't get any better than this! This can be your experience today. You don't need to drive anywhere, apply any sunscreen or walk barefoot on a hot, sandy beach. You just need to be available. Call on God, even now. Pray David's prayer, and might you come back to this peaceful place again and again.

TODAY'S PRAYER Dear Father, let me hear of Your unfailing love each morning, for I am trusting You. Show me where to walk, for I give myself to You. Teach me to do Your will, for You are my God. May Your gracious Spirit lead me forward on a firm footing. Amen.

Let's Make a Deal

TODAY'S VERSE "Trust in the Lord with all your heart; do not depend on your own understanding. Seek his will in all you do, and he will show you which path to take" (Proverbs 3:5-6).

TODAY'S THOUGHT When it comes to seeking God's will, we often fall into the role of Monty Hall on the old TV game show, "Let's Make a Deal." Larry Crabb, in his book *The Pressure's Off*, shares how we try to negotiate the Lord's will. He writes, "You negotiate; you do not worship. You analyze and interpret to gain control over what happens; you do not depend. You seek the 'better life' of God's blessing over the 'better hope' of God's presence." His advice was, "Seek only the blessing of His presence, and you'll know what to do." Solomon says that the secret to God's will is to trust in Him with all our heart and to seek His will in all we do. When we do, Solomon says that God will show us what to do. In another book, *The Papa Prayer*, Larry writes, "Know God so well that the deepest desire of His heart actually becomes the deepest desire of ours. That frees us to ask God for what we really want with the confidence that He'll move heaven and earth to grant our requests, because what we now want--matches what He wants." We don't need to make a deal with God. We don't need to try to balance a scale to get our way. We need to know Him. We need to spend time in His presence. As we do, He will direct us; He will guide our path.

TODAY'S PRAYER Father, I confess, I have sought Your blessings more than I have sought You. I have spent time seeking Your blessing more than Your presence. Lord, I want to know You. I want to seek You with all my heart. Please show me how. Please draw me to Yourself through the power and love of Your Holy Spirit. Dear God, take my life, take my mind, take my will. I want only You. Amen.

April 24
Be Real

TODAY'S VERSE "If we claim to be without sin, we deceive ourselves and the truth is not in us. If we confess our sins, he is faithful and just and will forgive us our sins and purify us from all unrighteousness" (1 John 1:8-9).

TODAY'S THOUGHT John wrote, "If we claim we have no sin." Who would ever claim that? Who in their right mind would think that they do not sin? The truth is that those of us in the church are close to doing that very thing. We come to a point where we feel we need to live a certain way in order to be a follower of Christ. Now, while there is virtue in trying to live a righteous life, we will never be sinless. So there becomes a temptation to try and hide any "sins" that we may have. There seems to be fear of humiliation or a shame that comes with falling from grace. This makes it hard for Christians to be honest and open with each other. Perhaps John's message today would be something like, "There are no perfect people in the Church, so don't pretend you are without sin. Go ahead and confess to God and each other. Christ is faithful to forgive you." In order to be real, we need to come to God and confess our sins, admit our needs and get the help we need. It is in sharing our struggles and helping each other that we experience true Christianity. Then we help others in the way we were helped. This is what people are looking for. They will think, "Finally, someone who is real! Someone who knows what I am going through and can help me." The sooner the community knows that there are no perfect people allowed at church, the sooner they will feel comfortable enough to come. The sooner you and I will invite them to experience the same grace, love, and forgiveness that we feel.

TODAY'S PRAYER Father, You know my situation. You know my shortcomings. Help me keep it real with You. Help me confess my sins so that I might experience Your freedom and forgiveness. And then, Father, help me help others, in the same way, You have helped me. Bring revival Lord to my church. Help us embrace our shortcomings, confess them one to another and accept Your forgiveness. Might we be a witness to Your grace throughout our community and to all who enter our doors. Amen.

Inner Strength

TODAY'S VERSE "I fall to my knees and pray to the Father, the Creator of everything in heaven and on earth. I pray that from his glorious, unlimited resources he will empower you with inner strength through his Spirit" (Ephesians 3:14-16).

TODAY'S THOUGHT I love the prayers that Paul prayed. His prayers give great insight into the will of God for His children. I believe that Paul models in his prayers, what we can pray for ourselves. So, what is Paul saying we can ask God for in this prayer? According to Paul, we can ask God to empower us with inner strength from His unlimited resources! Inner strength. What would it feel like to be empowered with inner strength? How would that change your day today? If you were empowered with inner strength, what would you do differently? I believe God wants to empower you with inner strength, and He certainly has the resources to do it. Do you have the faith to ask? Why not join Paul and ask God to use His glorious, unlimited resources to empower you with inner strength today.

TODAY'S PRAYER Dear Father, Creator of everything in heaven and on earth, I pray that today, from Your glorious, unlimited resources, You would empower me with inner strength through Your Spirit. Amen.

April 26
Roots

TODAY'S VERSE "The seed that fell on the footpath represents those who hear the message about the Kingdom and don't understand it. Then the evil one comes and snatches away the seed that was planted in their hearts. The seed on the rocky soil represents those who hear the message and immediately receive it with joy. But since they don't have deep roots, they don't last long. They fall away as soon as they have problems or are persecuted for believing God's word. The seed that fell among the thorns represents those who hear God's word, but all too quickly the message is crowded out by the worries of this life and the lure of wealth, so no fruit is produced. The seed that fell on good soil represents those who truly hear and understand God's word and produce a harvest of thirty, sixty, or even a hundred times as much as had been planted!" (Matthew 13:18-23).

TODAY'S THOUGHT Roots are crucial to the health of a plant. It's the way that plants get water and nourishment. Jesus used plants and roots as a metaphor for spiritual life. He pointed out that where you put your roots can make all the difference. Jesus shared about the futility of sowing seed on a path where the roots can't grow. This represents the evil one stealing away the truth from our heart. He says some seed falls on a rocky area where the roots can't grow deep. This represents a lack of commitment where spiritual fervor doesn't last long. Finally, Jesus talked about the seed that falls into the weeds, where the extraneous roots steal away nourishment. This represents the cares of this world or lure of things causing us to drift. Instead, the seed should be planted on the good ground. In Ephesians, Paul is praying for the church, that we would let our roots grow deep into the love that Christ has for us. How do we do this? By opening our heart to Christ's influence and trusting in Him. If we want to mature in Christ, then we must spend time in good soil. We need to pray, read His Word and meditate in His presence. Where are your roots?

TODAY'S PRAYER Father, I have not let my roots go down deep into your love. My commitment has wavered. I've let the cares of this world choke me out. Help me begin to go deeper with You. Help me know You more, hear You more and love You more. In Jesus' name, I pray. Amen.

True Significance

TODAY'S VERSE "How precious are your thoughts about me, O God. They cannot be numbered! I can't even count them; they outnumber the grains of sand! And when I wake up, you are still with me!" (Psalm 139:17-18).

TODAY'S THOUGHT Significance. How do you find it? The story goes that a man travels all around the world looking for treasure, and at the end of his life comes back to his home village to die. After he dies, the next person buys his house and finds diamonds in the backyard. He had a diamond mine in his backyard all the time. We look all around our own world to find love, acceptance, and significance. The truth is right in front of us. We are significant because God created us and loves us, period. David really believed that God thought about him. You can, too. How? By believing today's passage with your heart, not just your mind. Try it. "How precious are your thoughts about me, O God. They cannot be numbered! I can't even count them; they outnumber the grains of sand! And when I wake up, you are still with me!"

TODAY'S PRAYER Father, You are unfathomable, much more than I can ever comprehend. In all of your majesty, You created me. You know me, love me, and think of me. I am significant and precious in Your sight. Thank You so much, Lord. Help these thoughts fill my heart and shape my behavior today so I might return to You all my love and adoration. I praise You in Jesus' name. Amen.

Peace, Love, and Grace

TODAY'S VERSE Peace be with you, dear brothers and sisters, and may God the Father and the Lord Jesus Christ give you love with faithfulness. May God's grace be eternally upon all who love our Lord Jesus Christ" (Ephesians 6:23-24).

TODAY'S THOUGHT Paul knew how to end a letter. I can imagine him thinking, "What three things would my dear brothers and sisters in Christ need the most in the world? What would help them with any situation? What would give them the strength to carry on? What would be worth dying for? What would make life worth living?" This was more than the granting of three wishes. Paul prayed with the full knowledge that what he prayed could be our reality. He prayed that God would give you peace. He prayed that the Father and the Lord Jesus Christ would give you love. And finally, that God's own grace would be on you for all eternity. Peace, love, and grace. What could you do with that today? How much would you keep for yourself? How much would you give away? So, what do you do when someone offers you a gift? You take it. So today, might you take and be conscious of all the peace, love and grace God has for you.

TODAY'S PRAYER Father, thank You for Your peace, love, and grace that You have for me. I pray that today, I might really begin to experience the effect of Your peace, love, and grace in all that I do. In Jesus' name. Amen.

April 29
Search My Heart

TODAY'S VERSE "Have mercy on me, O God, because of your unfailing love. Because of your great compassion, blot out the stain of my sins" (Psalm 51:1).

"Search me, O God, and know my heart; test me and know my anxious thoughts. Point out anything in me that offends you, and lead me along the path of everlasting life" (Psalm 139:23-24).

TODAY'S THOUGHT The Bible says that David, "was a man after God's heart." What a tribute. Contrary to what we might think, this was not because David was perfect. He knew how easy he could fall into sin. He remembered how God had to wake him up from an immoral stupor through the rebuke of Nathan the Prophet. If anyone could have created the slogan, "No perfect people allowed," it was David. David had to give up the perception of perfection to renew a close relationship with God. When God convicted David of wrongdoing, David repented, asking God to have mercy on him. To stay in a close relationship with God, David decided to allow God to speak to him about his behavior. He prayed, "Search me, O God, and know my heart; test me and know my anxious thoughts. Point out anything in me that offends you, and lead me along the path of everlasting life." How about you? Do you feel far from God? Who moved? What is stopping you from coming back? Is it pride? Is it anger? Is it the false notion that you don't need to? Let us join David in becoming a man after God's heart, not through the false ambition of perfection, but through the daily, honest and open relationship with God that allows Him to search us, point out what we are doing wrong and then lead along the path of following Him.

TODAY'S PRAYER Father, I come to You today and pray what David prayed so long ago: "Search me, O God, and know my heart; test me and know my anxious thoughts. Point out anything in me that offends You, and lead me along the path of everlasting life." In Jesus' name, I pray. Amen.

April 30
True Light

TODAY'S VERSE "If you are walking in darkness, without a ray of light, trust in the Lord and rely on your God. But watch out, you who live in your own light and warm yourselves by your own fires. This is the reward you will receive from me: You will soon fall down in great torment" (Isaiah 50:10-11).

"Satan disguises himself as an angel of light" (II Corinthians 11:14).

TODAY'S THOUGHT When we are in the dark, we tend to think that any light will do. But that's not true. I started one night on a four-hour hike into a deep forest along a mountain trail. I had no choice, I had to go. But to my dismay, all I had was a flashlight with poor batteries. As the light failed, the walk ended up more like eight hours. You can't tell me that the kind of light you have doesn't make a difference. It was the hardest trek of my life because the light I had was no good. The prophet Isaiah is warning us that when it gets dark, we need trust in God, not our own fire. How often can we become deceived by good-sounding logic? Paul warns us that Satan comes to us masquerading as an angel of light! Today there are all kinds of self-help messages. While a lot of what is said is good, nothing can replace the light of God, His Word, and His presence. Spend time with Him. Use His light. Nothing else will light up your path like the light of Jesus.

TODAY'S PRAYER Jesus, You said that You are the light of the world! Please come today and direct my path. Show me the way. Keep me from falling prey to deceiving light and false direction. I commit myself and my journey to You. Amen.

Trust God in the Darkness

TODAY'S VERSE "If you are walking in darkness, without a ray of light, trust in the Lord and rely on your God" (Isaiah 50:10).

TODAY'S THOUGHT There is a difference in trusting God when things are going well and when everything seems to go all wrong. It can get so difficult. Sometimes we just end up in the dark. However, we are reminded by Isaiah that we can trust God in the darkness. Isaiah says that even "without a ray of light, trust in the Lord and rely on your God." David shares that we can never be anywhere that God is not present. He says that to God, the night shines as bright as day and that darkness and light are the same to him. Robert M'Cheyne wrote, "If I could hear Christ praying for me in the next room, I would not fear a million enemies! Yet distance makes no difference. He *is* praying for you." Neil Anderson has written many books on spiritual darkness, and in his book *Praying by the Power of the Spirit*, he writes about his own dark times. He had to lean on his faith. He had to make a choice to "never doubt in the darkness what God has shown me in the light." Where are you today? Are you in the light? If so, praise God and soak it in. Be thankful, learn at the feet of Christ so you'll have plenty to guide you in the dark. Are you in the dark today? Stop for a moment. Quiet yourself. Listen for His voice. He's there with you. Remember the light and walk in the darkness with the same faith. The light will come in the morning!

TODAY'S PRAYER Dear Father, it is so hard in the darkness. Thank You that nothing can separate me from Your love. Even here in the dark, You are with me. Help me to trust You. Help me not to doubt in the dark what You have shown me to be true in the light. Thank You, Lord, that even this will pass. The light will come in the morning. Amen.

Get Moving

TODAY'S VERSE "As Pharaoh approached, the people of Israel looked up and panicked when they saw the Egyptians overtaking them. They cried out to the Lord, and they said to Moses, 'Why did you bring us out here to die in the wilderness? Weren't there enough graves for us in Egypt? What have you done to us? Why did you make us leave Egypt? Didn't we tell you this would happen while we were still in Egypt? We said, 'Leave us alone! Let us be slaves to the Egyptians. It's better to be a slave in Egypt than a corpse in the wilderness!' But Moses told the people, 'Don't be afraid. Just stand still and watch the Lord rescue you today. The Egyptians you see today will never be seen again. The Lord himself will fight for you. Just stay calm.' Then the Lord said to Moses, 'Why are you crying out to me? Tell the people to get moving'" (Exodus 14:10-15).

TODAY'S THOUGHT It is so easy to complain. I think if we had steak for five days in a row, we would probably complain, "What … steak again?" The Jews had fled Egypt, not because of some clever plan cloaked in the darkness of night, but because of incredible miracles of God. Now God brought them to the edge of the Red Sea. Without faith, it looked like a dead end. It looked like an impossibility that they would ever escape. So, they did what comes so naturally: they complained. Their conclusion said it all, "It's better to be a slave in Egypt than a corpse in the wilderness!" Moses tried to console them, to no avail, so Moses did what he often did. He talked to God, face to face. God's answer was swift and to the point, "Why are you crying out to me? Tell the people to get moving!" What about you? Do you find yourself complaining about the situation you find yourself in? Do you have a hard time looking through the eyes of faith? There is a time to cry out to God and there is a time to get moving. Which is it for you?

TODAY'S PRAYER Father, I find it so easy to complain. How I must grieve Your heart! Forgive me. I find it so hard to trust. I feel stuck. Help me, Lord. You know my situation. I can't move without You. Have mercy on me! Give me a boost, hold Your rod up and part the seas. Help me get moving today and cross on dry ground. Amen.

Precious Promises

TODAY'S VERSE "I praise your name for your unfailing love and faithfulness; for your promises are backed by all the honor of your name" (Psalm 138:2).

"Because of his glory and excellence, he has given us great and precious promises. These are the promises that enable you to share his divine nature and escape the world's corruption caused by human desires" (II Peter 1:4).

TODAY'S THOUGHT If I were to create a secular society, one of my top rules would be, "Keep your promises." It is a building block of civil society. Is there anything more reassuring than a promise? Is there anything more demoralizing than a promise that is broken? In the spiritual realm, God is the promise keeper. Peter tells us that God has given us great and precious promises designed to help us be like Him. The Psalmist tells us that God's promises are backed by all the honor of His name. But do you know what God has promised you? As you read the scriptures, you begin to realize that His word is full of promises. He has promised that He would never leave you or forsake you. He has promised that He went to Heaven to prepare a place for you. He has promised that nobody can take you from Him. I asked earlier if there is anything more demoralizing than a promise that is broken. The only thing I can think of is the sorrow that we must bring God when we live as if He never promised us anything. Is that how you live? You can change that. Start today and begin to read His word. As you do, journal all the promises you find that apply to yourself. You will be amazed. Then start to live as if they are true. You will be blessed!

TODAY'S PRAYER Dear Father, thank You that You have given me many great and precious promises. Help me to learn more about them. Then help me to believe them and live my life accordingly. In Jesus' name. Amen.

Imitate the Love of Christ

TODAY'S VERSE "Imitate God, therefore, in everything you do, because you are his dear children. Live a life filled with love, following the example of Christ" (Ephesians 5:1-2).

"Love is patient and kind. Love is not jealous or boastful or proud or rude. It does not demand its own way. It is not irritable, and it keeps no record of being wronged. It does not rejoice about injustice but rejoices whenever the truth wins out. Love never gives up, never loses faith, is always hopeful, and endures through every circumstance" (I Corinthians 13:4-7).

TODAY'S THOUGHT You have heard it said, "Imitation is the best form of flattery." Have you ever watched a child imitate their father or mother? They are so serious. They pick up subtle nuances that we would never expect them to. They do not judge, they just act out what was acted out before them. This is what we have been asked to do. We are to imitate the love of Christ. We are to love the way He loved. Paul describes that kind of love. He says that love is patient, kind, not jealous, boastful, proud or rude. Love doesn't demand its own way, is not irritable and doesn't keep a record of wrongdoing. Love endures, doesn't lose faith, never gives up and is always hopeful. If we want to imitate Christ, we must love. Might Christ help us imitate His love today.

TODAY'S PRAYER Dear Jesus, help me to imitate You in everything I do. Help me to love the way You love. Guide me, direct me, fill me with Your Holy Spirit so I can follow Your example with those I meet today. Amen.

Be Strong and Courageous

TODAY'S VERSE "This is my command—be strong and courageous! Do not be afraid or discouraged. For the Lord, your God is with you wherever you go" (Joshua 1:9).

TODAY'S THOUGHT When we read Bible stories, we tend to feel that the people in the scriptures are supermen. The truth is, they were people just like you and me. If there is a difference, it's the fact that they heard from God and, in Joshua's case, decided to believe what God said. God chose Joshua to replace Moses as leader of the Jewish nation and lead them into the Promised Land. But God knew the task ahead, and he knew Joshua. He knew that Joshua was a normal person with passions, fears, and struggles. So, when God appointed Joshua as the leader, Moses met with him three times and told him to be strong and courageous. Then God called Joshua and Moses to appear before Him and personally told Joshua, "Be strong and courageous." Can you imagine the impact that would have had on Joshua? To have Moses tell him three times and then meet with God face to face, and hear God tell him the same thing? But that was not enough. After Moses died, God personally called Joshua and spoke directly to him four more times. Each time, God told Joshua to "be strong and courageous." What did God know about Joshua that would cause Him to tell Joshua, directly and indirectly, eight times that he was to be strong and courageous? He knew that Joshua was a man just like you and me and that he needed to put his feeble faith in a supernatural God. That is what Joshua did and God delivered him and the Jewish nation into the Promised Land. Remember today what God reminded Joshua of eight times: "Be strong and courageous! Do not be afraid or discouraged. For I AM with you wherever you go."

TODAY'S PRAYER Father, You know all about me. You know how I need You. Today, You have told me, like You told Joshua, not to be afraid and to be strong and courageous. Oh Father, tell me again and again, until, like Joshua, I get it. Today, I bring You my fears and my doubts, for You promised that You are with me wherever I am. Help me, Father, in my weakness, to be strong and courageous. Amen.

Don't Lose Your Soul

TODAY'S VERSE "And what do you benefit if you gain the whole world but lose your own soul?" (Matthew 16:26).

TODAY'S THOUGHT Jesus asked a question that has challenged people for centuries. His question has never been more relevant than it is today. He asked, "What will we benefit if we gain the whole world but lose our soul?" Isn't gaining the whole world what everyone seems to be striving for? Never in the history of man has it been harder to be content. The pressures of this world are amplified through print, television, movies, and internet. The convergence of media and information has escalated the speed of trends, fads, and popularity, making us even more susceptible to manipulation. We need to look certain ways, have certain things, go to certain schools, live in certain places. And if we cannot make it, then our children must. The words of Jesus stand in contrast to the media hype. They warn us to stop the madness! Jesus points out the fact that there is so much more to life than just the physical trappings and the praise of men. We have a soul! In this world, we live for 70, 80 years. Our soul, however, lives forever. This is the beginning of who we really are. God created more than your life, He created your essence. That essence is the real you, it is the soul. It never dies. It is eternal. You don't want to lose it to the next world. Jesus is an expert on the soul. Study what He has to say. Get to know Him, then live for Him. Jesus asked the question. One way or another, you must answer. "What do you benefit if you gain the whole world but lose your own soul?"

TODAY'S PRAYER Dear Jesus, I must admit I have jumped on a treadmill. I am running and running but not going anywhere. I look for significance, but it is nowhere to be found. I can feel my soul slipping away. Today, help me to see myself the way You see me. Help me to see myself as a living, breathing soul that You love and have created. Help me know You in a personal, intimate way. Help me find my true significance in You. Amen.

Spiritual Wisdom and Understanding

TODAY'S VERSE "So we have not stopped praying for you since we first heard about you. We ask God to give you complete knowledge of his will and to give you spiritual wisdom and understanding. Then the way you live will always honor and please the Lord, and your lives will produce every kind of good fruit. All the while, you will grow as you learn to know God better and better" (Colossians 1:9-10).

TODAY'S THOUGHT Do you desire to live a way that will always honor and please God? Do you want to produce every kind of good fruit with your life? These are high and lofty goals that Paul wrote for the church. These are goals that you and I need for our lives. But how? How do we achieve such spirituality? We do what Paul did. We should pray, and continue praying that God will give us a complete knowledge of His will and that we will know God better and better as we gain spiritual wisdom and understanding. It is through knowing God in this deep and intimate way that we will live the life He desires for us.

TODAY'S PRAYER Father, please give me a more complete knowledge of Your will for my life so I can live for you better and better. It is my desire to live a life that will always honor and please You, so I ask that You give a more complete knowledge of Your will and help me gain in spiritual wisdom and understanding. Amen.

The Unseen Real

TODAY'S VERSE "Therefore, we do not lose heart. Though outwardly we are wasting away, yet inwardly we are being renewed day by day. So, we fix our eyes not on what is seen, but on what is unseen. For what is seen is temporary, but what is unseen is eternal" (II Corinthians 4:16,18).

"I have set the LORD always before me. Because He is at my right hand, I will not be shaken" (Psalm 16:8).

TODAY'S THOUGHT The presence of God is a reality that we can experience. He is the God who is there. Unfortunately, we can go day after day and never be conscious of His reality. Leanne Payne, in her book *Listening Prayer,* writes, "It is especially easy for modern people to regard the supernatural world and activities as somehow less real than the world we behold with our senses. As twentieth-century Christians, we live in a materialistic age in which our systems of learning have long based their conclusions on scientific truth alone. The presuppositions of such systems have misled many generations of students, blinding them to the truths of God and the Unseen Real." Paul says that he did not lose heart because of the reality of fixing his eyes on what is unseen. The unseen reality of God renewed his heart, day by day. David said that he was not shaken by life's experiences because he experienced God at his side. How about you? Is God's presence a reality in your life? Do you renew your heart day by day because of the reality of His presence in your life? It's not too late. Start today to experience His reality. Spend time with God, talk to Him, ask Him to reveal Himself to you. When you do, you will find out that He really is the Unseen Real.

TODAY'S PRAYER Father, my life is so full of everything else but You. I spend so much of my time without any awareness of Your presence. I confess, I have been influenced by scientific rational thinking and find myself doubting Your reality. I have kept you at a safe distance, turned You into a religious relic. Forgive me. Today, reveal Yourself to me, Lord. Help me be conscious of Your presence. Help me renew my heart today by Your unseen reality. Amen.

What Do You Want Him to Do?

TODAY'S VERSE "She touched the fringe of his robe, for she thought, 'If I can just touch his robe, I will be healed'" (Matthew 9:20-21).

"Two blind men were sitting by the roadside, and when they heard that Jesus was going by, they shouted, 'Lord, Son of David, have mercy on us!' Jesus stopped and called them. 'What do you want me to do for you?'" (Matthew 20:30-32).

TODAY'S THOUGHT Deep down inside, you know there has to be more. There must be a relief from your pain. Perhaps like the woman in today's verse, you wonder, "What if I could just touch the fringe on His robe?" Like the two blind men on the side of the road, if you knew Jesus was coming, you would shout out to Him. In his book *The Church That Heals*, Doug Murren writes, "We need the miraculous in the church today. Postmodern people are too broken to be fixed through simple human caregiving; they need to be pieced back together through the Supernatural healing of Jesus through His body the church." What is it you need today? Where are you hurting? Today, Jesus is asking you the same thing that He asked the blind men: "What do you want me to do for you?"

TODAY'S PRAYER Jesus, I am sitting here today by the side of the road. I am in great need. I have shouted for mercy and You have heard me. Now, dear Lord, please hear my request. I simply come in faith to touch the hem of Your garment and be healed. (Take a moment and share with Jesus what it is you need Him to do.) Heal me I pray, in Jesus' name. Amen.

The Kingdom of Heaven Is Near

TODAY'S VERSE "Jesus went through all the towns and villages, teaching in their synagogues, preaching the good news of the kingdom and healing every disease and sickness" (Matthew 9:35).

"As you go, preach this message: 'The kingdom of heaven is near.' Heal the sick, raise the dead, cleanse those who have leprosy, drive out demons" (Matthew 10:7,8).

TODAY'S THOUGHT Jesus did the will of His father. He told His disciples to do the same thing. He gives us the same commission. Jesus said it best in John 14:10, 12. "Don't you believe that I am in the Father and that the Father is in me? The words I say to you are not just my own. Rather, it is the Father, living in me, who is doing his work. I tell you the truth, anyone who has faith in me will do what I have been doing. He will do even greater things than these because I am going to the Father." Today, you and I have been called to be about the same Father's business. We have been asked to go to the world and cry out, "The Kingdom of God is near." We are to go with the compassion of Christ and do the things He did. We are to pray that God would show forth His mighty power and do whatever we ask in the name of Jesus, so that it may bring glory to the Father. Today, ask God, "What would you have me do? What would you have me pray?" You are just as much His disciple as the original twelve. Follow Him.

TODAY'S PRAYER Father, I pray that Your Kingdom would be evident in my life today. Guide me, lead me, show me what You would have me do. Give me the courage and faith to trust You for mighty things and to be obedient to what You ask of me. I pray that I would honor You in all that I do today. Amen.

No Perfect People Allowed

TODAY'S VERSE "This is a faithful saying, and worthy of all acceptation, that Christ Jesus came into the world to save sinners; of whom I am chief" (I Timothy 1:15).

TODAY'S THOUGHT "No perfect people allowed!" I first heard this phrase in a message by John Burke, pastor of Gateway Church in Texas. I find it appealing because it allows us the freedom to be who we are in Christ. It is like the phrase, "Christians aren't perfect, they are forgiven." Yet why is it we come to church and pretend that everything is okay and never seek out the help we need? Could it be that when someone does something wrong, they so often end up being ostracized from the rest of the fellowship? We need to work on getting rid of the stigma of falling in our Christian walk and learn to help each other back up. People are looking for a Christianity where they can belong. Where they can be authentic and real with their life story. Paul tells us to "bear one another's burdens," not to pretend we don't have any. Paul ends his spiritual journey by admitting that he is the "chief of all sinners." As he goes through his journey, he changes focus on who Christ is and what He does with sin. Christ convicts, corrects, forgives, gives grace, and helps us get up after a fall and try again. We are not perfect but thank God, He has a perfect plan. Begin today, with all your struggles and imperfections, to live for Him and rejoice in His unconditional love for you.

TODAY'S PRAYER Lord, I am tired of trying to be perfect. I cannot do it. Instead, I humbly accept Your grace and forgiveness. Thank You, Lord, for accepting me with all my imperfections. In Jesus' name. Amen.

This Little Light of Mine

TODAY'S VERSE "You are the light of the world—like a city on a hilltop that cannot be hidden. No one lights a lamp and then puts it under a basket. Instead, a lamp is placed on a stand, where it gives light to everyone in the house. In the same way, let your good deeds shine out for all to see so that everyone will praise your heavenly Father" (Matthew 5:14-15).

TODAY'S THOUGHT Light. You never really appreciate it until you are in the dark. We take light for granted. I remember one night having to hike into a deep forest on the side of a mountain. I had to get to a destination by morning and all I had was a dim flashlight. All night long, I appreciated every ray that emanated from the head of that lifesaving light. The next day, on the way back, I saw that I had walked for miles along the top of a deep ravine. Without the light, I am sure I would have perished. As Christians, we are the light of the world. We are the illumination on the path that leads through the wilderness along the dangerous ravine. Jesus reminds us that we must not hide the light, but instead should put it where everyone can see by its brightness. He concludes with this command: "In the same way, let your good deeds shine out for all to see so that everyone will praise your heavenly Father." Today, you have a choice. You can contribute to the darkness of those around you or you can be the light. There is no neutral ground. When God gives us the opportunity today, might we shine with the love of Christ that God will get the praise and glory.

TODAY'S PRAYER Father, I pray that today You will shine Your light through me as You guide me to the darkness that You want me to shine upon. Help me see the needs around me and respond with Your love and compassion so others will praise You today. Amen.

Don't Work in Vain

TODAY'S VERSE "Unless the Lord builds a house, the work of the builders is wasted. Unless the Lord protects a city, guarding it with sentries will do no good" (Psalm 127:1).

"For we are God's workmanship, created in Christ Jesus to do good works, which God prepared in advance for us to do" (Ephesians 2:9).

TODAY'S THOUGHT It is so easy to try and do everything by ourselves. Perhaps we don't trust others. Perhaps we feel we need to get ahead and no one cares as much as we do. Maybe deep down, we enjoy the praise and recognition we get from being a rugged individual. Or, if we fail because we try to do everything by ourselves, perhaps even negative attention is better than no attention at all. When is the last time you did something "with the Lord?" Notice I didn't say "for" the Lord. I said "with" the Lord. We need God, plain and simple. It is vain to try and do things without Him. He loves you. He cares for you. God wants to work for and with you to do His will. Paul reminds us, "For we are God's workmanship, created in Christ Jesus to do good works, which God prepared in advance for us to do." Doing His good works, in His time and in His strength, is what we were created for. It is where we will be the most fulfilled. It is where we will have the greatest peace. Today, work with God. Find out what He wants you to do and join Him. Or, if you have things you must do already, invite God to partner with you. If you do, it will not be in vain or wasted.

TODAY'S PRAYER Father, I realize that so much of what I have done has been on my own. So much of what I have done has been in vain. I am so sorry. Today I realize that I am Your workmanship and that You created me to do Your good works. Thank You so much. Today, Father, I ask You to take charge of my life. I invite You to guide me in all I do. I commit this day and all of its activities to You. In Jesus' name. Amen.

Behold His Beauty

TODAY'S VERSE "One thing have I desired of the LORD, that will I seek after; that I may dwell in the house of the LORD all the days of my life, to behold the beauty of the LORD, and to inquire in his temple" (Psalm 27:4).

TODAY'S THOUGHT I remember when I first saw my wife. People had told me about her. They said that we would be a great couple. One friend, who was trying to match us up, brought me a magazine article with her picture in it. That was it. I was smitten. I beheld her beauty. It was more so when I finally met her. While we were dating, I would catch myself looking at her. Still today, I am moved by her presence. This is more than a visual experience. It is emotional and existential. Why? Because I fell in love with her. Did you know that you can behold God in the same way? You can. God has given us an *inner eye*, that spiritual ability to connect with Him in a deep and personal way. David knew this, so he made it his most passionate desire. He wrote, "One thing have I desired of the LORD, that will I seek after; to behold the beauty of the Lord." If you can do that, everything else in life will fall in line. Today, stop and ask God to help you "behold His beauty." Commit yourself to spend time in His presence, read His word, meditate on His goodness and you will begin to fall in love with God.

TODAY'S PRAYER Father, help me begin to behold Your beauty. Help me know You, hear You, fellowship with You. Help me trust You, commit myself to You, help me love You. Lord, I know this is a process, but it is one I deeply desire. Start today, Father, to guide me into a deeper relationship with You. Amen.

May 15
How Great Is God

TODAY'S VERSE "LORD, I have heard of your fame; I stand in awe of your deeds, O LORD. Renew them in our day; in our time make them known" (Habakkuk 3:2).

TODAY'S THOUGHT Have you ever read a verse of scripture that seems to express the longing of your heart? This verse expresses mine. Every time I read the scripture, I end up marveling at God's deeds. How magnificent. How mighty. As I read the life of Jesus, I cannot help but think of how merciful and full of love He is. And yet, as I see my life, as I see the Church today, as I see our country I cannot help but pray what Habakkuk prayed, "Renew your deeds in our day; in our time make them known." I believe God has, to some degree, stayed His hand. I believe He is waiting for the church to believe that He is mighty today and not just in the past. He is waiting for us to lay down our materialism, our preoccupation with success, fame, and riches. I believe He is waiting for those of us who go to church on Sunday to want His Lordship on Monday. We need the prayer of Habakkuk to flood our churches, to be on the lips of our people. It needs to be our passion, our plea, and our deepest desire. We need the Lord. We need His mighty power in our life. Today, marvel at all that God has done in the past and then ask Him to do it again in your life. He is waiting for us to ask.

TODAY'S PRAYER Father, how I marvel at Your mighty deeds. How I stand in awe of all that You have done. Dear Lord, I need Your power in my life. I come today and ask that You would again do Your mighty deeds. Renew them again and make Yourself known to my world. Work in my life today that others might see and stand in awe of You. Amen.

Hope Does Not Disappoint

TODAY'S VERSE "We rejoice in the hope of the glory of God. Not only so, but we also rejoice in our sufferings, because we know that suffering produces perseverance; perseverance, character; and character, hope. And hope does not disappoint us because God has poured out his love into our hearts by the Holy Spirit, whom he has given us" (Romans 5:2-5).

TODAY'S THOUGHT Births and funerals. Health and disease. It seems that life has its contrasts. On one hand, we have the Promised Land, on the other, we have the wilderness. None of us go through life unscathed. We all have trials and difficulties. Some self-inflicted, others inflicted upon us. Paul knew that the temptation during difficulties is to complain and give up, so he wrote to the church in Rome to encourage them during their time of persecution. Paul admits to them that on one hand, we have our hope of heaven, and on the other hand, we have suffering in this life, but he instructs us in both circumstances to rejoice. I understand the rejoicing in the hope of heaven, but why would Paul say that we should rejoice in our sufferings? Paul says we should rejoice in our sufferings because of "hope." Hope is the word that makes all the difference. You see, our suffering produces perseverance, which produces character, which results in hope. But what really makes hope spectacular is what Paul writes next. Five words: "Hope does not disappoint us!" Hope in Christ will never fail. Today, you may have disappointment. You may have difficulties. But friend, today you also have hope!

TODAY'S PRAYER Father, today, where there is darkness, help me see hope. Where there is pain, help me feel hope. Where there is disappointment, help me realize hope and where there is doubt, fear, and anxiety, help me to know hope. Father, thank You that You promised that Your hope will not disappoint us. I receive Your hope today. In Jesus' name. Amen.

Choose Today

TODAY'S VERSE "Choose today whom you will serve. Would you prefer the gods your ancestors served beyond the Euphrates? Or will it be the gods of the Amorites in whose land you now live? But as for me and my family, we will serve the LORD" (Joshua 24:15).

TODAY'S THOUGHT Choose today whom you will serve. Many people treat Christianity as if it was a once-and-for-all decision. We decide to receive Christ as our Savior and that is it. We are born again, and then we go on autopilot. But the term *born* indicates that it is the beginning of a life-long process, not the end! Christianity starts with a single choice but is followed by a lifetime of choosing to live for Him. The trouble is our life becomes such a routine that we make choices out of habit. Worse, we don't even see our behavior as a choice anymore. We are just responding as if we were programmed. We need to wake up to the fact that we do have choices. If you have been going down the wrong road, you can stop today and *choose* to go a different direction. Have you been depressed? The good news is that you can *choose* to be happy. Have you struggled with wrong choices? You can CHOOSE to come to God with your problem and He will help you make the right choices. You have a choice because God gives it to you. All the power of God is available and waiting for you to make a choice. What will you choose today?

TODAY'S PRAYER Father, thank You that I do have a choice. I can choose to follow You every day. Help me see all the opportunities ahead of me. Help me to see all of the hundreds of actions I make every day as choices. Thank You that with Your Holy Spirit, I am not powerless, I don't have to be the victim of negative habits. I pray that today, Father, You will help me, guide me, and give me the strength to choose wisely in everything I do. In Jesus' name. Amen.

God Loves Me

TODAY'S VERSE "This is real love—not that we loved God, but that he loved us and sent his Son as a sacrifice to take away our sins" (I John 4:10).

"For God loved the world so much that he gave his one and only Son so that everyone who believes in him will not perish but have eternal life" (John 3:16).

"But God demonstrates his own love for us in this: While we were still sinners, Christ died for us" (Romans 5:8).

TODAY'S THOUGHT It is one thing to *say* you love someone. It is another to *really* love them. You see, the real language of love is not found in some poetic phrase. The language of love is in our actions. Love needs to be a verb. So, when I say, "God loves you!" I am referring to much more than some simple sentiment. I am referring to the fact that you are important to God. You are special to Him. Paul shares that "God demonstrates His love for us in this: While we were still sinners, Christ died for us." When we are at our worst, when we are farthest from Him, His love for us is still there. God sent Jesus to be the sacrifice for our sinfulness, so we could have a legitimate relationship with Him; so we could experience His love and begin to express our love back to Him. Have you received His love? Have you made it personal? If not, acknowledge the fact that He loves you today. Thank Him for providing a way for you to come before His Holiness, cleansed, forgiven and as His child. In John 1:12, Jesus said it best: "Yet to all who received him, to those who believed in his name, God gave the right to become children of God." If you believe that He died on the cross for you, then receive His death as a substitute for you by acknowledging it as a fact and thanking Him for it today.

TODAY'S PRAYER Father, I have heard the words, "God loves me" before. Today, I want to make it personal. I want You to know how thankful I am that You sent Jesus to be my substitute, so I could come before You holy and blameless. So that I could be "born again" as Your child. Today, I receive these words into my heart, "God loves me!" Help me to really understand it and all the joy that it brings. In Jesus' name, I pray. Amen.

May 19
Rejected Wisdom

TODAY'S VERSE "This is what the LORD says: 'Stop at the crossroads and look around. Ask for the old, godly way, and walk in it. Travel its path, and you will find rest for your souls.' But you reply, 'No, that's not the road we want'" (Jeremiah 6:16).

TODAY'S THOUGHT There is a bitter truth in this passage. The truth is, so often we're just playing spiritual games with God. We come to a crossroad in life where we need to ask for wisdom. We go through the spiritual motion of wanting His wisdom, but as soon as the pressure is off, as soon as we think we're in the clear, we choose to go our own way again. We're torn between God and the world. We waver, and our own worldly desire usually wins. How can we break this cycle? How can we really understand God's wisdom for our life and then follow it? Fall down at His feet, tell Him the truth, ask for forgiveness and then ask Him to direct, guide and empower you to follow Him. It's by spending time with God, listening to Him and accepting the guidance of His Holy Spirit. We follow Him one crossroad at a time. We live for Him one request for wisdom at a time. We start to say "Yes" to Jesus one day at a time. Why not start today?

TODAY'S PRAYER Father, so often I have good intentions. I want to follow You. I ask for wisdom. I come to the crossroads with all the intention of going down the right road. And then something happens. I get torn inside and start to doubt. I start to waver, to be tempted to go another way, and soon I am far from the wisdom I so desperately sought. Help me, Lord. I want to follow You. I ask You to guide me today. Help me to have Your wisdom for today and follow it. Today, Lord, I choose to follow You. Amen.

The Victory Is His

TODAY'S VERSE "Perhaps the LORD will help us, for nothing can hinder the LORD. He can win a battle whether he has many warriors or only a few" (I Samuel 14:6).

TODAY'S THOUGHT We all have our wars to fight. Saul and his 600 men were trying to defeat the mighty Philistine army with thousands of soldiers. It was a bitter war. Saul and his 600 men were pinned down and trapped. Saul's son, Jonathan, summoned his armor bearer and felt that they should go and fight the army. His famous battle cry was, "Perhaps the LORD will help us, for nothing can hinder the LORD. He can win a battle whether he has many warriors or only a few!" With faith, Jonathan and his armor bearer went to the Philistine outpost and took on twenty soldiers. Then something miraculous happened. The Philistines' vast army in the camp became confused, panicked and afraid. God added an earthquake, and all the army fled, being chased by the Israelites. In the midst of difficult times, we need to be reminded that "Nothing can hinder the Lord." When the odds seem overwhelmingly against us, we must remember, "He can win a battle whether he has many warriors or only a few!" Today, count on the Lord. Let Him help you in your own private conflict. He can win the battle!

TODAY'S PRAYER Father, You know my personal battles. You know how overwhelmed I can get. Lord, I know that nothing can hinder You. You can indeed give me personal victory, whether I have many resources or only a few! Today, I submit myself and my situation to You and ask that You would provide for me in miraculous ways. Amen.

May 21
A Conversation with God

TODAY'S VERSE "But as for me, I watch in hope for the LORD, I wait for God my Savior; my God will hear me" (Micah 7:7).

TODAY'S THOUGHT He hears our prayers. He hears, and the very fact that He hears assures us that He, in turn, answers us. Prayer is not a one-way street. Prayer was never meant to be a list of demands or a message we leave on an answering machine. Prayer is a conversation. Leanne Payne, in her book *Listening Prayer*, writes, "That our God is faithful to hear and answer all prayer is something I want to shout from the housetop." Dallas Willard, in his book *Hearing God*, writes, "A biblical Christian is not just someone who holds certain beliefs about the Bible. He or she is also someone who leads the kind of life demonstrated in the Bible: a life of personal, intelligent interaction with God." We worship the God who listens. We serve the God who answers. Our God desires a conversation. Isn't it time you really talked to Him? Today, talk to God. Share with Him your concerns, desires, and hopes. But don't just pray. Converse with Him. Ask Him questions and listen for answers.

TODAY'S PRAYER Father, today I come to You to have a conversation. You have called me your friend, so I come as a friend. As I pour out my heart to You, as I strike up a conversation, tune my heart to hear Your reply. Fill my heart with Your peace, joy, and hope. Might I experience Your loving presence during our time together. In Jesus' name, I pray. Amen.

May 22
The Battle Is in the Mind

TODAY'S VERSE "We demolish arguments and every pretension that sets itself up against the knowledge of God, and we take captive every thought to make it obedient to Christ" (2 Corinthians 10:5).

"Fix your thoughts on what is true, and honorable, and right, and pure, and lovely, and admirable. Think about things that are excellent and worthy of praise" (Philippians 4:8).

TODAY'S THOUGHT When it comes to the many struggles in life, the real battle is often in the mind. James writes, "What causes fights and quarrels among you? Don't they come from your desires that battle within you?" (James 4:1). That is why Paul tells us to demolish those thoughts that stand against what God wants for us. We are in a spiritual battle and need to take every stray thought captive and repent, correct it the way God would have us correct it. If I am hating someone, I need to capture the hateful thoughts, realize that they are wrong, ask forgiveness and choose not to hate. Paul also gives us a second way to win the victory in the battle for our mind. He says that we need to discipline our thinking, so it focuses on thoughts that are worthy of praising God. Those thoughts that are true, honorable, right, pure, lovely, admirable and excellent. Anger, bitterness, hate, jealousy, fear, anxiety; these negative emotions can literally kill us. They are joy robbers; they suck the life right out of us. Greed, selfishness, pride, and thoughts that worldly keeps us from living for God. The good news is that God has not left you powerless. You have a choice. Take responsibility for your thought life. Capture the negative thoughts and focus on the good ones. Today, choose your thoughts wisely.

TODAY'S PRAYER Father, so much goes on in my head. Help me today, dear Jesus, to bring every thought captive and realign them to where they are true, honorable, right, pure, lovely, admirable and excellent. In Your name, I pray. Amen.

Make Every Effort

TODAY'S VERSE "Always be humble and gentle. Be patient with each other, making allowance for each other's faults because of your love. Make every effort to keep yourselves united in the Spirit, binding yourselves together with peace" (Ephesians 4:2-3).

TODAY'S THOUGHT Can you imagine if everyone in the church would take these words to heart? What a witness to God's love we would be. Paul is sharing how we should behave as a church. He writes that we are to always be humble, gentle and patient with each other. This is not easy. That is why he says that we need to make allowance for each other's faults and to make "every" effort to be united and bound together in peace. How about today? Who is it that bothers you? Who gets under your skin? When you catch yourself talking bad about someone, who is it? What commitment can you make to be humble, gentle and patient with that person? What efforts can you put forth in the next week to keep yourself united with them in the Spirit? This is where it needs to start. May God grant you the courage and strength you will need today to step up and make every effort to be united and at peace.

TODAY'S PRAYER Father, I desire to be humble, gentle, and patient with those that bother me. Help me focus on Your love so I can make allowances for the faults of others. Help me, Lord, to make every effort to be united in the Spirit, binding myself to others with the bonds of peace. Amen.

Anxiety or Peace?

TODAY'S VERSE "Cast all your anxiety on him because he cares for you" (1 Peter 5:7).

"You will keep in perfect peace all who trust in you, all whose thoughts are fixed on you" (Isaiah 26:3).

TODAY'S THOUGHT As hard as we try, we can't control everything. Circumstances happen, situations arise, consequences catch up with us. Anxiety or peace? Because of God, we do have a choice. God makes all the difference in the world! Peter tells us to cast all our care on God. I love the imagery. You throw something light but cast something heavy. We are to take our heavy load of worry and anxiety, use all our strength and faith, and cast it onto Jesus. Let Him take it. Why? Because He cares for us. Why? Because He is able to keep us in perfect peace. Isaiah shared the secret to peace. He said to fix our thoughts on God and trust Him. What is it that you are worried about today? Cast it onto Jesus. Trust Him with it. Fix your thoughts on His love for you.

TODAY'S PRAYER Father, I thank You that I can cast all my cares on You. I thank You that You care for me and that You are able to keep me in perfect peace. Take my situation, I trust You with it. I choose to take my focus off my worries and fears and put it on You and Your love. Give me Your peace today. Amen.

To-Do Today

TODAY'S VERSE "Be joyful always; pray continually; give thanks in all circumstances, for this is God's will for you in Christ Jesus" (1 Thessalonians 5:16-18).

TODAY'S THOUGHT Not sure what to do today? Don't know which direction to go in or where to start? In today's verse, Paul has given us a tremendous "to do" list. In fact, he is emphatic about our doing it. He uses the words, *always*, *continually* and *in all circumstances*. Look at what he says we should do. "Be joyful always!" We think of joy as an emotion, but in fact, many times joy is an act of the will. We choose to see the glass half full, the trip almost finished, and hope right around the corner. We see hope and experience the presence of Christ in our lives and choose joy! Pray continually. Prayer is more than an occasional ritual. It is the communication that comes out of a vibrant real relationship. It is a conversation with the living God that goes on all day. God really is with us and we talk to Him continually. "Give thanks in all circumstances." Giving thanks is that expression of gratitude we give to God when we decide to give Him the glory for the good around us and trust Him with the bad. When things go right, we praise, and when we are not sure about our circumstances and are upset, it is the voice of reason that says, "I thank you, God, that you are trustworthy." Today, add to your list of things to do: be joyful, pray, and give thanks.

TODAY'S PRAYER Father, above all else today, I choose to be joyful. I also commit myself to pray throughout the day as things come to my mind. And Father, today I will deliberately be conscious of giving You thanks in all my circumstances. Help me to this end I pray, in Jesus' name. Amen.

Choices

TODAY'S VERSE "Trust in the LORD with all your heart; do not depend on your own understanding. Seek his will in all you do, and he will show you which path to take" (Proverbs 3:4-6).

"Now faith is being sure of what we hope for and certain of what we do not see" (Hebrews 1:1).

TODAY'S THOUGHT There are many choices to make in life. How do we integrate our faith into the major life decisions we make? First, we see in this verse that we are to "trust in the Lord with all our heart." This is more than *head knowledge*. It is experiential knowledge. This *knowing* has gone past our brain into our experience so that it has finally resided in our inner being. It is not a blind faith; rather, it's what the author of Hebrews calls being "sure of what we hope for and certain of what we do not see." It is out of our relationship with God that we "seek His will in all we do" and God is faithful to lead us and show us which path to take. What is it that you need help with? What is it that you need to decide? Seek God's help today. Pray over the issue at hand. Seek counsel, apply wisdom, pray much, and then allow Him to guide you. Let Him work in your heart and mind. He promises He will.

TODAY'S PRAYER Father, some decisions are so hard. I find myself so many times baffled at what to do. Situations where I have dug myself into a hole, consequences of other people's sins, circumstances beyond my control, these have often left me rocking. Father, help me trust You with all my heart today. Increase my faith. Impart Your wisdom to me and lead me in the way I should go. I pray this in the precious name of Jesus. Amen.

No Condemnation

TODAY'S VERSE "So now there is no condemnation for those who belong to Christ Jesus" (Romans 8:1).

TODAY'S THOUGHT It is one thing to forgive someone else. How do we forgive ourselves? How do we get rid of a guilty conscience? Conviction is one thing. We need conviction. The job of the Holy Spirit is to help us live the life that God created us for. Jesus said that He had to leave the earth. His job of dying for our sins would be over, but then the Holy Spirit would come and convict of sin, righteousness, and judgment. When we feel convicted, we repent, ask forgiveness and accept the forgiveness. At least, that is how it is supposed to work. But for many, it doesn't stop there. Instead, there is a nagging condemnation. An ugly worthlessness, a sense of hopelessness that we can never be loved, let alone forgiven. A shame that is so hard to overcome that our soul becomes numb. My friend, let me assure you, God does not use shame. He does not condemn. Lift your head, go ahead, lift up your head and look into the eyes of Jesus. You will see nothing but unconditional love for you. Hear these words of Paul today, let them resound deep into your heart, breathe them in: "There is no condemnation for those that belong to Christ Jesus." Know today that you are forgiven, you are loved. So, forgive yourself, be healed, be free from any false guilt. Accept His unconditional love.

TODAY'S PRAYER Father, today I quit trying to earn Your love. I let go of all the thoughts, all the negative self-images, all the nagging doubts and condemnation that is stopping me from accepting Your unconditional love. Instead, as I sit here, fill me with Your forgiveness. Overwhelm me with the joy You have over me. I thank You that You are not ashamed of me and that I am precious in Your sight. Today, I am washed clean in Your grace, forgiveness, and love. In Jesus' name. Amen.

Forgiveness

TODAY'S VERSE "Make allowance for each other's faults, and forgive anyone who offends you. Remember, the Lord forgave you, so you must forgive others" (Colossians 3:13).

TODAY'S THOUGHT Forgiveness is at the root of Christianity. It is the cornerstone of our beliefs. Christ came so we could be forgiven of all our sins. So, is it any surprise that forgiveness is the basis of a healthy human existence? No one gets through life unscathed. All of us have to forgive someone at one time or another. And it can be very difficult. But we need to understand that the consequences of unforgiveness can be worst than the offense we need to forgive. Sickness, mental illness, stress and poor life choices can all be the result of a bitter unforgiving spirit. Are you hurt, bitter, angry, gripped by the inability to forgive? Leanne Payne, in her book *Listening Prayer*, says, "We do not forgive evil. We hate evil. But we find the grace to forgive those in the grip of evil, those who did the evil against us." According to Neil Anderson, in his book *Bondage Breaker*, "Forgiveness is not forgetting what happened. Rather, it is agreeing to live with the consequences of another person's wrongdoing, it is acknowledging the hurt and hate." When you do, something deeply spiritual happens. God can suddenly help you see His deep love and forgiveness for you and His Holy Spirit gives you the ability to forgive, even when you won't feel like it. He will help you make the choice to forgive. Set yourself free, choose to forgive today.

TODAY'S PRAYER Father, forgiving those that have hurt me is hard. Bring to my mind today, those that I need to forgive. Then help me, by Your grace, to be honest about my hurt and hate and then to deliberately choose to forgive them, just as You deliberately died on the cross and forgave me. Set me free today from the bondage of unforgiveness. Amen.

Don't Give Up Doing Good

TODAY'S VERSE "So let's not get tired of doing what is good. At just the right time we will reap a harvest of blessing if we don't give up" (Galatians 6:9).

TODAY'S THOUGHT It is hard work doing good. It seems like there is always a shortcut, a reason to delay, an easier way. It is easier to complain than to fix something. It is easier to quit than to go the extra mile. We find ourselves asking, "If this is so good, why is it so hard?" Besides, there is no way you will ever get paid for all you are doing; most of the time, your efforts will go unrewarded. And yet we do good because it is the right thing to do. It is His will, it is what Jesus would do. Nobody knew this more than the Apostle Paul. He pens these words for our encouragement, "Don't get tired of doing good! You will reap a harvest of blessing, just don't give up!" What good are you doing? What have you started but need to get back to? Are you discouraged? Do you feel like giving up? Talk to God about it today. Let Him know. Ask Him for strength and joy. Ask Him to give you a glimpse of the possibilities, and then get back up and continue. You will see the end, there will be a blessing ... don't give up.

TODAY'S PRAYER Lord, You know where I am at. You know the good I am trying to do. You know my struggle. I cannot see the end. I need Your help. I need Your strength. I recommit myself today to doing the good that You have called me to do. Lord, I want to see the harvest of blessing. Amen.

Tongue and Temper

TODAY'S VERSE "Understand this, my dear brothers and sisters: You must all be quick to listen, slow to speak, and slow to get angry. If you claim to be religious but don't control your tongue, you are fooling yourself, and your religion is worthless" (James 1:19, 26).

TODAY'S THOUGHT James doesn't pull any punches. He knows how easy it is to pretend we are living for Christ. We have all the right outward behavior. We know the right phrases, go to the right programs, and do the right ministries. But James doesn't talk about any of that. Instead, he gets right to the heart of Christianity. He says that we must be quick to listen, slow to speak and slow to get angry. How different would this world be if all would heed what James has said? How many fights, feuds, and even wars have been fought because people would not control their tongue or emotions? How worthless has our Christianity seemed to others because we did not allow James's admonition to permeate our behavior? If Jesus would be Lord and Master of our life, then He must be Lord and Master of our tongue and temper. If this has been a weakness, confess it to Christ and ask for the help of His Holy Spirit. He will guide you. Today, might we give our emotions to Christ. When given an opportunity today, might we be quick to listen, slow to speak and slow to get angry.

TODAY'S PRAYER Father, You know how many times I have been so swift to speak and get angry. You how I have not listened to others the way I should. I confess my poor habits and ask, dear Lord Jesus, that You would forgive me and fill me with Your Holy Spirit. Give me the discipline I need today to be quick to listen, slow to speak, and slow to get angry. Amen.

Focus on Him

TODAY'S VERSE "Have nothing to do with sexual immorality, impurity, lust, and evil desires. Don't be greedy, for a greedy person is an idolater, worshiping the things of this world. Now is the time to get rid of anger, rage, malicious behavior, slander, and dirty language. Don't lie to each other, for you have stripped off your old sinful nature and all its wicked deeds. Put on your new nature, and be renewed as you learn to know your Creator and become like him" (Colossians 3:5-10).

TODAY'S THOUGHT Just say no! Okay, maybe it's not quite that easy. But you must admit that the attitude you take into a situation helps shape the outcome. If we can read this list that Paul gives us and determine that with God's strength we are going to say "No" before we get into a challenging situation, it will help. Paul uses phrases like "Have nothing to do with" and "get rid of." This indicates that God expects us to take some initiative. What I like the best about today's passage is the phrase, "Be renewed as you learn to know your Creator and become like Him." So, do we get victory over these sins because we focus on them and fight diligently to overcome, or because we focus on God and try to be more like Him? Sure, it is some of each, but I really believe that a positive focus will always win over the negative. Try what Paul suggests, focus on God, get to know Him, let Him mold you more into His likeness, and He will help you take care of any negative behavior. It's like the old saying, "Love God and do as you please."

TODAY'S PRAYER Lord, You know I want to live a life that pleases You. I don't want to be sexually immoral, evil or greedy. I don't want to be angry or full of slander or dirty language. I don't want to lie. Help me today to focus on You. Help me to know You, to love you, to commune with You, and I will trust You with all the other behaviors. Help me today to be more like You. In Jesus' name. Amen.

This Day

TODAY'S VERSE This is the day the LORD has made; let us rejoice and be glad in it. Give thanks to the LORD, for he is good; his love endures forever" (Psalm 118:24, 29).

TODAY'S THOUGHT In most cases, there is a choice. Even if there is no other way out of a situation you still can choose how you react to the inevitability of the event. Paul writes in Galatians 5:22-23, "But the fruit of the Spirit is love, joy, peace, patience, kindness, goodness, faithfulness, gentleness, and self-control." Here, we have a broad range of godly reactions to our situation. Add to that list faith, hope prayer. How else can we react when the Psalmist suggests, "This is the day the LORD has made; let us rejoice and be glad in it"? I know how hard life can be. I know there are difficulties, horrific situations, and sometimes a seemingly hopeless situation—but God has made this day. Today is yours. What you do with it may have human limitations, may have the deck stacked against it, but know this: nothing, nothing, nothing can take you out of the love that God has for you, and you can rejoice and be glad in this day.

TODAY'S PRAYER Father, I know I have a choice. Today, I choose You. I choose to rejoice and be glad in this day. Give me this day my daily bread. Lead me this day and keep me from falling into temptation. Dear Father, this is a day You have made. With Your strength, I will rejoice and be glad in it. Amen.

As His Child, We Bear His Name

TODAY'S VERSE "Imitate God, therefore, in everything you do, because you are his dear children. Live a life filled with love, following the example of Christ" (Ephesians 5:1-2).

TODAY'S THOUGHT The story goes that a young boy was brought before Alexander the Great for stealing a horse. Alexander saw how young he was and heard his story and decided he would be lenient. Getting ready to release him, Alexander asked the young boy, "What is your name?" He replied, "Alexander, sir." Alexander the Great was furious and asked him again, "What is your name?" The boy, this time with fear in his voice, said, "Alexander, sir." In anger, Alexander the Great threw the boy to the ground, pointed at him, and said, "Boy, change your conduct, or change your name." I wonder...are we a good representative of the name of Christ, or would the cause of Christ be better served if we did not call ourselves a Christian? Being His child is a privilege and an honor. So that we don't bring any reproach to His name, our goal should be to live a life of love just like He did. How can we be a good representative of His name today?

TODAY'S PRAYER Dear Jesus, I know that I bear Your name and haven't imitated You the way that I should. I haven't been the best representative of who You are. Help me live out Your love in everything I do today, so Your name will get the glory and honor it deserves. Amen.

A Citizen of Heaven

TODAY'S VERSE "You are a chosen people. You are royal priests, a holy nation, God's very own possession. As a result, you can show others the goodness of God, for he called you out of the darkness into his wonderful light. Once you had no identity as a people; now you are God's people. Once you received no mercy; but now you have received God's mercy" (1 Peter 2:9-10).

TODAY'S THOUGHT I grew up as an American, but without much of an ethnic heritage. On the other hand, two of my best friends did. Steve Camarata was Italian and Ron Torigan was Armenian. I enjoyed learning about their heritage, foods, and customs. I always loved their family gatherings and the sense of belonging to a common past and future. I have often felt that is what Christianity should be about. As Christians, if God is our father, then we are all related through Him and our citizenship is not just of this world, but of the one to come. In this passage, Peter is talking to all of us who believe. All of us who call on the name of Christ for our salvation. We are a chosen people! But we are not to keep this truth to ourselves. It is God's will that all people become part of His forever family. Because we are God's chosen people, Royal Priests, a Holy Nation, Peter wrote, "You can show others the goodness of God, for he called you out of the darkness into his wonderful light." It is marvelous that once we were outside God's family, but then we saw the light, and now we belong to Him. Let's share this great privilege with others so they, too, can enjoy being a citizen of Heaven.

TODAY'S PRAYER Dear Lord Jesus, once I was without mercy and forgiveness in my life. Then You came along and called me into Your kingdom. Thank You for forgiving me of all my sins and making me Your child. Help me, even today, to share with others that do not know You, how they can come to know You as their personal Savior, how they too can enter Your forever kingdom. Amen.

Praise Him

TODAY'S VERSE They sang: "Blessing and honor and glory and power belong to the one sitting on the throne and to the Lamb forever and ever" (Revelation 5:13).

Praise the LORD! Praise God in his sanctuary; praise him in his mighty heaven! Praise him for his mighty works; praise his unequaled greatness! Let everything that breathes sing praises to the LORD! Praise the LORD" (Psalm 150:1-2, 6).

TODAY'S THOUGHT We often have so many pressing issues that it is easy to come to God and pour out our requests without saying anything of praise toward God. But when we forget to praise God, it is us who misses a blessing. It is ironic that we come to bless God with our praises and we are blessed in the process. Derek Prince once said, "If we only have ten minutes to pray, eight of them should be spent in praise!" There is so much we can praise God for today. Praise Him for His power. Praise Him for His glory. Praise Him for His provision. Praise Him for His love toward us. Praise Him for His death and resurrection. Praise Him for being our Almighty God. Who are we that God would allow us to even utter His name in praise, yet He does. He desires our praise and gratitude. Today, lift your voice in praise to Him. Let everything that is in us praise the Lord!

TODAY'S PRAYER Father, I confess I have not praised You as I should. I become so occupied with this life that You have given me. So busy that I forget to stop and thank You for all you have done for me. So busy that I forget to praise You for who you are. Today, I come to say, "Thank You!" Thank You for dying on the cross for my sins. Thank You for all your provision. Thank You for loving me and taking care of me. I stop now to praise You for Your majesty and power, for Your Holiness and unfailing love. I love You, Father God, and praise You today in the name of my Lord and Savior, Jesus Christ. Amen.

Come to God with Confidence

TODAY'S VERSE "Let us then approach the throne of grace with confidence, so that we may receive mercy and find grace to help us in our time of need" (Hebrews 4:16).

"This is the confidence we have in approaching God: that if we ask anything according to his will, he hears us. And if we know that he hears us—whatever we ask—we know that we have what we asked of him" (1 John 5:14-15).

TODAY'S THOUGHT Confidence. There are many ways you can approach God. You could be fearful, apathetic, humble, arrogant, with faith or without it, confused or assured, angry or in worship. You can also come to God with full assurance and confidence that He loves you and will answer your prayer. In her book *Listening Prayer,* Leanne Payne writes, "In a day when we are out of touch with the soul and its way of communicating and interacting with God, we have to learn anew how to receive from Him." She continues, "It is really simple. Through an act of the will we release our faith in confidence and receive what we have asked for, thanking God in advance for the answer." This happens as we dialog with God about His will. "What is it you want, Father?" we ask. And when He answers (and He will in His time), then we can go to God with confidence, knowing He will do His will. John says it this way, "This is the confidence we have in approaching God: that if we ask anything *according to his will*, he hears us. And if we know that he hears us—whatever we ask—we know that we have what we asked of him." What do you want to ask God for today? Come to Him with confidence and talk to Him about it.

TODAY'S PRAYER Father, help me learn to be more intimate with You and to have confidence, even today, in who You are and how much You love me. Lord, You know my situation. You know my needs. Help me to know what Your will is in these matters, so I can pray accordingly and thank You in advance for Your answer. In Jesus' name, I pray. Amen.

A New Person

TODAY'S VERSE "Salvation is not a reward for the good things we have done, so none of us can boast about it. For we are God's masterpiece. He has created us anew in Christ Jesus, so we can do the good things he planned for us long ago" (Ephesians 2:9-10).

TODAY'S THOUGHT Motives can be complex. So much of what we feel and do is because of what we believe. What we believe creates our motives. A negative self-image can create a motive that drives us to do what we think will make us acceptable in other people's eyes. What about God's eyes? If our eternal destiny is at risk, doesn't it make sense that we do all we can to earn our way into God's favor? Yet that is exactly what Paul was trying to argue against. Paul writes, "Salvation is not a reward for the good things we have done, so none of us can boast about it." You see, if holiness is the only thing that will satisfy a Holy God, then I can never earn my way to heaven. That is why Jesus had to be my substitute. His perfect life was traded for my jaded one. Now I am a child of God and Heaven because I took the citizenship He offered me. He made me a new person. Have you taken His offer to become His child? You can today. Then you know what you will find out about doing good? It's not to earn God's love, it's because you have it.

TODAY'S PRAYER Thank You, Lord Jesus, for dying on the cross for me. I know I need Your perfect life as a substitute for my own sinful one. I understand You died for me, and today I accept Your free gift of salvation. Amen.

June 7
Show Me the Way

TODAY'S VERSE "Trust in the LORD with all your heart; do not depend on your own understanding. Seek his will in all you do, and he will show you which path to take" (Proverbs 3:5-6).

"My child, pay attention to what I say. Listen carefully to my words. Don't lose sight of them. Let them penetrate deep into your heart, for they bring life to those who find them, and healing to their whole body. Guard your heart above all else, for it determines the course of your life" (Proverbs 4:20-23).

TODAY'S THOUGHT Is the Bible just an ordinary book to you? Just some old religious sayings? Perhaps a few good stories, but really, nothing to take seriously? If so, let me challenge you to reconsider your view. You see, there is a wisdom that only comes from God. It comes from reading His Word, meditating on it and committing yourself to what it says. This wisdom is the secret to life! Today, heed what Solomon is saying when he writes, "Trust in God, don't lean on our own understanding." Pay attention to what His word says, listen closely, let it penetrate deep into your being and God will bless you. And guess what the results will be? God will direct your way. His word will give you life and healing. Your reading and understanding will help you guard your heart and determine the course of your life. Start today, make a commitment to read and study God's word, the Bible.

TODAY'S PRAYER Father, You know my life, my situation, and circumstances. You know my emotions and my health. I need You. I need Your wisdom. I need Your understanding in order to make it through the day. Help me guard my heart by reading Your word. Let Your words that I read sink down deep into my soul and guide me, protect me and give me direction. Show me the way I should go even today, I pray. In Jesus' name. Amen.

Power and Majesty

TODAY'S VERSE "We did not follow cleverly invented stories when we told you about the power and coming of our Lord Jesus Christ, but we were eyewitnesses of his majesty" (2 Peter 1:16).

TODAY'S THOUGHT The Bible makes it plain that there is a spiritual battle going on for the souls of mankind. It is more than good versus bad. Part of the satanic plan is to confuse people about God's plan. We are warned that Satan often comes as an *angel of light*. For centuries, fiction has imitated the supernatural. Fairytales, myths, folk stories with magical powers and superheroes not only imitate the supernatural, they plant a seed of doubt in believing that the Bible is true. After all, a fairytale is make believe, so why believe the stories told in scriptures. Peter knew this was happening. That is why he insisted that we know that he and the other disciples were not following some clever invented story. Instead, they were sharing about what they witnessed. They witnessed the very power and majesty of Christ. Majesty, that splendor of character, greatness, authority and sovereign power that Christ exhibited in the way He lived. What if you and I could say with Peter that we were eyewitnesses of this same power and majesty today? We can, you know. We can experience the real, living Christ today, just like the disciples. Ask Christ if it is true. Go ahead—talk to Him about His power and majesty. Ask Him to reveal Himself to you. Today, begin a deeper walk with Him. If you do, you too will join Peter and the millions of others who, through the centuries, have known His power and majesty.

TODAY'S PRAYER Father, I want to know You in all Your power and majesty. I want to be an eyewitness to the same kinds of things that Peter experienced. Help me believe. Increase my faith. Make Your supernatural presence a reality in my life. I pray this in Jesus' name. Amen.

Where Do You Go?

TODAY'S VERSE "So, let us come boldly to the throne of our gracious God. There we will receive his mercy, and we will find grace to help us when we need it most" (Hebrews 4:16).

TODAY'S THOUGHT Where do you go when there is trouble? There are a lot of choices. We can run to our friends. Friends who listen and understand and help us when we need it are a true blessing. But not all of us have those kinds of friends. Sometimes, it is easier for us to simply run away. This can be in many different forms. It can be procrastination—you know, where we will always get to some solution later. It could be an addiction, to simply anesthetize ourselves from the situation. It could be plain running full steam ahead, ignoring any problems and focusing on achievement or materialism. There is a better way. Today's scripture gives us another option. One that makes good sense. The author of Hebrews writes, "So let us come boldly to the throne of our gracious God. There we will receive his mercy, and we will find grace to help us when we need it most." You notice the verse doesn't say to be timid. It says to "boldly" come to God. And what do we get when we find ourselves in His presence? Mercy and grace. Two of the most beautiful words in the Bible. Mercy is not giving us what we deserve. Grace is *giving us what we do not deserve*. Thank God today that He has His mercy and grace available for you.

TODAY'S PRAYER Father, thank You for Your love for me. Thank You that You have promised me that I can come boldly to You, anytime—day or night. I can come boldly with my problems, my issues, my concerns, and weaknesses. I come to You now, dear Father. Hear my needs, hear the deep inner thoughts and concerns of my heart. Please make me conscious of Your wonderful mercy and grace that You have promised to me. In Jesus' name, I pray. Amen.

Focus on Believing

TODAY'S VERSE "Now to him who is able to do immeasurably more than all we ask or imagine, according to his power that is at work within us, to him be glory in the church and in Christ Jesus throughout all generations, forever and ever! Amen." (Ephesians 3:20-21).

TODAY'S THOUGHT Which are you: the glass is half empty or the glass is half full? When it comes to reading today's verse, it really makes a difference. It's easy to let our *glass half empty* attitude bring down a *glass full and running over* type verse. What do you think when you read, "Him who is able to do immeasurably more than all we ask or imagine"? Bill Johnson, in his book *When Heaven Invades Earth*, writes, "Faith is not the absence of doubt. It is the presence of belief." So maybe today we shouldn't worry about our doubts. It's okay to have them. We all do. But for today, perhaps we should just focus on believing what God has said. He *can* do more than you and I can ever imagine. Ask God to help you believe this today. Give Him your worries, fears, and problems. Let Him control your life. He is more than able!

TODAY'S PRAYER Father, today, instead of trying to rid myself of doubt, I choose to believe You are able to do more than I can ever imagine. Today, I choose faith. Today, I choose to trust You. Today, I choose Your love for me and will live today in this hope, that You are alive and are able. In Jesus' name. Amen.

Trust in His Love

TODAY'S VERSE "Let all who fear the LORD repeat: 'His faithful love endures forever.' In my distress, I prayed to the LORD, and the LORD answered me and set me free. The LORD is for me, so I will have no fear. What can mere people do to me? Yes, the LORD is for me; he will help me" (Psalm 118:4-7).

TODAY'S THOUGHT What a marvelous passage. Our faith is in a God who knows. Our faith is in a God who is able. Our faith is in a God who cares. Our faith is in a God whose love endures forever! A tragic situation faced our family. My middle son was in critical condition after being hit by a car. My youngest son was shaken to the core, and that night before he went to sleep asked me to pray with him. I prayed with all my heart. Afterward, as I was leaving, he asked me, "That won't really make a difference, will it?" I know he believed, but he was as fearful as I was. I looked at him and said, "Yes, I believe it makes a difference. I always pray for God's power. I ask for His power, but I trust in His love." Like the Psalmist, we, too, can pray in our distress and the Lord, He will answer. The Lord is for you, you can trust in His love.

TODAY'S PRAYER Lord, I don't know everything that is going on. I can't see the future. I know I often waiver in my faith. But Lord, I know in my distress I can call upon You. Help me with those special burdens I am carrying. Most of all, help me today to really trust in Your love. Amen.

Our Purpose

TODAY'S VERSE "Love the LORD your God with all your heart, all your soul, all your strength, and all your mind.' And, 'Love your neighbor as yourself" (Luke 10:27).

TODAY'S THOUGHT We search for our place in this world. What is my purpose? Why am I here? How can I make sense of this life? These are questions that all of us ask. And then you come across today's verse. What a succinct answer to our philosophical dilemma. What is our purpose? To love God, but not with some idealistic romantic sentimentality. Rather, we are to love God with all our heart, soul, strength and mind! This is a radical love that comes from deep inside of us. As He permeates our life, we find the inner resources to love Him even more. God has also created us with the purpose to love others as we do ourselves. What is our higher calling? Is there a job description loftier than to be God's ambassador of love? Someone once said, "Love God and do as you please." At first, it sounds like an oxymoron, but upon reflection, if we love God the way He has asked us to, we would not do anything that would contradict that love. That means when we love our family, we are loving God. When we work hard at work, we are loving God. When we are polite to that stranger, we are loving God. When we love our spouse, we are loving God. When we enjoy watching the sunset, we are loving God. Might we start today, loving God with our whole heart, soul, strength, and mind, and love our neighbor as we do ourselves.

TODAY'S PRAYER Dear Heavenly Father, help me right now become conscious of Your love for me. Help me know Your love so intimately, that every part of me becomes permeated with it. Then I will be able to love You with my whole heart, soul, strength, and mind, and those around me like I love myself. Help me love You this way even today, through and in the power of Your Holy Spirit. Amen.

Correct Your Course

TODAY'S VERSE "But your sinful behavior has separated you from God" (Isaiah 59:2).

"When he finally came to his senses, he said to himself, 'I will go home to my father and say, "Father, I have sinned against both heaven and you"'" (Luke 15:17-18).

TODAY'S THOUGHT Attitudes and behavior. How easily they can get us off course. Left unchecked, we can find ourselves far from where we wanted to be. It's like that in sailing. You don't get to the other side of the lake in a straight line. Storms, waves and the wind all send you off course. Instead, you must constantly adjust your sails and correct your course to reach your destination. In life, it is our sinful behavior and attitudes that separate us from God. It was this way in the parable of the Prodigal Son. It was the son who decided to leave home and rebel against the father. But there is hope. Jesus said that the son was at a low point, feeding the pigs, and finally came to his senses. He thought of his father's love and mercy and decided to go back home. Do you feel far from God today? Do you feel off course? Come to Him. Come to repentance, come in true sorrow and ask for His forgiveness. Ask Him to help you correct your course. When you do, listen to the promise Joel makes, "He is merciful and compassionate, slow to get angry and filled with unfailing love."

TODAY'S PRAYER Father, You know my attitudes and behavior. You know how I have wandered far from You. But today, Father, I have come to my senses. I want to come back. I thank You for Your mercy and compassion, Your forgiveness and unfailing love for me and I choose to accept that love and forgiveness right now. I choose now, in the power and help of Your Holy Spirit, to correct my course. Amen.

Powerful Possibilities

TODAY'S VERSE "I also pray that you will understand the incredible greatness of God's power for us who believe him. This is the same mighty power that raised Christ from the dead and seated him in the place of honor at God's right hand in the heavenly realms" (Ephesians 1:19-20).

TODAY'S THOUGHT How would it change your life if you really understood the power God has for you? Can you imagine someone only living on $20,000 a year when they had a million dollars given to them and placed in their bank account? It would be foolishness to have a million dollars and never understand all that you could do with it. Yet what must God think when He has deposited into our life account His incredible power, and we never avail ourselves of it, we only live on a fraction of what He has supplied us with? How different would our life be if we really begin to understand how He wants us to use His power? Pray today that God will open your eyes to all that He wants to do in your life through His powerful possibilities.

TODAY'S PRAYER Dear Father, help me to understand all the power You have for my life. Help me see how I am a steward of that power, how You want to use Your power in and through my life. Please Lord, open my eyes to the possibilities that Your power can have for my life, then give me the faith today to use it. In Jesus' name. Amen.

June 15
Praise Him Today

TODAY'S VERSE "I will exalt you, my God and King, and praise your name forever and ever. I will praise you every day; yes, I will praise you forever. Great is the LORD! He is most worthy of praise! No one can measure his greatness" (Psalm 145:1-5).

TODAY'S THOUGHT Have you ever praised the Lord? No, I mean really praised the Lord? It could have been a quiet, sweet praise that brought tears to your eyes. Perhaps it was a shout-out-loud, hand clapping exuberance. If you haven't been praising the Lord lately, today would be a great time to start. David said that he praised God every day. Why? Because David knew that God was worthy of his praise! We, too, can praise God. Just start to think of all the goodness in your life. Think of all that you have. Think of those most precious to you. Think of the fact that today you are alive, and if you are alive, God has a purpose for you. If that is not enough, think of the fact that God loves you unconditionally. He has forgiven you for all the wrong you have ever done through the sacrificial death of His Son. Finally, think of how almighty God is. Think of how awesome He is. His wisdom, majesty, power, and greatness are without limit. So, what is stopping you? Right now, stop and praise the Lord. Tell Him how much you love Him. Tell Him how great and majestic He is and how thankful you are to have a relationship with Him. He is worthy of our praise.

TODAY'S PRAYER Almighty, glorious, everlasting, majestic God. I come now to bow before You. I come to praise Your Holy name. I come to lift my voice from the depth of my soul and say, "Halleluiah." I thank You for who You are and for what You have done in my life. I thank and praise You for all that I have and for all that I am. I thank You for Your love for me, for Your death on the cross for me, and for the gift of Your Holy Spirit. I praise You God for Your greatness. I praise You God and affirm how great You are. Truly, You are worthy of all my praise. Amen.

Answered Prayers

TODAY'S VERSE "We have placed our confidence in him, and he will continue to rescue us. And you are helping us by praying for us. Then many people will give thanks because God has graciously answered so many prayers for our safety" (2 Corinthians 1:11).

TODAY'S THOUGHT Prayer. How many times are we tempted to think that it doesn't matter? How many times does it feel as if our prayers are bouncing off the ceiling, not affecting any outcome? Yet we see in today's verse that Paul is saying, "You are helping us by praying for us." Now, Paul knew where the real credit belonged. He confesses that his confidence is in God, who continues to rescue him, but he is quick to add that praying to God is a catalyst that often causes the power of God to prevail. God designed it that way. Our almighty, all-knowing, all-powerful God has chosen to allow His power to be used at the point of our involvement. He chose you and me to be His co-laborers, His agents in this world charged with the responsibility of invoking His power. After all, Jesus himself taught us to pray, "Your kingdom come, Your will be done on earth as it is in Heaven." Paul said, "Many people will give thanks because God answered so many prayers for our safety!" Let me ask you, how many people will give thanks because you prayed on their behalf? It's not too late! Start praying today. Pray for your family, pray for your friends. Pray for those at work. Pray for your church. When you are done, pray some more. God desires our prayers. He desires to work out His will in harmony with our requests.

TODAY'S PRAYER Dear Jesus, I feel like Your disciples who asked You to teach them to pray. I am so ignorant, so inexperienced, so naïve about prayer. Holy Spirit, teach me, guide me, instruct me. Help me to know what to pray. Give me the faith to trust You. Today, embolden my heart to pray in a way that brings You glory and works on behalf of those that so desperately need Your touch. Amen.

God Will Rescue You

TODAY'S VERSE "We were crushed and overwhelmed beyond our ability to endure, and we thought we would never live through it. In fact, we expected to die. But as a result, we stopped relying on ourselves and learned to rely only on God, who raises the dead. And he did rescue us from mortal danger, and he will rescue us again. We have placed our confidence in him, and he will continue to rescue us"   (2 Corinthians 1:8-10).

TODAY'S THOUGHT Sometimes, life gets so hard. You wonder how you will make it. And then you come to a passage of scripture like today's and become encouraged deep down in your soul. Paul was overwhelmed beyond his ability to endure, but through it, he learned not to rely on himself but to rely on God. God who is so powerful that He can raise the dead! As a result, Paul put all his confidence in God who he knew would rescue him again. What about you? Is there something that is wearing you down? Do you, or someone you love, need rescuing? If so, come to God today. Bring your situation to Him who is faithful. Place your confidence in Him and He will continue to rescue you.

TODAY'S PRAYER Father, thank You that I can come to You with my deepest sorrow, my gravest situation, and my greatest fears. I thank You that I can put my confidence in the fact that You will hear my prayers and rescue me. I commit myself to You today and will rely on You to provide all my needs. In Jesus' name. Amen.

Healed Healers

TODAY'S VERSE "God is our merciful Father and the source of all comfort. He comforts us in all our troubles so that we can comfort others. When they are troubled, we will be able to give them the same comfort God has given us" (2 Corinthians 1:3-4).

TODAY'S THOUGHT I love the term "wounded healer." It was coined by Henri Nouwen in his book by the same name. It conjures up the image of a person that comes alongside someone and shares healing with great understanding, compassion and empathy. Why? Because they have been in the same situation. They share the same wounds and scars. They know the other person's pain. But Paul is going a step farther than just being a wounded healer. He is suggesting that we be a "healed healer!" There is great empathy and compassion in being wounded and helping another with their wound, but besides empathy and compassion, there is hope, health, and wholeness offered by a healed healer. Paul states that God is the merciful father and the source of all comfort. As we come to Him and receive comfort, we are to go and give this same comfort to others. As God heals us, we share that healing. Should we be full of empathy? Yes, much so. Should we be compassionate? Yes, we of all people. Should we be patient, kind and understanding? If we are not, then we have forgotten that it was by His grace that we were healed. When God comforts us, we are grateful, humbled and full of joy. Make His comfort complete by going and comfort others in the same way. May we never forget His mercy. May we never forget to treat others in the same way He has treated us.

TODAY'S PRAYER Dear Father, God of all comfort. Thank You for the many times You have comforted me. Forgive me for not being as compassionate and patient as I should toward others. Forgive me for forgetting how much You have done for me. Help me today to extend that same comfort to others that You have given to me. Help me love those that You bring into my path today in the same way that You love me. Amen.

Ask for Wisdom

TODAY'S VERSE "My child, listen to what I say and treasure my commands. Tune your ears to wisdom, and concentrate on understanding. Cry out for insight, and ask for understanding. Search for them as you would for silver; seek them like hidden treasures. Then you will understand what it means to fear the LORD, and you will gain knowledge of God. For the LORD grants wisdom! From his mouth come knowledge and understanding" (Proverb 2:1-6).

"If you need wisdom, ask our generous God, and he will give it to you. He will not rebuke you for asking" (James 1:5).

TODAY'S THOUGHT In I Kings, the third chapter, God asks Solomon, David's son and the new King of Israel, "What do you want?" Solomon gives an eloquent response and asks for wisdom. God was impressed and blessed Solomon beyond measure. I admire Solomon's choice. He could have asked for riches, fame, land, skills, athletic ability, immortality; a myriad of choices were his to ask for, but he chose wisdom. He knew that with wisdom comes so much more. With wisdom comes knowledge and understanding. It is more precious than hidden treasure. The best news is that God will give it to us freely if we ask for it in faith. What do you need wisdom about today? Is it a relationship, job situation, financial worry, medical choice or family issue? God hears your request. Search for wisdom, cry out for insight, seek for it and God will grant your request. Like James said, "If you need wisdom, ask our generous God, and He will give it to you."

TODAY'S PRAYER Dear Almighty, all-wise God. I need Your wisdom today. I need You to speak to me, to show me Your way, to give me Your knowledge and understanding. I cannot live the way You want me to without it. I want it more than riches, fame, or success. Thank You that you said if I need wisdom I can ask You and You will give it to me. So, Father, I come now, bowing before You, asking for wisdom, knowledge, and understanding. Thank You for hearing my prayer. I ask in the precious name of Jesus. Amen.

June 20
The Promised Land is Waiting

TODAY'S VERSE Then Caleb silenced the people before Moses and said, "We should go up and take possession of the land, for we can certainly do it." But the men who had gone up with him said, "We can't attack those people; they are stronger than we are." And they spread among the Israelites a bad report about the land they had explored" (Numbers 13:30-32).

TODAY'S THOUGHT Attitudes can change everything. You know the story. Moses sent spies into the Promised Land to see what it was like. All twelve men saw the same thing but came back with different conclusions. Two saw possibilities born out of faith and hope in God's love and power. The others saw defeat, death, dying and doom. The people believed the second story. Why is that? Why can we believe the death, dying and doom story so much easier than the land of milk and honey? What is it that keeps us from believing in the goodness of God? We don't doubt whether He can do good, we doubt whether He wants to. Dallas Willard, in his book *Hearing God*, shares why even the miracles of Jesus could not convince some people of His love and Lordship. Willard writes, "Our preexisting ideas and assumptions are precisely what determine what we can see, hear or otherwise observe." You see, Caleb's report could not change what the people already believed in their heart, that God did not really love them, and they were better off taking care of themselves. What do you think? Seeing a miracle won't change it. A good report won't change that deep-down doubt. Only repentance and a relationship can. Repent of unbelief, doubt, and fear, and then spend time with God. Don't quit. Every day, get to know Him until you sense His concern and His deep passion and love for you. Come to Him today, ask Him to show you His love. He will. The Promised Land is waiting.

TODAY'S PRAYER Oh Father, You know my heart. You know my doubts, fears, negative thoughts. I have had them all my life. I repent Lord. I want to believe. Help me correct my thinking. Help me know You more and more until my inner thoughts reflect the faith and love that You created me for. In Jesus' name. Amen.

How Do You Wait?

TODAY'S VERSE "Be still before the LORD and wait patiently for him" (Psalm 37:7).

TODAY'S THOUGHT Waiting can be hard, especially when we find ourselves in difficult situations. To waiting, we often add fretting. We create deadly combinations: waiting plus stewing, waiting plus conniving, waiting plus brooding. Instead, David adds *God* to the waiting. David tells us to be still before the Lord and wait patiently for Him. That means if we are going to add anything to waiting, it should be wait plus faith; wait plus prayer; wait plus hope; wait plus the peace that passes all understanding. Is there something that you are having trouble waiting for? Are you fretting, stewing, conniving or brooding? If so, give it to Jesus. Be still before Him and wait in faith, hope, and peace.

TODAY'S PRAYER Father, it is so hard to wait. Forgive me for fretting, stewing, conniving and brooding. Help me instead, to trust You. I surrender my situation to You. Today I will wait in faith, hope, and peace. Amen.

Filled with the Knowledge of God

TODAY'S VERSE For this reason, since the day we heard about you, we have not stopped praying for you and asking God to fill you with the knowledge of his will through all spiritual wisdom and understanding. And we pray this in order that you may live a life worthy of the Lord and may please him in every way: bearing fruit in every good work, growing in the knowledge of God, being strengthened with all power according to his glorious might so that you may have great endurance and patience, and joyfully giving thanks to the Father, who has qualified you to share in the inheritance of the saints in the kingdom of light" (Colossians 1:9-11).

TODAY'S THOUGHT Being filled with the knowledge of God is crucial to our Christian experience. But how does this happen? How are we filled with the knowledge of God? F.B. Meyers writes, "God's impressions within and His Word without are always corroborated by His providence around, and we should quietly wait until those three focus into one point." We gain knowledge as we quiet ourselves to listen to God, read His Word for understanding, and follow His leading as it is played out. Dallas Willard, in his book *Hearing God* shares, "So our union with God—His presence with us, in which our aloneness is banished, and the meaning and full purpose of human existence is realized—consists chiefly in a conversational relationship with God while we are each consistently and deeply engaged as His friend and collaborator in the affairs of the kingdom of Heaven." This's what Paul is saying. As we listen to God, muse on His word, and practice His presence as we go about living for Him, He will give us wisdom and knowledge, the fruit of good works and all the strength and power we need. Start today. Talk to God, read His Word and converse with Him as you go about your day. Does it get any better than that?

TODAY'S PRAYER Dear Father, is it true? Can I really be filled with Your knowledge and wisdom? Can my life bear good works? Can I really have Your strength and power in my life? This is what I desire. Please help me, Lord, with the discipline I need to quietly spend time listening to You and reading Your word. Amen.

What Do You Want Me to Do?

TODAY'S VERSE Jesus went through all the towns and villages, teaching in their synagogues, preaching the good news of the kingdom and healing every disease and sickness. When he saw the crowds, he had compassion on them, because they were harassed and helpless, like sheep without a shepherd. (Matthew 9:35-36).

TODAY'S THOUGHT Jesus saw the needs of His creation and traveled through towns and villages with compassion and help. Viv Grigg, in his book *Companion to the Poor*, has said it better than anyone I have ever read. "There is a drum-beat beating in my head day after day, a beat that impels me forward into long hours of discipline and constant work. It is the cry of those saved from their sins, only to be entangled again by that same sin—by the tentacles of their poverty, drawing them down, down, down till they are totally lost to this earth. We must work and direct our undivided energy and unflagging zeal to provide economic stability for these, our brothers and sisters in Christ. We must avoid being so busy working among the poor that we forget to deal with the problems of the slums themselves. The biblical response to poverty caused by sin is to preach the gospel to the sinner, but the biblical response to sin caused by poverty is to destroy the curse of poverty." Might we do both! Jesus did.

TODAY'S PRAYER Dear Jesus, I see Your compassion and I am humbled. Forgive me, for I have not cared like I should. I haven't been that involved in helping those in need. I want to make a difference, but how? What do You want me to do? Speak to me and show me, Lord. Even today, help me to see the needs around me through Your eyes. Then help me act on what You show me. I pray this Jesus, in your compassionate name. Amen.

Baby Steps

TODAY'S VERSE "For this very reason, make every effort to add to your faith goodness; and to goodness, knowledge; and to knowledge, self-control; and to self-control, perseverance; and to perseverance, godliness; and to godliness, brotherly kindness; and to brotherly kindness, love. For if you possess these qualities in increasing measure, they will keep you from being ineffective and unproductive in your knowledge of our Lord Jesus Christ" (2 Peter 1:5-8).

TODAY'S THOUGHT Have you bought the lie? Do you sit around wishing there was something you could do with your spiritual life? Do you feel helpless to live the kind of life that Christ has asked you to? Well, there is good news! You and I do not have to be a victim of satanic attacks or the pull of our old nature. God, in His Word, has suggested a better way. He tells us to make every effort to "add to your faith goodness; and to goodness, knowledge; and to knowledge, self-control; and to self-control, perseverance; and to perseverance, godliness; and to godliness, brotherly kindness; and to brotherly kindness, love." Every effort, I can live with that. Every effort means that we really try. It acknowledges that there may be setbacks, but that's okay. Get up, and make every effort again! That is what Peter means when he writes that we need to possess these qualities in increasing measure. He is talking about baby steps. We make every effort ... when we fall, we get up and make every effort again. When we do, look at the hope, look at what God promises. He says if we make every effort to increase our faith, goodness, knowledge, self-control, perseverance, godliness, brotherly kindness and love in baby steps, it will keep us from being ineffective and unproductive in our Christian walk. Today, you can claim this promise for yourself. Don't buy the lie. You can live for God today. You can make a difference, one baby step at a time.

TODAY'S PRAYER Dear God, I want to live for You, but I acknowledge that I keep tripping up. Help me take my faith and add to it, goodness, knowledge, self-control, perseverance, godliness, brotherly kindness and love in baby steps. Holy Spirit, convict me, guide me and give me the discipline to begin these baby steps today. In Jesus' name, I pray. Amen.

Do You Really Know Him?

TODAY'S VERSE "Grace and peace be yours in abundance through the knowledge of God and of Jesus our Lord. His divine power has given us everything we need for life and godliness through our knowledge of him who called us by his own glory and goodness" (2 Peter 1:2-3).

TODAY'S THOUGHT Do you know Christ? I don't mean, know *of* Christ, but do you *know* Christ to the point that knowing Him deeply influences your life? Look at today's verses. Peter is saying that we will experience an abundant amount of grace and peace through our knowledge of Christ. He then goes on to say that our knowledge of Christ will set loose the power of God and give us everything we need for life and godliness. I love that phrase, "Everything we need for life and godliness!" Some things? Almost everything? No, everything we need for life! This is no small claim. Peter is saying that our knowledge of Christ is crucial to everything we need in life. So, what does knowledge mean? Peter was using the Greek word that means a full knowledge, a deep participation by the knower in the object known so that it powerfully influences him or her. This is more than an acquaintance or a casual relationship. It is a passion to know, really know God. It is a hunger for His word, a longing to spend time in His presence, an openness to dialog freely with Him and listen to His voice. There is so much to gain by knowing Him, really knowing Him. You can start to know Him more today. He is waiting for you to try.

TODAY'S PRAYER Dear God, I confess my lack of spiritual knowledge. I have not taken the time I should to really know You. I haven't been real with You nor have I let You be real with me. But today, I want to start. I want to know You, really know You. I want to hear Your voice. I want to sense Your presence in my life. I want Your scriptures to come alive in my mind. Father, I want to know You as Father. Help me know You, I pray in Jesus' name. Amen.

Peace

TODAY'S VERSE "You will keep in perfect peace all who trust in you, all whose thoughts are fixed on you" (Isaiah 26:3).

TODAY'S THOUGHT Peace. It has many meanings. I heard a story of a man who commissioned a contest to see who could best paint a picture of peace. He would hang the entries in a gallery and let the townspeople vote on which picture best portrayed it. Beautifully painted sceneries with sunsets and ocean scenes draped across the gallery walls. Majestic mountains with beautiful colors were brought to the gallery and hung. Other painters submitted paintings of birds flying in the air, old people with peaceful smiles on their faces and children playing. People were hard-pressed to decide which was more peaceful. Finally, the day before voting, the last entry was being hung. As people saw it, they didn't quite understand why it was submitted. It was a picture of a turbulent river with a violent current smashing against the river canyon walls. Dark, ominous clouds were overhead. Felled trees littered the river's bank, and the wind was bending a tree in the foreground. Then someone pointed out in the branch of the tree was a little bird. The bird was whistling, enjoying the spray of the river below. Not worried about the river, the bird was in perfect peace. When the vote was finished everyone agreed that that was the most peaceful picture. Peace during peaceful times is one thing. Peace during life's troubled, stormy times is another. May God keep us in perfect peace today, as our minds trust in Him.

TODAY'S PRAYER Father, I pray for Your peace to fill my heart today. Thank You for Your unfailing love for me. Thank You for being my Father. I choose to fix my thoughts on You today, to trust You and commit every worry into Your capable hands. Amen.

Using Your Spiritual Gift

TODAY'S VERSE "Now about spiritual gifts, brothers, I do not want you to be ignorant. To one there is given through the Spirit the message of wisdom, to another the message of knowledge by means of the same Spirit, to another faith by the same Spirit, to another gifts of healing by that one Spirit, to another miraculous powers, to another prophecy, to another distinguishing between spirits, to another speaking in different kinds of tongues, and to still another the interpretation of tongues. All these are the work of one and the same Spirit, and he gives them to each one, just as he determines" (1 Corinthians 12:1, 8-11).

TODAY'S THOUGHT Can a carpenter build a house without tools? Can a farmer plant a field without seed? Can a professional athlete compete without the necessary skills? Why is it that we feel we can serve God to our fullest, do all that He has for us to do and see mighty deeds done in His name if we do not use the spiritual gifts He has given us? Look at the Church today. What's missing? Is there healing, miracles, a sense of God speaking to us? Is there great faith, godly knowledge or wisdom? Are we seeing great and mighty things done in the name of Jesus? Is injustice halted, the sick healed and the poor rescued? If these deeds sound more at home in a fairy tale than our church, perhaps we need to start using our spiritual gifts. God never expected us to do His work on our own. He sent the Holy Spirit to equip us, empower us and give us gifts to be used. God told us, through Paul, that He did not want us to be ignorant concerning spiritual gifts. Might we learn more about our own spiritual gifts today.

TODAY'S PRAYER Father, I know that You gave me the Holy Spirit to equip me for Your service. You said that You give all Christians a spiritual gift. Help me know what my spiritual gift is. Help me use it so I can do the work You called me to do in the fullness of Your power. Amen.

Do Over

TODAY'S VERSE "Have mercy on me, O God, according to your unfailing love; according to your great compassion blot out my transgressions. Wash away all my iniquity and cleanse me from my sin. For I know my transgressions, and my sin is always before me. Against you, you only, have I sinned and done what is evil in your sight so that you are proved right when you speak and justified when you judge. Create in me a pure heart, O God, and renew a steadfast spirit within me" (Psalm 51: 1-4, 10).

TODAY'S THOUGHT How many times have you wanted to do something over? "If I could just take back what I said." "If I could take the test again." "If I had one more chance!" In golf, it is the *mulligan*. In Monopoly, it is the *get out of jail* card. On Wheel of Fortune, it is the *free spin*. How many times do we need a do-over? King David needed one. He had committed adultery, resulting in the woman becoming pregnant. To make it worse, he had her husband killed! God sent Nathan the Prophet to David to rebuke him. David came under severe guilt and repented. Instead of running from God, he ran toward God. He openly admitted his sins and asked God for forgiveness. He experienced the love of God and complete forgiveness. His behavior is a wonderful example for us. He depended on God's unfailing love and look at what he asked for. Mercy, blotting out of his sins and cleansing his heart. David agreed with God, that he was guilty. But he also agreed with God, that His love is unfailing. Next was the do-over. David prayed, "Create in me a pure heart, O God, and renew a steadfast spirit in me!" Why not start over like David today? Make David's prayer your own.

TODAY'S PRAYER Dear Righteous Father. I know that You know all about me. You know my wrongdoing. I agree with You that I am guilty of so many things. I come now to confess that I need Your total forgiveness for all that I have done. I need a do-over. Please create in me pure heart. Please renew a right spirit in me. I come to You to start afresh right now. In Jesus' name. Amen.

He Will Never Forget You

TODAY'S VERSE "Can a mother forget the baby at her breast and have no compassion on the child she has borne? Though she may forget, I will not forget you! See, I have engraved you on the palms of my hands" (Isaiah 49:1, 6, 15).

"God has said, 'Never will I leave you; never will I forsake you'" (Hebrews 13:5).

TODAY'S THOUGHT The union between a mother and her little child is incredible. I watched my daughter-in-law interact with our new six-week-old granddaughter, doting over her. It was so tender. Our granddaughter laid there wiggling, smiling, making funny faces and squealing. I love the squeals! What an illustration. Like a mother's love, God's love for you is born out of creating you. God has formed you and has a unique love for you. But that is where the comparisons between God and a mother end. You see, it is possible for a mother to neglect her child. Incomprehensible as it may seem, a mother may even abandon and forget her child. But not God! He promises that He will never, never, never forget you! How can you be sure? He has engraved your name on His hands. He has etched you into the very flesh of His hands, a place He will never forget. Today, choose to rest in this truth; He knows your name, He loves you, He will never leave you or forsake you.

TODAY'S PRAYER Father, I thank You that I can trust You. Help me with my doubts, fears, and insecurities. Like a child, I reach out to You. Help me see Your hands with my name, my very being, engraved in them reaching toward me. Thank You that I am safe in Your love. Thank You that You promised that You will never forget me, leave me or forsake me. Amen.

I Can Only Imagine

TODAY'S VERSE "No eye has seen, no ear has heard, no mind has conceived what God has prepared for those who love him" (1 Corinthians 2:9).

TODAY'S THOUGHT Whenever our family has moved, my wife and I have worked together on finding a house. However, when we moved to Georgia, I was out there for two months before her. My son came with me and we looked for homes. He found one on the MLS listing and went to meet the people. He called me at work and said that he found the house for us. He was right. It was love at first sight. It was rustic, in the woods, and had a lot of potential. Of course, that meant it needed a lot of work. Somehow, though, I could see the finished home in my mind's eye. I was very excited and sent my wife a rendering of what I proposed. I promised her that I would get the house fixed up. I kept my word. I put in trails, two ponds, a guest apartment, bird sanctuary, plumbing, electric work, a deck and new floors. I painted, cleaned and put in gardens. I have never enjoyed a project more than that one. I really wanted my wife to love it like I did. Well, she fell in love with the house, too. Now imagine what Jesus feels like. He said that He went to prepare a place for us. And what a place it must be! Paul says that "No eye has seen, no ear has heard, no mind has conceived what God has prepared for those who love him." As the popular Christian song says, "I can only imagine!"

TODAY'S PRAYER Jesus, I thank You that You have gone on ahead to prepare a place in eternity for me. I cannot imagine what You must have in store. I only know that You love me and no one can even begin to conceive how great it will be to spend eternity with You. Let me live today with eternity in mind. Thank You, Lord Jesus. Amen.

All the Strength You Need

TODAY'S VERSE "If anyone serves, he should do it with the strength God provides" (I Peter 4:11).

"I can do everything through Him who gives me strength" (Philippians 4:13).

"I love you, O LORD, my strength" (Psalm 18:1).

TODAY'S THOUGHT Strength is the energy that God gives us to complete a task. It is what helps us endure to the end. Strength is also what helps us resist negative forces. What better place to get stronger than from God? He is able to provide all the strength we need to do what He calls us to do. Need to love someone who is unlovely? Ask Him for strength. Need to forgive someone who hurt you deeply? Ask Him for strength. Does something seem impossible? Ask Him for strength. Is fear crippling you or depression strangling you? Ask Him for strength. Paul said, "I can do everything through Christ who gives me strength." We can experience the same reality that Paul did. And when we do, we will be able to say with David, "I love you, O Lord, my strength!"

TODAY'S PRAYER Almighty God, I need Your strength. I can't live the life You want me to without it. Help me, Father. Give me all the strength I need to do all that You ask me to do this day. I thank You for hearing this prayer. I will step out in faith and go forward in the power and strength of Your might. Amen.

Staying on Course

TODAY'S VERSE "All Scripture is God-breathed and is useful for teaching, rebuking, correcting and training in righteousness" (2 Timothy 3:16).

TODAY'S THOUGHT God has not left us alone to wander through this world as helpless victims. He has given us His word to instruct and guide us. God does not wait until we make a mistake and then discard us. He has given us His word to rebuke and correct us. God does not leave us the way we are. He has given us His word to train us. Life is like a journey. There is a trail we can follow that will get us through the wilderness. Through His word, God shows us the trail to go on. His word also lets us know when we wander from the trail. The Bible also shows us how to get back on the trail again. Finally, the scriptures show us how to stay on the trail and not wander off. Read His word. Make a part of your daily routine. Through it, He will teach you everything you need to know about living this life.

TODAY'S PRAYER Father, I thank You for Your word. Please help me understand what the scriptures are saying. Help me apply it to my life. Holy Spirit, use the Bible and teach me, rebuke me, correct me and train me. Help me be the person You desire me to be. Amen.

Experiencing His Presence

TODAY'S VERSE "I will bless the LORD who guides me; even at night, my heart instructs me. I know the LORD is always with me. I will not be shaken, for he is right beside me" (Psalm 16:7, 8).

TODAY'S THOUGHT There is one prayer that has made all the difference in my life. It is one I need to pray over and over again. It is a form of discipline, for if I don't pray this prayer, I will not keep my spiritual vitality. The prayer is simple and yet powerful. It is, "Lord make me conscious of your presence." Being conscious of God's presence makes all the difference in the world. Because David was conscious of the fact that God was always with him, right beside him, he was not shaken during life's struggles. Instead, God guided him and instructed his heart at night. How about you and me? What if today we were conscious of God right next to us? What if we knew that He was in the same room we were? What if we sensed that He heard our thoughts and prayers and would to answer the questions we have? What if we experienced His comforting presence when we are under pressure? What if we knew He was present to hold our hand when we had that extremely challenging task to do? God is. God is always with us. Let us be conscious of His presence in all that we do today.

TODAY'S PRAYER Dear God, thank You for being with me constantly. Please make me aware of Your presence today. Help me to see how relevant You are to my life. Help me experience Your presence, to really know that You are always with me, in fact right beside me. Father, open my eyes to see You, my ears to hear You and my heart to sense Your very presence. In Jesus' name. Amen.

A Solid Foundation

TODAY'S VERSE "Do your best to present yourself to God as one approved, a workman who does not need to be ashamed and who correctly handles the word of truth" (2 Timothy 2:15).

"Therefore, everyone who hears these words of mine and puts them into practice is like a wise man who built his house on the rock. The rain came down, the streams rose, and the winds blew and beat against that house; yet it did not fall, because it had its foundation on the rock" (Matthew 7:24-25).

TODAY'S THOUGHT It matters what you build your life on. Both Jesus and Paul agreed that you need to build your life on the truth of the Bible. Not just knowing the truth, but living the truth. Jesus said, "Everyone who hears these words of mine and puts them in practice is like a wise man who built his house on the rock." Paul wrote that we should be a "workman that does not need to be ashamed, who correctly handles the word of truth." If we want our lives on firm ground, then we need to be grounded in His word. We need to read the Bible, study it and then apply it to our life. We need to live what we read. When we do, we will find that life will stand the tests of time.

TODAY'S PRAYER Lord Jesus, I want to live my life on solid ground. I want to be able to stand firm when I go through hard times. Help me to read Your word and understand its meaning. Help me to live what You tell me to do. I want to be a workman that does not need to be ashamed, who correctly handles Your word of truth! Amen.

What Have You Asked For?

TODAY'S VERSE "Until now you have not asked for anything in my name. Ask and you will receive, and your joy will be complete" (John 16:24).

"You do not have because you do not ask God. When you ask, you do not receive, because you ask with wrong motives, that you may spend what you get on your pleasures" (James 4:2-3).

TODAY'S THOUGHT I'm not sure which is sadder—a person who never gets a chance to have what he or she desires or a person who had all the chances in the world and never took one. Here we are with a God who is all-wise, all-powerful and all-loving. We also have Jesus Himself saying, "Until now you have not asked for anything in my name. Ask and you will receive, and your joy will be complete." And yet what do we do? What have we asked for lately? Jesus is not talking about a magic lamp that we rub three times and make wishes for our own pleasure. We aren't to ask God for things with wrong motives. Instead, Jesus is suggesting that we have a fellowship with His Father, which is so rich and deep that we end up aligning our will with His. When we know His will, it will bring us deep joy and great pleasure to ask God for it. We will be about the business of making His will done on earth as it is in Heaven. What at home, work or in your church can you ask God for? What can you ask for your family, friends, and coworkers that would be in alignment with His will? Pray that God will give you insight into His will and a Holy boldness to ask for it. When you do, you will receive, and your joy will be complete.

TODAY'S PRAYER Dear Father, I ask You to help me know what to pray for. Help me to know Your will for my life and for my family. Help me to know how to pray for my friends and co-workers. Help me pray for my relationships, career, and ministry. Speak to my heart and then give me the faith to ask. Help me not to be like the person who had so many chances in life but never took one. Help me to ask You for something special today! Amen.

He Will Intercede

TODAY'S VERSE "Therefore, he is able, once and forever, to save those who come to God through him. He lives forever to intercede with God on their behalf" (Hebrews 7:25).

"In the same way, the Spirit helps us in our weakness. We do not know what we ought to pray for, but the Spirit himself intercedes for us with groans that words cannot express" (Romans 8:26).

TODAY'S THOUGHT Have you ever had anyone intercede for you? In some circumstances, you need someone with special qualifications who is specifically equipped to represent your needs—perhaps a lawyer, customer service representative, a trusted friend or a medical professional. When you get the right person with the right skills, it's a beautiful thing to watch. When they're inept or insincere, watch out! Now here we are, trying to live our life—one person among billions of others. We have great needs, not only in this life but in the life ahead. We need help, but who will help us? Who can understand our plight? Who would care enough for us to do something? Who would have the power to effect any change? Thank God, the Father for His Son Jesus and His Holy Spirit. They are the ones interceding for us. Jesus intercedes for our sins with His own blood and the Holy Spirit intercedes for our weaknesses and needs in this life. Even when we don't know how to pray, the Holy Spirit passionately groans and pleads our case to God the Father. What compassion, what mercy. Even now, confess to Jesus your deepest needs. Come to Him with your hidden secrets, your most perplexing problems, your most heinous sins. He will intercede, and when He does, He will bring peace and deep joy to your heart.

TODAY'S PRAYER Dear Lord Jesus, I come to You as I am, desperate and needy for Your touch. I need Your help. You know my situation. I need You and Your Holy Spirit to intercede for me to God the Father. To Him, who can do all things. To Him, who is all love and all power. Dear Jesus, I give You my life today. Guide me, direct me, fill me with Your peace and power. I pray this in Your name, Lord Jesus. Amen.

How Do We Behave?

TODAY'S VERSE "Lead a life worthy of your calling, for you have been called by God. Always be humble and gentle. Be patient with each other, making allowance for each other's faults because of your love. Make every effort to keep yourselves united in the Spirit, binding yourselves together with peace. Get rid of all bitterness, rage, anger, harsh words, and slander, as well as all types of evil behavior. Instead, be kind to each other, tenderhearted, forgiving one another, just as God through Christ has forgiven you" (Ephesians 4:1-3; 31-32).

TODAY'S THOUGHT How can it get any clearer than this? Paul is commanding us to live like Christians should. This is not a *once and for all* choice, but rather, a daily decision to live the way Christ wants us to live. We are to be humble, gentle, forgiving, loving and patient. We are to get rid of bitterness, rage, anger, harsh words and slander. Throw it off! Stop. Instead, we are to be tenderhearted, forgiving and kind. How will we live during the next twenty-four hours? What are we going to choose to do today? We'll have opportunities all day to choose. But our choices need to be grounded in the Holy Spirit. Paul writes in Galatians that the fruit of the Holy Spirit, which is the by-product of living under the direction of the Holy Spirit in our life, is love, joy, peace, patience, kindness, goodness, faithfulness, gentleness, and self-control. We need to make living this way our goal. We need to ask the Holy Spirit to produce His fruit in our lives today. He will.

TODAY'S PRAYER Oh, Holy Spirit. I need to get rid of all the negative emotions and behaviors in my life. But I can't without You! I need You to produce Godly behavior in my life. I want love, joy, peace, patience, kindness, goodness, faithfulness, gentleness and self-control to be my normal experience. I want to be a witness to others of Your love through my behavior. Come, Holy Spirit. Convict me, correct me, forgive me, inspire me, teach me, guide me and fill me. Might I live completely under Your control. Might my life bear the fruit that only You can produce. Amen.

Our Real Purpose

TODAY'S VERSE "For we are God's workmanship, created in Christ Jesus to do good works, which God prepared in advance for us to do" (Ephesians 2:10).

TODAY'S THOUGHT Some people search a lifetime for a purpose. Why am I here? Where can I find meaning? We look for this *bigger-than-life* significance and we can't find it. We search for something that will fill this hollow feeling inside. There is a craving in our soul that we can't satisfy, a thirst that we cannot quench. It's like the song says, "we are looking for love (purpose) in all the wrong places." All the while the Bible gives a fundamental answer to the secret of life satisfaction. Paul sums up our purpose in one simple verse. You and I will never be happy, never feel fulfilled until we figure out what Paul is saying. He says that you and I are the workmanship of God. A specific personally made creation by Almighty God Himself. More than that, we were created for this one simple thing, to do good works! That's it. Our meaning, purpose, life satisfaction comes from living for God, from loving in His name, from doing good because He created us specifically to do good. What joy, what purpose, what meaning to know that we are hand-picked agents of God's goodness in this world. Do you believe this? Are you living this? If not, you can start today!

TODAY'S PRAYER Dear God, help me to fully understand what it means to be Your workmanship, created for good works. Help me to comprehend that You really know me, love me deeply and have specifically called me to be Your representative in this world. Thank You for such a glorious calling. Help me today to do Your good works which You prepared me to do before I was even born. You are my creator, I am Your servant. Thank You, Lord. Amen.

Wait on the Lord

TODAY'S VERSE "Wait for the LORD; be strong and take heart and wait for the LORD" (Psalm 27:14).

TODAY'S THOUGHT Sometimes you have to wait. But it is so hard. I had planted a whole new batch of elephant ears and caladiums in a shady path I made in the woods behind my house. I watered them faithfully, and after a couple weeks, I started to walk around to see if they were beginning to sprout. I couldn't find any sign of life. Day after day, I looked—nothing! I was starting to become angry. I kept asking myself, "Why haven't they broken ground yet?" Then anger turned to fear. "What if they were dead?" I thought. Finally, one day, when I was walking the path to see if any of the plants had sprouted up, a thought occurred to me. "None of my looking was going to make the plant sprout one second sooner than God had planned." I laughed and thought how much that was just like life. We don't like to wait. We want what we want, and we want it now! But we refuse to realize that waiting is more than waiting. So often, waiting is also becoming more understanding. Waiting is learning to be empathic. Waiting is gaining knowledge or building character. Waiting can often lead to situations where God gets all the glory. The plants did come up, each in their own time. They were beautiful. Likewise, so will our lives, as we are strong, take heart and wait on the Lord.

TODAY'S PRAYER Lord, I find it so hard to wait. I really want to trust You, but I need Your help. Help me today Father to be strong, to take heart and to wait on You. Amen.

A Sense of Blessing and Well-Being

TODAY'S VERSE "Even if my father and mother abandon me, the LORD will hold me close" (Psalm 27:10).

TODAY'S THOUGHT At first glimpse, this verse may not seem like it has much depth. But if we really understand its meaning it can change our lives. In his book *Experiencing Healing Prayer*, Rick Richardson shares, "From our mother we get our sense of being and well-being. From our father, we get a sense of blessing." The trouble is that none of us go through our childhood unscathed. No parent can completely meet all our needs. If our mother or father is controlling, absent, abusive, distant or exhibits any number of other negative traits, it can result in a struggle with affirmation and self-esteem. But what can we do? Do we have to be a victim of a fallen world? Today's verse gives us the answer. "Even if our father and mother abandon us, the Lord will hold us close." When we understand our true relationship with God, we will be able to receive our sense of being and well- being from Him. When we really comprehend how much He loves and approves of us, we will live our life with a deep sense of blessing that He has for us. Celebrating who we are in Christ can help us rise above our circumstances and go beyond the limits of our childhood.

TODAY'S PRAYER Father, I thank You for your deep, deep love for me. I thank You that You created me for a purpose. I thank You that I am not a mistake. Because of Your love for me, I can really feel good about myself. I receive a sense of well-being from knowing that I am a blessing to You. Thank You, Lord, that no matter what my past, what my parents may have done, I can come to You with my needs. When I do, You will hold me close. Amen.

The One Thing

TODAY'S VERSE "One thing I ask of the LORD, this is what I seek: that I may dwell in the house of the LORD all the days of my life, to gaze upon the beauty of the LORD and to seek him in his temple" (Psalm 27:4).

TODAY'S THOUGHT Have you ever gone somewhere and hated to leave? Have you ever enjoyed something so much that you did not want it to stop? Is there anything in your life that has become that "one thing"? This is what David felt about his relationship with God. If we had to choose a word to describe David, it would be the *worshipper*. David really loved God. He was sold out to Jehovah. So much so that if he had to choose just one thing, it would be to worship God all the time. What about you? What role does the worship of God play in your life? Is it just an hour of church on Sunday? That wasn't enough for David. If he could, he would have stayed in the Temple of God worshipping all the time! The good news is that we don't have to go to a Temple to worship God. We are the temple. Our body is His temple and our heart is an altar for worship. We can stop anytime, anywhere and gaze upon His beauty in the quietness of our own soul. Bring your praise and adoration to Him in your own temple throughout the day and night. Let loving God and living for Him become your *one thing*.

TODAY'S PRAYER Lord, I admit I have been preoccupied with so many things that worshipping You has taken a back seat in my life. I am so sorry. I do love You. I really do want to get my priorities right. Help me know and love You more and more until worshipping You becomes the *one thing* in my life. Amen.

Fully Aware of Your Presence

TODAY'S VERSE "The LORD is my light and my salvation—whom shall I fear? The LORD is the stronghold of my life—of whom shall I be afraid?" (Psalm 27:1).

TODAY'S THOUGHT Sometimes we just need to answer the questions. It may seem that the answers should be obvious. "Who should I fear?" It is almost rhetorical, yet sometimes our eyes are blinded to the truth. I remember seeing a little boy who thought he was lost start screaming. He cried hysterically, and yet his father was right next to him. The little child was so overcome with fear of abandonment, he cried so hard that he could not see his father right in front of him. It wasn't until the dad picked him up and hugged him for a few moments that the boy took comfort in his father's arms. Fear is like that. When we fear, it blocks out all other reality. Here is God, our light, and salvation, and yet we act as if we are lost in utter darkness. We are in the stronghold of God's love, and yet fear blinds us from the reality of our salvation. Is this your reality? What is it that you fear? Rebuke it right now. Look into the eyes of Jesus, let his light penetrate your mind and heart. Let him be your stronghold, arise and walk in peace.

TODAY'S PRAYER Dear Father, I admit that I let my emotions overwhelm me. I do not allow myself to fully understand what it means that You are my light, salvation, and stronghold. Forgive me, Lord. I want Your peace. I want Your joy. I want to know You more fully. Even today let me experience Your presence in my life. Even today, Lord, I ask You to make me fully aware of Your love and power. I give myself to You, Jesus, I will not be afraid. Thank You, Lord! Amen.

July 13
His Unconditional Love

TODAY'S VERSE "Look at my Servant, whom I have chosen. He is my Beloved, who pleases me. I will put my Spirit upon him, and he will proclaim justice to the nations. He will not fight or shout or raise his voice in public. He will not crush the weakest reed or put out a flickering candle. Finally, he will cause justice to be victorious. And his name will be the hope of all the world" (Matthew 12:18-21).

TODAY'S THOUGHT You can tell a religion by the God it follows. We follow Jehovah, who made Himself a man in the person of Christ Jesus. He could have chosen to come as a ruler, a dictator, a mighty military leader or a tyrant. Instead, He came to earth in the person of Jesus. Isaiah says that Jesus came to proclaim justice. He came to be our hope. He did not come to crush the weakest reed or put out a flickering flame. What a picture Isaiah is painting. Here we are; often messy, needy and weak. We get beat up, confused, tempted and tired. What does Jesus do? Does he step all over us? Does he crush the reeds? No, not even a faint brush to disturb them. Does he rant and rave? Does he blow out the littlest bit of a flame that we have left? No, he does nothing that would cause the flame to go out. His name is Hope! Hope today in His unconditional love for you.

TODAY'S PRAYER Dear Father, what a picture of Your love for me! I need Your love. I need Your understanding, Your mercy, and Your total forgiveness. I fully receive them right now. I praise You for Your kindness, I shout with joy even now for Your unconditional love for me. Thank You, Jesus. My hope is in You! Amen.

Here Am I

TODAY'S VERSE "Jesus went through all the towns and villages, teaching in their synagogues, preaching the good news of the kingdom and healing every disease and sickness. When he saw the crowds, he had compassion on them, because they were harassed and helpless, like sheep without a shepherd. Then he said to his disciples, 'The harvest is plentiful but the workers are few. Ask the Lord of the harvest, therefore, to send out workers into his harvest field'" (Matthew 9:35-38).

"Then I heard the voice of the Lord saying, 'Whom shall I send? And who will go for us?' And I said, 'Here am I. Send me'" (Isaiah 6:8).

TODAY'S THOUGHT Matthew 9 reads like a journal of supernatural power. Jesus heals a paralyzed man, raises a dead girl and gives sight to two men. He is exhausted, feeling cramped in by all the throngs of people coming to him for help. Even after all this, Jesus goes from town to town, teaching, preaching and healing every disease and sickness. But then there is a dramatic shift in strategy—Jesus sees all the people harassed, helpless and needing help, and then tells His disciples to pray that God would send you and me to help Him do His work. Do you get it? Jesus didn't come here to help and heal everyone by Himself. He came to redeem mankind, begin the process of helping mankind find the way, truth, and life, and then commissions you and me to take His power and ministry to the entire world. He has empowered you and me to aid Him in bringing His message of salvation and healing to a desperate world. The world where you and I live out our existence. Might our response be like Isaiah, "Here am I. Send me!"

TODAY'S PRAYER Dear Lord, I thank You for your tireless mission of love that reached out to me. Today I hear Your voice saying, "Whom shall I send? Who will go?" How else can I respond to Your love but say, "Lord Jesus, I want to join You in Your work. Here am I. Send me!" Amen.

More Than a Father

TODAY'S VERSE "And because we are his children, God has sent the Spirit of his Son into our hearts, prompting us to call out, 'Abba, Father'" (Galatians 4:6).

TODAY'S THOUGHT What a tender thought. Paul was very deliberate in using "Abba Father." This is a more affectionate term that simply saying, *Father*. The real translation of Abba Father is the word "*daddy*." Imagine, God invites us to call Him, our affectionate Father, Daddy. Can you say that? Have you thought of him that way? Paul says that as God's children, he has given us His Spirit, and the job of the Spirit is to help us fall more and more in love with the Father until we can call him "Daddy." Will you let him do that? Will you begin to meditate, to really stop and consider that he is your loving Father? Imagine his deep love for you. Imagine yourself coming into his presence, calling him "Daddy." Ask God to help you know this reality deep in your heart. After all, God has sent the Spirit of his Son into our hearts, prompting us to call out, "Abba, Father."

TODAY'S PRAYER Dear Father, I want to call You "Daddy." I hear it in my head, but it isn't quite in my heart. I invite You Holy Spirit to speak to my heart, to help me feel the Father's love, to know the Father's love. Prompt me Holy Spirit to call God, "Dear Father, Dear Daddy." Amen.

New Thinking Habits

TODAY'S VERSE "And now, dear brothers and sisters, one final thing. Fix your thoughts on what is true, and honorable, and right, and pure, and lovely, and admirable. Think about things that are excellent and worthy of praise" (Philippians 4:8).

TODAY'S THOUGHT It is so easy to let our thoughts run away from us. You know, the inward chatter that goes on all day. The voice when you get up in the morning, the musing on the drive to work, the stewing over events on the way home. Inner thoughts are powerful. They create emotions, which in turn cause actions. Paul is saying that we must take ownership of our inner dialog. It is so easy to be negative, anxious, angry, doubtful, bitter or carnal in our thinking. Instead, we need to be responsible for what we think and deliberately focus on true, honorable, right, pure, lovely, admirable, excellent and praiseworthy thoughts. What a difference this discipline would bring to our life.

TODAY'S PRAYER Father, I give You my thought life. I want You to be Lord of both my conscious and unconscious part of my being. You know my thought process. You know my habitual thinking patterns. I bring them to You. I ask that You help me today, begin a habit of focusing on true, honorable, right, pure, lovely, admirable, excellent and praiseworthy thoughts. Amen.

Your High Calling

TODAY'S VERSE "Imitate God, therefore, in everything you do, because you are his dear children. Live a life filled with love, following the example of Christ" (Ephesians 5:1-2).

TODAY'S THOUGHT We search for purpose and significance. We strive to secure a meaningful job or vocation. But in reality, there is no higher calling on earth than being God's child and imitating Him by living a life filled with love. This is the ultimate purpose to which God has called each one of us.

TODAY'S PRAYER Father, I thank You that You have made me your child. I thank You that You have given me the most important job on earth, which is to live a life filled with love. I admit I can't do this without You. I need Your Holy Spirit to help me live a life of love, today. Amen.

Stop and Praise Him

TODAY'S VERSE "Let all that I am praise the LORD; with my whole heart, I will praise his holy name. Let all that I am praise the LORD; may I never forget the good things he does for me. He forgives all my sins and heals all my diseases. He redeems me from death and crowns me with love and tender mercies. He fills my life with good things. My youth is renewed like the eagle's" (Psalm 103:1-5).

TODAY'S THOUGHT Charles Spurgeon wrote; "I don't which is more incredible, God's faithfulness or man's forgetfulness!" It is so easy to forget all that God has done for us. We get so preoccupied. Our lives get so crazy that we can go whole days, weeks, perhaps months without thanking God for his presence and provision. But today is a new day! Today, we can say with David, "Let all that I am praise the Lord!" Today, we can thank him with our whole heart. Right now, we can lift our eyes to heaven and shout, "Thank You God for all your blessings!" He forgives our sins. He crowns us with love and tender mercies! He fills our lives with good things. Stop and spend a moment thanking him for all he is and has done for you.

TODAY'S PRAYER Dear God, I praise You today with my whole heart. Everything that is in me says, "Praise You, God!" I thank You for Your tender mercy. I thank You for Your love and provision. I thank You for forgiving all my sins. Forgive me for forgetting so easily. Truly, Father, You are worthy of all my praise. I worship You now with praise and thanksgiving, In Jesus' name. Amen.

What Do You Believe About God?

TODAY'S VERSE "And without faith, it is impossible to please God because anyone who comes to him must believe that he exists and that he rewards those who earnestly seek him" (Hebrews 11:6).

TODAY'S THOUGHT What we believe about God makes a difference. Is He an overbearing parent, never pleased with us? Is He our celestial genie whose purpose is to give us our wishes on command? Is He a senile old man, unable to really comprehend what we are thinking or doing? Is He sadistic, getting pleasure from making our lives miserable? Perhaps a mad scientist that started this experiment but has lost control, not able to influence any desirable outcome? If we are honest with ourselves, we will see a little bit our own beliefs in these scenarios. The author of Hebrews says if we want to please God, then we must believe that He is the God of the Bible, not something that we make up. Not some misconceptions that we bring with us from childhood. He is the God who created the world and loves us with a never-ending love. He is the God that rewards those that earnestly seek Him. Start today to earnestly seek Him. Study the Bible, pray, meditate on his goodness. He is the God who desires to be known as He really is. Seek the truth about Him today.

TODAY'S PRAYER Dear God, I confess I do not really know You as I should. I haven't spent the time it takes. I haven't shared my real heart with You. I haven't waited long enough to hear Your voice. Forgive me, Heavenly Father. I really do want to know You. Please reveal Yourself to me through Your word and in my prayers. Today, I commit myself to know You more. Amen.

Love Is More Than a Four-Letter Word

TODAY'S VERSE "Love is patient, love is kind. It does not envy, it does not boast, it is not proud. It is not rude, it is not self-seeking, it is not easily angered, it keeps no record of wrongs. Love does not delight in evil but rejoices with the truth. It always protects, always trusts, always hopes, always perseveres. Love never fails" (1Corinthians 13:4-8).

TODAY'S THOUGHT I read this list of love's attributes and I feel so inadequate. I am guilty of using the word love so insincerely, halfway using its true definition. Love is more than a four-letter word. I use the same word to describe my attitude toward a sports team or favorite dessert that I use to describe my devotion toward my spouse or God. Love is more than saying, "I love you." More than a romantic feeling, love demands my doing something. It is more walk than talk. It's the kind of love the world is dying for. Today, I invite you to join me. Let's read the list of love's attributes over again, and make it our goal today to love those around us in this radical Christ-like manner. With His help, you and I can love those around us in the way Christ would have us love them.

TODAY'S PRAYER Lord, loving the way You love is not easy. I cannot do it by myself. I ask You to help me today love those around me with the patience, kindness, sacrifice, and dedication that You love me with. Thank You for Your love; help me to love others. In Jesus' name, I pray. Amen.

Help Me Believe

TODAY'S VERSE "Now faith is being sure of what we hope for and certain of what we do not see" (Hebrews 11:1).

"Immediately the boy's father exclaimed, "I do believe; help me overcome my unbelief" (Mark 9:24).

TODAY'S THOUGHT Faith is not easy. If it was, it wouldn't be faith. However, the more we get to know the object of our faith, the more we can "become sure of what we hope for and certain of what we do not see." How well do you know God? Do you spend time with Him? Do you trust Him? It's not always what we *believe* that affects our lives; sometimes it is what we *don't* believe. If you do not believe God loves you deeply; if you do not believe that He will do all He says He will; if you do not believe that He will never leave you or forsake you, then your prayer needs to be, "I believe Lord. Help me overcome my unbelief."

TODAY'S PRAYER Dear Lord, there is much I believe about You. But there are also some critical issues that I am wrestling with. Help me today give them back to You. I stand before You now and cry out with all my heart, "Help me, Lord! Help me overcome those things that I am having a hard time believing. Help me keep it real with You and grow to know, love, trust and believe You more and more." In Jesus' name. Amen.

Help Me

TODAY'S VERSE "Help, LORD" (Psalm 12:1).

"In my distress, I called to the LORD; I cried to my God for help. From his temple he heard my voice; my cry came before him, into his ears" (Psalm 18:6).

TODAY'S THOUGHT Sometimes the most significant prayers are the simplest. "Help me!" It is the cry of the heart that God hears. What is it that your soul needs? What is the longing of your heart? Talk to Him, pour out your heart. He will listen.

TODAY'S PRAYER Father, thank You for the invitation to pour out my heart to You. I cry out for Your help. Help me where I don't even know I need help. Help me where I cannot reach. Help me in ways that only You can. Help me with Your power, Your love, and Your wisdom. I commit myself to Your loving care. In Jesus' name. Amen.

You Are His Delight

TODAY'S VERSE "The LORD your God is with you, he is mighty to save. He will take great delight in you, he will quiet you with his love, he will rejoice over you with singing" (Zephaniah 3:17).

TODAY'S THOUGHT Some thoughts are so powerful, they can change your life. Or at least, they should. This verse is that way. If you can read, "He will take great delight in you, he will quiet you with his love, he will rejoice over you with singing" and not feel special, not feel like God adores you, not be moved to gratitude and thankfulness for His attention toward you, then you need to read it again. If you can read, "The Lord your God is with you, He is mighty to save you" and not feel secure, special and in a safe place, then you need to stop, ask God to speak to your heart and read this verse over. Today's verse can change your life if you let it.

TODAY'S PRAYER My dear Lord and Mighty God. Who am I that You would shower me with such attention? And yet, even with my doubt and feeble faith, today I choose to believe You. I choose to believe that I am a delight to You and that You rejoice over me. Quiet my heart with Your love. Help me see Your smile of acceptance with my imagination. Let me sense Your warm embrace of love and hear my name in Your singing. Amen.

More Than This World

TODAY'S VERSE "He has also set eternity in the hearts of men" (Ecclesiastes 3:11).

TODAY'S THOUGHT There is something about this world that causes us to yearn for the next. We were never meant to live here without belief in the next. God, created us for more than just this. He created us to be eternal. A soul that never dies. He has etched it deep into our hearts. C.S. Lewis wrote, "If I find in myself desires which nothing in this world can satisfy, the only logical explanation is that I was made for another world." The good news is that Christ came to make a way to prepare for the next life. He is the only one who lived in both. He is God and human in one. He made a way, through His death, for us to co-exist with a Holy and Almighty God. So much so that we now can come to God and call Him Father. That's what children do. They call their father, "Father," and they long to be home. Listen to that inner voice and respond to your Father in Heaven.

TODAY'S PRAYER Dear Father, I do hear another voice. It is from a distant land, and I do long to know more about it. There has to be more than what I can see around me. I come today and ask You to make me more conscious of Your presence. More aware of Your power and mystery. I invite Your heaven to invade my earth and help me become a citizen of both. Awaken my soul to Your heavenly reality. In Jesus' name. Amen.

Be a Messenger of Encouragement

TODAY'S VERSE "Let everything you say be good and helpful so that your words will be an encouragement to those who hear them" (Ephesians 4:29).

TODAY'S THOUGHT What a wonderful calling. What a tremendous privilege is ours. God has called us to be an encourager. Encouragement. It can change a person's life or alter the destiny of families. Nations can rise and fall. Alright, maybe not that dramatic, but who can deny the power of encouragement? How many of us have been overwhelmed, about ready to give up, and someone stopped and in a loving moment poured encouragement all over us? Is there anything more refreshing? God loves the whole world and He has chosen you and me to be His messenger of encouragement. Might He lead us to someone in need of encouragement today.

TODAY'S PRAYER Dear Father, I thank You for all the times You have sent encouragement my way. I pray that today, You might help me be an encourager to someone who so desperately needs it. Give me eyes to see people the way You do and to say things that are good and helpful so that my words today might be an encouragement to those who hear them. Amen.

Do Not Lose Heart

TODAY'S VERSE "Therefore we do not lose heart. Though outwardly we are wasting away, yet inwardly we are being renewed day by day" (2 Corinthians 4:16).

TODAY'S THOUGHT The heart. That part of us that balances out the rational thinking part of us. It is the center of mystery, passion, hope, wonderment, love. It is that part of us that reacts to the love of Christ. It is what keeps us alive. God told the Jews that He would take out their stony heart and give them a heart that is alive! He has done that for us. Unfortunately, we can ignore our heart. We can get so busy, so worried, so carnal that we forget that God wants our heart. Paul warns us, "Do not lose your heart!" The question is, "How?" Paul gives us that answer, too. He says, "By renewing your heart, day by day." Devotions, meditating, praying, spending time with God is the way to renewal. Today, stop and come to Him. Give Him your heart. Ask Him to renew it. If the worries of the world, the lure or temptations of riches, or the eagerness to get ahead has your heart in cardiac arrest, go to code blue. "Stand back" and let Jesus resuscitate your heart right now.

TODAY'S PRAYER Jesus, creator of my heart, I come to You now in desperate need of heart renewal. You know how I have let time slip by. I have not protected my heart. I can feel it becoming callous. Forgive me. Oh, Spirit of God, right now, I ask to renew my heart. Give me the peace, joy, love, passion, hope, and steadfastness that comes from a heart renewed by You day by day. Amen.

It's Your Choice

TODAY'S VERSE "Choose today whom you will serve… but as for me and my family, we will serve the LORD" (Joshua 24:15).

TODAY'S THOUGHT Choices. Every day we are called upon to make choices. Some insignificant, some with heavy consequences. There are some choices in life that lead us down certain paths. Marriage, vocation, other major choices all have ramifications for our future. But it is the everyday choices that determine how we live out the marriage, vocation or our other major choices. That is why what you chose today is so important. You may have started down a path and strayed off. Today, you can choose to turn around. You may have habitual choices that have been negative. Today, you can choose to go another direction. You have the power to choose. You can choose to love. Likewise, happiness is a choice. God is constantly calling out to us, "Choose me." God and our choice, what a powerful combination. Choose today whom you will serve, for not to choose is to choose already.

TODAY'S PRAYER Dear God, please help me. I admit I haven't always chosen wisely. Give me wisdom, discernment, and self-discipline to make the right choices today. Most of all today, dear Lord, I choose You. I choose to love You and live for You. In Jesus' name. Amen.

An Open Door

TODAY'S VERSE "Search me, O God, and know my heart; test me and know my anxious thoughts. See if there is any offensive way in me, and lead me in the way everlasting" (Psalm 139:23-24).

"Behold, I stand at the door and knock. If anyone hears My voice and opens the door, I will come into him and dine with him, and he with Me" (Revelation 3:20).

TODAY'S THOUGHT Who are we? Who are we that the God of the universe would be interested in a relationship with us? Yet, this is exactly what these verses imply. It is an open invitation to you and me to sit with God and pour out our heart. It is a tremendous opportunity to allow Him to know our most inner thoughts, emotions, and imaginations. We can come to Him without reservation and trust that He cares; that He is interested; that He is able to show us any needed correction and that He will lead us in the way we should go. Do you have that kind of relationship with God? If not, you can start today. He stands at the door of your heart and knocks. Open it, invite Him in and start to let God know who you are.

TODAY'S PRAYER Dear Father, it is so hard to say, "Search my heart." I don't want to slow down. I don't want to be vulnerable. But, if I cannot trust You with my heart, who can I trust? Forgive me for running from You. Help me be still. Help me trust You as I say, "Holy Spirit, I come now and open the door of my heart to You. Come in, search me, know my thoughts and lead me in the way You want me to go." Amen.

Heaven on Earth

TODAY'S VERSE "I am the resurrection and the life, He who believes in me, though he may die, yet he will live" (John 11:25).

"Your Kingdom come, Your will be done on earth as it is in Heaven" (Matthew 6:10).

TODAY'S THOUGHT It is impossible to truly understand this life without considering the next life. If we are to comprehend God's will on earth, then we must be conscious of His kingdom and let it influence our thoughts and actions. You see, nothing really makes sense in this world without a heavenly perspective. Thank God that Jesus was the bridge between the two worlds. He is the resurrection to the next world and the key to life in this one. So today, take time to invite His Kingdom to invade yours. Make room for heaven in your life. Ask God to make you conscious of His presence right now and to influence all you think and do this day.

TODAY'S PRAYER Father, I confess I have had my head on the ground, busy focusing on my life in this world. I haven't taken the time to think of Your heavenly perspective. I invite You now to invade my presence and help me see life from Your perspective. Thank You for Your resurrection and how it provides the way for me to live with You for all eternity. Help me to start living in eternity right now. I pray as You taught me, Lord Jesus, "Your Kingdom come, Your will be done on earth today, as it is in Heaven." Amen.

Give This Day to God

TODAY'S VERSE "Let the morning bring me word of your unfailing love, for I have put my trust in you. Show me the way I should go, for to you I lift up my soul. Rescue me from my enemies, O LORD, for I hide myself in you. Teach me to do your will, for you are my God; may your good Spirit lead me on level ground" (Psalm 143:8, 10).

TODAY'S THOUGHT Do you start your day hearing a word from God about His unfailing love? Do you start your day trusting in Him? Do you ask Him for direction, protection, and instruction for the tasks that are ahead of you this day? If not, what is stopping you now? No matter what your yesterdays were, no matter what you fear for tomorrow, there is nothing stopping you from committing this day to God. You can begin a new habit of thanksgiving and expectation today.

TODAY'S PRAYER Father, in the quietness of this moment, let me hear You confirm Your unfailing love for me. Right now, I put my complete trust in You. Please, dear God, show me the way I should go, for I lift up my soul up to You. Rescue me from any trouble today, O LORD, for I hide myself in You. Teach me to do Your will, for You are my God; may Your Holy Spirit lead me today. Amen.

Go and Do Likewise

TODAY'S VERSE "The Lord gives justice to the oppressed and food to the hungry. The LORD frees the prisoners. The LORD opens the eyes of the blind. The LORD lifts up those who are weighed down. The LORD loves the godly. The LORD protects the foreigners among us. He cares for the orphans and widows, but he frustrates the plans of the wicked" (Psalm 146:7-9).

TODAY'S THOUGHT Is this the God we see in the Bible? Is this the God we pray to? Where do we find this God in our Christian lifestyle? The truth is, the God we worship in the Bible has always taken the poor, downtrodden and displaced people seriously. He expects us to do the same. We serve God when we serve others. Ask God to show you ways you can serve the needy. He cares. Do we?

TODAY'S PRAYER Lord, I confess I need to be more compassionate. I need to be more proactive in helping the lonely, hurting and distraught. Please show me ways I can start to love those in need the way You do. Even today, lead me to someone I can help. In Jesus' name. Amen.

We Can Be Confident in His Help

TODAY'S VERSE "So, we say with confidence, 'The Lord is my helper; I will not be afraid. What can man do to me?'" (Hebrews 13:6).

TODAY'S THOUGHT Have you ever said anything with confidence? It is different than saying "I think so," "Perhaps," "Maybe," or "We'll see." Confidence connotes a certainty, an assurance that what we believe is true. Because we believe in a God that will never forsake us, a heavenly Father who will never abandon us, we can have confidence that this same God is our helper, our strength, our shield, our shelter in the storm, our rock of ages, our mighty fortress, our protector, our hope, our Savior. Yes, we can say with confidence, "Today, I will not be afraid!"

TODAY'S PRAYER Thank You, Mighty God, that You have chosen to be my helper. You have reached down to me and have assured me that You care, that You will always have my soul in Your hand. I thank You with a confidence in my heart that what You say is true and every thought, fear, apprehension, and doubt that stands against this confidence is a lie. I accept Your help today. I will trust You and not be afraid. Amen.

Never Forsaken, Never Alone

TODAY'S VERSE "God has said, 'Never will I leave you; never will I forsake you'" (Hebrews 13:5).

TODAY'S THOUGHT Loneliness; abandonment; alienation; separation; betrayal; desertion. These are words that cut right to the heart. Because of our human relationships, all of us, to one degree or another, have experienced these negative emotions. The great news is that when you become His child when you are born again, you enter into a permanent relationship with almighty God. He becomes your loving Father who loves you (yes, you!) so much that He has made a tremendous promise. God has written, for all to read, that He will never, never, never, never, never, never leave you or forsake you. Never! Why? Because when He chose to love you unconditionally, it was settled—end of the discussion. No changing His mind, ever. You are His child forever.

TODAY'S PRAYER Dear Heavenly Father, is it really true? I want to believe it with my mind and with my heart! Help me really see how much You love me. Thank You that You promise that You will never leave me or forsake me because of Jesus. Amen.

Daily Practice

TODAY'S VERSE "It is good to praise the LORD and make music to your name, O Most High, to proclaim your love in the morning and your faithfulness at night" (Psalm 92:1-2).

"The joy of the LORD is your strength" (Nehemiah 8:10).

TODAY'S THOUGHT You can't eat one meal and say that is enough for the rest of the month. It is not good enough to take one breath and quit. Most of life seems to have a rhythm, a sustainability that comes from repeated processes. Praise and joy are the same way. It is not good enough to have had joy once upon a time. You can't live a victorious Christian life on memories of better days. No, with God, every day has its measure of mercy and grace. Every day has the presence of the God. The question is, are we aware of it? If we are going to get all we can out of life, then we need to make a conscious effort to be aware of the presence of God. What better way than to proclaim His love in the morning and when the day is over—purposely reflecting on His faithfulness.

TODAY'S PRAYER Praise You, dear God, for Your love for me. Thank You for Your faithfulness. Help me to sing Your praises, to have a heart of gladness and a spirit of thankfulness for all You have done for me. Help me to proclaim Your love every morning and Your faithfulness every night. Might Your joy be my strength today. Amen.

August 4
Bring It to Jesus

TODAY'S VERSE "So then, since we have a great High Priest who has entered heaven, Jesus the Son of God, let us hold firmly to what we believe. This High Priest of ours understands our weaknesses, for he faced all of the same testings we do, yet he did not sin. So, let us come boldly to the throne of our gracious God. There we will receive his mercy, and we will find grace to help us when we need it most" (Hebrew 4:14-16).

TODAY'S THOUGHT Sometimes you need a helping hand. You need someone who understands what you are going through and can help you navigate difficult times. Jesus is that intercessor. He is God, with all the power and wisdom we need, yet because of His volunteer time spent on earth in human form, He knows exactly what we are going through. He knows all our limitations, frailty and emotions, and how to work with them and live a victorious life. He can guide us down the same path of faith, strength, hope, and love that He took. So, let's do what the author of Hebrews suggests. Let's come boldly to our gracious God and ask Him for the help we need today. We will find Him gracious, compassionate and able to help us when we need it the most.

TODAY'S PRAYER Dear Jesus. I come to You because You know all about me. You know my situation. You know my thoughts, my frustrations, and my desires. You know my needs. I come to You because You the Almighty God and can do all things. And yet with all Your Holiness, You are still endlessly compassionate toward me. You promised that if I come to You that You will help me when I need it the most. I come to You now. I give You this day with all of its challenges, struggles, and complexities. Make me conscious of Your presence as You meet the deepest needs of my heart and life today. Amen.

Perfect Peace

TODAY'S VERSE "You will keep in perfect peace all who trust in you, all whose thoughts are fixed on you" (Isaiah 26:3).

TODAY'S THOUGHT Perfect peace. I have a hard time comprehending that. Perfect peace. I take a deep relaxing breath just thinking about it. That is what God is promising us if we trust in Him. Why? Because He is trustworthy! He can be trusted. But trusting is more than just saying we trust Him. Isaiah qualifies the kind of trust we need to have perfect peace. It is the trust that keeps our thoughts fixed on God. Fixed on His love. Fixed on His compassion. Fixed on His grace. Fixed on His provision. Fixed on His promises. Fixed on His almighty power. Today, let's experience that perfect peace. We can start right now, by fixing our thoughts on Him and keeping them there throughout the day.

TODAY'S PRAYER Dear Lord, I desire Your perfect peace! Please help me trust You by focusing my attention on You and all that You will provide to get me through this day. Please, Lord, when my thoughts wander and peace begins to flee, nudge me, help me to refocus on You again. Thank You, in Jesus' name. Amen.

Try to Grasp This

TODAY'S VERSE "I pray that you, being rooted and established in love, may have power, together with all the saints, to grasp how wide and long and high and deep is the love of Christ, and to know this love that surpasses knowledge—that you may be filled to the measure of all the fullness of God" (Ephesians 3:17-19).

TODAY'S THOUGHT Paul had a second prayer for the Ephesians. This time, he is asking God to invade our imagination. He wants to turn on the wide-screen HDTV in our head and help us understand something that can't be fully comprehended, at least without God's power. Paul prays that God would use His power to help us see and understand, to grasp how magnificent God's love is for us.

TODAY'S PRAYER Dear Father, I open my mind to your Holy Spirit and ask Him to come in all His power and help me grasp how much you love me! Fill me right now with the glorious realization of who You are and who I am in You. Amen.

Increase Your Inner Strength

TODAY'S VERSE "I pray that out of his glorious riches he may strengthen you with power through his Spirit in your inner being" (Ephesians 3:16).

TODAY'S THOUGHT Over 2000 years ago, Paul the Apostle prayed this prayer for the church in Ephesus. He prayed that God would use His mighty resources to strengthen them with *power* in their *inner being*. Can you think of anything that we need more than that? All around us, there is strife, stress, conflicts, and confusion. We often find ourselves going up and down emotionally. It is easy to get sucked into this world's problems and forget that there is a God who cares, who loves us and who can strengthen us. To make it in this world, we need a mighty reservoir of strength on the inside, where we really live. And according to Paul, it is the job of the Holy Spirit to make this all happen. The good news is the Holy Spirit will give us the strength we need on the inside. Ask Him to strengthen you with His power today.

TODAY'S PRAYER Dear Holy Spirit, I know you are real. You are God, in Spirit form, that comes and takes residence in us upon our conversion. I confess I have ignored you. I repent and ask your forgiveness. I ask you now, Oh Holy Spirit, to come in all your power and give me strength today in my inner being. Might I live in the fullness of your power even now. In Jesus name. Amen.

Learn to Live Before You Die

TODAY'S VERSE "For to me, living means living for Christ, and dying is even better" (Philippians 1:21).

TODAY'S THOUGHT We often hear this verse quoted at funerals. And yet I wonder how often we think of the first part of this verse. Paul wanted us to know that Heaven awaits us, but he never intended to diminish the importance of "living means living for Christ." Do we live as if that part of the verse is true? If Paul reviewed what we did yesterday or looked at today's schedule, if he walked around our home, talked to our family or those we work with, would he be able to say that *life* to us was *living for Christ*? We will all die. It is very important to know our eternal destiny. Trusting in Christ as our Savior is indeed the only way to heaven. But please, God put us on this earth first in order that we would live for Him. Let's learn to live for Christ before we die.

TODAY'S PRAYER Dear Father, I know that your death for me on Calvary took care of my eternal destiny. It's not the dying that is troubling me right now, it is the living. Help me understand how you want to bless my life. Help me get my priorities right. I give to you my today. Please guide me in all I do. Today, I choose to live for you. In Jesus name. Amen.

Take Comfort, Then Give It Away

TODAY'S VERSE "For when we came into Macedonia, this body of ours had no rest, but we were harassed at every turn—conflicts on the outside, fears within. But God, who comforts the downcast, comforted us by the coming of Titus" (2 Corinthians 7:5-6).

TODAY'S THOUGHT It is difficult to make it a week without feeling hassled. Frustrations, aggravations, conflicts, temptations seem to be at every turn. Paul the Apostle certainly knew what it was like. Listen to his language. "Harassed at every turn—conflicts on the outside and fears within." And yet Paul shares with all confidence that he was comforted by God as reflected in his phrase, "God who comforts the downcast." No matter what we go through, we can go through it knowing that God is committed to our comfort. He understands, cares, and comforts. And notice one of the ways God comforts. He uses people like you and me to comfort others. God used Titus to be a comfort to Paul. Today, be comforted by God. Let your soul be at peace. But don't stop there. Go and help comfort someone else. Be a Titus to someone who is desperate need of help.

TODAY'S PRAYER Lord comfort my heart today. Might I find peace, joy, patience, and hope in your love. Might I find all I need in the love you have for me. At the same time, Dear Father, help me comfort others in the way you have comforted me. Amen.

Why Would He Ask?

TODAY'S VERSE "When Jesus saw him lying there and learned that he had been in this condition for a long time, he asked him, 'Do you want to get well?'" (John 5:6).

TODAY'S THOUGHT This time, Jesus came to the Pool of Bethesda, where many who were sick were hoping to get better. For 38 years this man was crippled, laying on his pallet, alone and not able to get into the fabled healing water. Thirty-eight years. When Jesus came along, instead of asking the man, "What do you want me to do?" Jesus asked, "Do you want to get well?" The answer should be obvious. But is it? Perhaps the crippled man has long since given up. Perhaps he has tied his significance to being a victim. What if bitterness has dug its root deep into his soul? Getting well isn't always an easy choice. How about you? What is hurting you? What is your disease? Is it bitterness, anger, depression, financial distress, addictions, failed relationships? How is your heart? Jesus is asking, "Do you want to get well?" The Healer is at the door; what will your answer be?

TODAY'S PRAYER Dear Lord, thank you that you care. Thank you that you have walked by today. Thank you that you have asked me if I want to be healed. My answer is "yes," Lord. Please show me my need and heal it. I give my need to you. I give you my heart. I give you myself, body, soul, and spirit. Great physician, heal me. Amen.

August 11
What Do You Want Jesus to Do?

TODAY'S VERSE "Jesus stopped and called them. 'What do you want me to do for you?' he asked" (Matthew 20:32).

TODAY'S THOUGHT Two blind men were on the side of the road and heard Jesus coming. They cried out for Jesus to stop and have mercy on them. The disciples tried to stop them, but they cried out louder! Jesus saw their faith and earnestness and said, "What do you want me to do for you?" They said, "We want to see." Jesus had compassion on them and gave them their sight. How excited do we get about Jesus? How eagerly do we desire to have Him walk our way? What is it that we want Jesus to do in our life? Today, stop and have a conversation with Jesus. Talk to Him about your needs. Cry out to Him. He is there, He will listen. What do you want Jesus to do?

TODAY'S PRAYER Lord Jesus, I come to you needy. I come to you crying out for your mercy. Help me to know how to answer your question, "What do you want me to do?" Give me faith to believe and a readiness to receive what you have for me. Amen.

It's Your Move

TODAY'S VERSE "I am convinced that nothing can ever separate us from God's love" (Romans 8:38).

TODAY'S THOUGHT A man was going down the road and saw a sign that read, "Do you feel far from God?" He thought about the question and was pondering how far he felt from God when he saw a second sign which read, "Who moved?" How about you? Do you feel far from God? Today's verse assures us nothing can ever separate us from the love of God, but that doesn't mean that we can't ignore His love or take it for granted. If we feel far from God, then it is because we have moved. Move back, move toward God today. Accept His love, thank Him for it and worship Him. Renew your love relationship with God today.

TODAY'S PRAYER Father, I confess I often do feel far from you. I know it is because I have moved away. Forgive me. Instead, right now, I choose to embrace your love, to accept it. Open my eyes so I become convinced that nothing can ever separate me from your love. Because of Jesus and in His name. Amen.

What Do You Remember?

TODAY'S VERSE "I remember my affliction and my wandering, the bitterness and the gall. I well remember them, and my soul is downcast within me. Yet this I call to mind and therefore I have hope: Because of the LORD's great love we are not consumed, for His compassions never fail. They are new every morning; great is Your faithfulness" (Lamentations 3:19-23).

TODAY'S THOUGHTS What we choose to dwell on impacts our thinking and eventually our actions. What do you think of? What do you remember? Like the author of Lamentations, are we lamenting? He was dwelling on the negative, and sure enough, his soul was downcast. Is our soul down today? The good news is that he learned the secret to abundant living. He discovered how to have hope. He decided to meditate on this fact: We are not consumed! We are still living. God is not finished with us yet! Besides that, God's compassion toward us never fails. His compassionate thoughts toward us are new every morning. And he concludes: Great is God's faithfulness! Dwell on God's compassion toward you. Let it give you hope today.

TODAY'S PRAYER Dear Father, forgive me for dwelling on the negative. I stop now to give you thanks. Thank you that this morning you had compassionate thoughts about me. You are the Almighty God and, yet You think tenderly toward me every morning. Help me really believe that. Let it shape my thoughts today. Thank you for your faithfulness. Amen.

His Grace Is All You Need

TODAY'S VERSE "But He said to me, 'My grace is sufficient for you'" (2 Corinthians 12:9).

TODAY'S THOUGHT Paul the Apostle was distraught. He had asked God three times to help alleviate a situation that was plaguing him. Each time, God said, "No." Instead, Paul shares that God told him, "My grace is sufficient for you." Grace—what a word! It means God's concern, His favor, His provision and His friendship; all this, without any merit on our own that would cause Him to act favorably toward us. It is from the depth of His unconditional love for us that He helps us in the inner person. He will do whatever it takes to get us through to the other side. His grace is sufficient for anything you bring to Him today. Will you accept His grace today?

TODAY'S PRAYER Lord, I come to you needy. Please make me conscious of your grace to me today. I come with an empty cup and ask that you fill it today with your grace. Let me drink of it. Let it go down deep into my soul until I can say with confidence, "Your grace is sufficient for me." Thank you, Lord! In Jesus' name. Amen.

Don't Fool Yourself

TODAY'S VERSE So, get rid of all the filth and evil in your lives, and humbly accept the word God has planted in your hearts, for it has the power to save your souls. But don't just listen to God's word. You must do what it says. Otherwise, you are only fooling yourselves" (James 1:21-22).

TODAY'S THOUGHT With today's multitasking world, it is hard to focus on anything for more than five minutes. Interruptions have become a fact of life. Emergencies, just-in-time deadlines, we make judgments on the fly and hope that they stick. Well, if we are going to make it spiritually, we have to be intentional. It isn't good enough to hear the Bible, a verse here, a sermon there. We need to know the word of God. And then, most importantly, we need to do it. Start today, make a commitment to study the Bible and apply it to your life.

TODAY'S PRAYER Dear Holy Spirit, I know that it is your joy to help me learn the word of God and apply it to my life. I invite you to be my teacher, guide, and mentor. Please help me start today to make the Bible a priority in my life. Amen.

Quick to Listen, Slow to Speak, Slow to Get Angry

TODAY'S VERSE "Understand this, my dear brothers and sisters: You must all be quick to listen, slow to speak, and slow to get angry. Human anger does not produce the righteousness God desires" (James 1:19-20).

TODAY'S THOUGHT Quick to listen, slow to speak, slow to get angry. How different would our life be if we would follow this simple advice? How more effective would we be in our job, ministry or dealing with those in our family? What opportunities to heal and bless others would be ours if we would submit to this behavior code? Today, we can make a choice. Choose to listen. Choose to think before we speak. Choose to pray before we act out our anger. With God, all things are possible.

TODAY'S PRAYER Dear Heavenly Father, I ask for your help this day to watch my tongue and emotions. Help me to really listen to others. Help me to be careful before I speak and help me control my temper. Fill me with your Holy Spirit so I can be more like Your Son, Jesus. Amen.

Overcoming Temptations

TODAY'S VERSE "No test or temptation that comes your way is beyond the course of what others have had to face. All you need to remember is that God will never let you down; he'll never let you be pushed past your limit; he'll always be there to help you come through it" (I Corinthians 10:13, *The Message*).

TODAY'S THOUGHT Life is hard. It is easy to be tempted to take the easy way out. Easy to complain. Easy to give up. But what a slippery slope we walk on—lying, cheating, substance abuse, gambling. These are the temptations we hear about the most. But what about the temptation to hate, become depressed or ungrateful? You see, we are all tempted to behave in a way we shouldn't. What's your temptation? Do you feel hopeless to overcome? Are you in total denial? Whatever your temptations are today, God knows and is waiting for you to come to Him for help. "He will never let you be pushed past your limit, He will always be there to help you come through." Call on Him today.

TODAY'S PRAYER Dear Father, you know the temptations I face. I have been in such denial. I have felt so helpless at times. I can't do this life without you. I need your help. Thank you for promising that you will always be there to help me come through. Oh, my Heavenly Father, I wait for you to help me. Help me today. I pray in the name of Jesus Christ Your Son, my Savior. Amen.

Mercy and Forgiveness

TODAY'S VERSE "Have mercy on me, O God, because of your unfailing love. Because of your great compassion, blot out the stain of my sins. Wash me clean from my guilt. Purify me from my sin" (Psalm 51:1-2).

"If we claim we have no sin, we are only fooling ourselves and not living in the truth. But if we confess our sins to him, he is faithful and just to forgive us our sins and to cleanse us from all wickedness" (I John 1:8-9).

TODAY'S THOUGHT Forgiveness. It is the most exciting concept in the Bible. God loves you and me so much, but our negative attitudes, the wrongs that we have done, the things that we have failed to do, these and more have separated us from our Holy God. But today's verses offer great news. This scripture assures us that if we confess our sins, repent of our negative ways and ask for His forgiveness, He will forgive and treat us as if we have never done wrong at all. His love is unconditional. His desire to forgive is insatiable. He is faithful and just to forgive our sins and to cleanse us from it all.

TODAY'S PRAYER Lord Jesus, it is hard for me to believe that You never tire of forgiving me. Help me believe it. You know me, You understand me, and even with all my tendencies, You choose to love me with a never dying love. I confess my sin today. Please forgive me, cleanse me and help me rise in true freedom, forgiveness, and joy to serve You. Amen.

Trust, Delight, and Commit

TODAY'S VERSE "Trust in the LORD and do good; dwell in the land and enjoy safe pasture. Delight yourself in the LORD and he will give you the desires of your heart. Commit your way to the LORD; trust in him and he will do this" (Psalm 37:3-5).

TODAY'S THOUGHT There is a spiritual rhythm in these three verses. It really speaks to the soul. It is like drinking a tall, cool glass of water after coming in from a steamy hot day. Somehow trust, delight, and commit seem to go together. Today, start with trusting God. Give everything over to Him. Let go, trust Him. Then stop and delight in Him. Feel His love. Let Him give you deep joy. Delight in His presence. Finally, bow before Him and commit everything to Him. Put your life in His hands. And you know what? He says He will give us the desires of our heart. It doesn't get better than this!

TODAY'S PRAYER Dear Father, I come to You now and trust You with all my concerns and worries. You are God and I give myself to You. I choose to delight in You. I ask You to fill me with a deep joy today. I want to love You with all my heart. I commit this day to You and all that will transpire. I commit myself joyfully into Your hands. Thank You that you have promised that if I trust, delight and commit, You will give me the desires of my heart. Amen.

Which Comes First, the Fruit or the Tree?

TODAY'S VERSE "But the fruit of the Spirit is love, joy, peace, patience, kindness, goodness, faithfulness, gentleness and self-control" (Galatians 5:22-23a).

TODAY'S THOUGHT Love, joy, peace, patience, kindness, goodness, faithfulness, gentleness, and self-control. What a list. It is easy to focus on each attribute and begin to feel overwhelmed by the challenge to master each one. But that is not what today's verse is suggesting. Rather, it is saying that the list of attributes is the result of living in the Spirit. In nature, if we want fruit, we need to nourish the tree it comes on. Fruit is only produced when the tree is healthy. Likewise, when we fellowship with the Spirit, live in harmony with His direction, and follow His leading every day, the Spirit's fruit will be produced in our lives. As the Holy Spirit instructs, rebukes, guides, and comforts us, if we respond to His voice, we will experience His fruit.

TODAY'S PRAYER Dear Holy Spirit, I want Your fruit, which is love, joy, peace, patience, kindness, goodness, faithfulness, gentleness, and self-control, to grow in my life. I know that is only possible through letting You guide my life. Help me hear Your promptings. Let me experience fellowship with you today. Guide me in all things. Fill me Holy Spirit. In Jesus name, I ask it. Amen.

August 21
It's About Forgiveness

TODAY'S VERSE "The LORD is compassionate and gracious, slow to anger, abounding in love. He will not always accuse, nor will he harbor his anger forever; he does not treat us as our sins deserve or repay us according to our iniquities. For as high as the heavens are above the earth, so great is his love for those who fear him; as far as the east is from the west, so far has he removed our transgressions from us. As a father has compassion on his children, so the LORD has compassion on those who fear him" (Psalm 103:8-13).

TODAY'S THOUGHT If I had to pick one word to describe Christianity, it would be "forgiveness." There is something about God's love and forgiveness that is unique to Christianity. Jesus made it possible to really experience it. Read the verses again and then ask yourself, "Do I really believe that these verses apply to me?" This personalization is where change comes from. What you read in the Bible won't change your life if you choose not to believe it. God says, "As high as the heavens are, so great is my love for you." If you know Jesus as your Savior, then really know that your sins—yes, all of them—are forever forgiven and forgotten.

TODAY'S PRAYER Thank you, Jesus, for dying on the cross so that all of my sins can be forgiven. Take my heart and draw me to Yourself even now. Surround me with Your love and forgiveness while I wait for you. Help me to really know and appreciate Your love and forgiveness, in all of its fullness, throughout this day. In Jesus' name. Amen.

August 22
We Need to Walk the Talk

TODAY'S VERSE "What good is it, my brothers, if a man claims to have faith but has no deeds? Can such faith save him? Suppose a brother or sister is without clothes and daily food. If one of you says to him, 'Go, I wish you well; keep warm and well fed,' but does nothing about his physical needs, what good is it? In the same way, faith by itself, if it is not accompanied by action, is dead. But someone will say, 'You have faith; I have deeds.' Show me your faith without deeds, and I will show you my faith by what I do'" (James 2:14-18).

TODAY'S THOUGHT There is a great need in our world, but we are so busy we don't see it. We are so inwardly focused, so concerned about our own welfare, that we don't stop to help others. That is not the way of Christ! Our churches should be making huge differences in our communities, but we don't. When will this change? It can change today if you and I decide to do something. Today, we can make a difference in someone's life if we just open our eyes and hearts. May God help us to "walk our talk."

TODAY'S PRAYER Lord Jesus, help me see other people's needs with Your eyes. Bring someone into my life today that needs help. Give me the mercy to stop, the wisdom to know what to do and then the love to do it. Thank you, God, for all You have done for me, help me do for others. Amen.

Are You Conscious of His Love for You?

TODAY'S VERSE "If God is for us, who can be against us...who shall separate us from the love of Christ?" (Romans 8:31b; 35a).

"For I am convinced that neither death nor life, neither angels nor demons, neither the present nor the future, nor any powers, neither height nor depth, nor anything else in all creation, will be able to separate us from the love of God that is in Christ Jesus our Lord" (Romans 8:38-39).

TODAY'S THOUGHT This is one of the greatest promises in the Bible. It is true for every child of God. Nothing...nothing...nothing can separate you from the love of God. You may feel like His love is distant. You may have doubts. You may be in circumstances where it seems like God is nowhere near, but the truth remains. His love is with you and He is conscious of you right this very moment! Stop and recognize his presence. Be still and know that He is your God.

TODAY'S PRAYER Almighty God, my Heavenly Father. I renounce all negative beliefs that lead me to think that You do not care or have abandoned me. I pray that You will, this very moment, make me conscious of Your presence. Fill me with Your Holy Spirit and help me to really understand that nothing has or ever will separate me from Your love. Thank You for your great love for me. Amen.

Turn on the Light

TODAY'S VERSE "I sought the LORD, and he answered me; he delivered me from all my fears" (Psalm 34:4).

TODAY'S THOUGHT Fear comes in different shapes and sizes. To be sure, there are full-blown phobias and crippling fears that can interrupt our life, but for most of us, fear is more insidious. Fears of rejection, insignificance, and abandonment may not interrupt our life, but they can sure direct the way we think and act. You see our thoughts, motives, and behavior are constantly shaped by either faith or fear. The Psalmist found the secret. He said that if we seek the Lord, He will deliver us from all our fears. Turn on the light of faith and the darkness of fear will dissipate. Decide to seek God today. Move away from fear and toward faith.

TODAY'S PRAYER Lord, I want to trade my fears for faith. Today, when fear comes to my attention, I will seek You. I will seek You with all of my heart. Thank You that you promise to deliver me. Amen.

Ask for Wisdom

TODAY'S VERSE "If any of you lacks wisdom, he should ask God, who gives generously to all without finding fault, and it will be given to him" (James 1:5).

TODAY'S THOUGHT Sometimes you hit a wall. Something comes along and has you completely baffled. You have no answers. Nothing makes sense. There doesn't seem to be any reason to what is happening. What can you do? James offers a solution. He says, "Ask God for wisdom." Stop, wait on God, cry out to Him and meditate. God promises that He will generously give us wisdom.

TODAY'S PRAYER Dear Father, I need wisdom. I need Your guidance and understanding. You have promised that you will give wisdom to me generously, so I come to You in faith, asking You to give me that wisdom today. In Jesus name. Amen.

Everything We Need for Life and Godliness

TODAY'S VERSE "His divine power has given us everything we need for life and godliness through our knowledge of him" (2 Peter 2:3).

TODAY'S THOUGHT How many times have we felt inadequate in a situation? If only there was something that could help us. It's easy to feel this way about our spiritual life. How can we live for God? How can we live this Christian life the way He wants us to? By ourselves, we can't. But the good news is, He has given us everything we need for life and godliness. How? Through knowing Him and His promises. Today, spend time and get to know God. Talk to Him. Ask Him to reveal Himself to you. If you will spend time getting to know God, you will find that He does indeed have everything you need for life and godliness.

TODAY'S PRAYER Dear God, I want to live the life You want me to, but I can't do it by myself. I need You. I need Your promises. Reveal Yourself to me today and in the days to come, so I can get to know You more and more and live the life You desire for me. Amen.

Help, I'm Falling and Can't Get Up

TODAY'S VERSE "When I said, "My foot is slipping," your love, O LORD, supported me. When anxiety was great within me, your consolation brought joy to my soul" (Psalm 94:18-19).

TODAY'S THOUGHT Have you ever lost your footing? My son Nathan did. I went rock climbing with my two oldest boys. Nathan was climbing above me. He was almost to the top of our little climb and his feet slipped. I was below on a ledge, and as he came sliding down the face, I was able to catch him. We hugged, and I sent him back up, where he completed the climb. I don't know who was more scared, Nathan or me. I love my son and did everything I could to stop him from hurting himself. Our feet slip, don't they? Every day, anxiety, pressure, complexities of life assault us and knock us off balance. The good news is we have a Father waiting to catch us and help us back up the trail.

TODAY'S PRAYER Father, when my feet slip, I am so thankful for Your help and support. When I am troubled today, I ask that You make me conscious of Your presence and bring a deep joy to my soul. Amen.

Are You a Light?

TODAY'S VERSE "I have come into the world as a light so that no one who believes in me should stay in darkness" (John 12:45-45).

"I am the light of the world" (John 9:5).

"You are the light of the world. A city on a hill cannot be hidden. Neither do people light a lamp and put it under a bowl. Instead, they put it on its stand, and it gives light to everyone in the house" (Matthew 5:14-15).

TODAY'S THOUGHT What is the purpose of light? It's to invade darkness! What have we done? We have built islands of light and hidden it from the darkness. We have hoarded the light. Might we hear God's call to be *givers* of the light! Rise up; use your spiritual gifts. Give away the light. Invade the world's darkness. Today, give away hope, peace, love, joy, and patience!

TODAY'S PRAYER Oh Father, Maker of light, You have invaded my dark heart, but I am guilty of hoarding the light. Forgive me. Help me to invade the darkness and give away Your light. Might everything around me light up. Amen.

August 29
Love God

TODAY'S VERSE "You must love the Lord your God with all your heart, all your soul, all your strength, and all your mind" (Luke 10:27).

TODAY'S THOUGHT God created us for a relationship with Him. His purpose is for us to love Him. Specifically, we are to love Him with all of our heart, soul, and strength. But how do we do this? In his book *Sacred Companions,* Dr. Benner writes, "To know God we must think of Him, not simply about Him. We must learn to spend time gazing at Him, being still before Him and focused on Him. And we must learn to listen to Him. These disciplines of loving attention form the basis of the development of a love relationship with Him." But what do we do if we find it difficult to love God with all of our heart? Dr. Benner suggests "God doesn't want me to try to be more loving. He wants me to absorb His love so that it flows out from me. And so, I return again to knowing myself as deeply loved by God. I meditate on His love, allowing my focus to be on Him and His love for me, not me and my love for Him." Today, let your love for God grow by taking time to be still before Him and focus on His incredible love for you.

TODAY'S PRAYER Father, thank You for Your love for me. Help me to understand it more fully so I can learn to love You with my whole heart. Amen.

Fear

TODAY'S VERSE "Such love has no fear because perfect love expels all fear. If we are afraid, it is for fear of punishment, and this shows that we have not fully experienced his perfect love" (1 John 4:18).

TODAY'S THOUGHT Not all fear is equal. There is legitimate fear and false fear. God wants to free us from both. With true fear, we need to lean on His love and power. With false fear, we need to lean on the truth. False fear is the anxiety and panic we feel over something that in reality should not trouble us. It's built on a lie. For example, fear of abandonment, rejection, and failure are often the result of feeling unlovable and broken. These are lies. The truth is that we are loveable and are not damaged goods. We may stop from trying something new because we fear failure. Why? Because we believe if we fail, we'll be rejected or abandoned. Indeed, someone with conditional love may reject us, but that doesn't mean we're unlovable. It does not negate God's unfailing love for us. God's love trumps those that reject us based on performance. Their rejection is not the final word—God's is! That's what John meant when he wrote, "Perfect love expels all fear." Today, consider how much of what you do is motivated by fear. Consider the lies you believe and the fear of false consequences that push you into a panic. Bring them all to the cross of Calvary. Let God's perfect love expel all your fears and especially your false fears.

TODAY'S PRAYER Father, help me with fear. I need your wisdom to know the truth and not believe lies that send me into a panic. More than wisdom, I need to know Your perfect love. Help me live in that love without fear. In Jesus' name. Amen.

Value

TODAY'S VERSE "So don't be afraid; you are more valuable to God than a whole flock of sparrows" (Matthew 10:31).

TODAY'S THOUGHT We are valuable to God! Why is it that I wrestle with that so much? Why can't I accept the fact that God's love defines my value, not my performance, material belongings or status? I have value because God says I do! It's the lack of believing in our value that causes us to create a false self. In *The Deeper Journey*, M. Robert Mulholland Jr. writes, "As our false self-manages our life, we fear that we might not be valued. If our false self's identity is rooted in our performance, then our value must be rooted in how well we perform. To the extent our false self-guides our life, we fear others. Life with others is a constant threat to our false self. Others are constant threats to that fragile structure we have created to provide ourselves with identity, meaning, value and purpose." Jesus came to declare how valuable we are. He would not have wasted His life and died the horrible death He did for something of little value. No, He came to redeem the most valuable thing to Him in the whole universe— the human race. Today, know that you are loved by God. Know that you are valued by Him.

TODAY'S PRAYER Father, thank You that You love me and created me with value. Might the thought that I am valuable to You change my life today and set me free from the fear and bondage of trying to earn Your love. In Jesus' name. Amen.

September 1
Forgiveness

TODAY'S VERSE   "Praise the LORD, O my soul, and forget not all his benefits who forgives all your sins" (Psalm 103:2-3).

TODAY'S THOUGHT   What a beautiful plan! God creates us for fellowship with Him. Like with Adam and Eve, God allows our free will so we can choose to love Him and follow His ways. All the while, God knows our human condition and that we're tempted to stray from Him and His holy standard. Yet because of His perfect unconditional love for us, He does not require us to be perfect, just forgiven. This is possible through the substitutionary death of Jesus Christ on the cross. Because of Christ, God is able to forgive us for every transgression. John writes, "If we confess our sins, he is faithful and just and will forgive us our sins and purify us from all unrighteousness." Today, confess anything that is between you and God. Get your conscience clear with Him. When you do, God promises to forgive.

TODAY'S PRAYER   Father, thank You for the Holy Spirit that convicts me of things that are wrong in my life. Thank You for Jesus Christ, who took my place on the cross. Guide me today and help clear my conscience with You. In Jesus' name. Amen.

Praise God

TODAY'S VERSE "Let all that I am praise the Lord; with my whole heart, I will praise His Holy name" (Psalm 103:1).

TODAY'S THOUGHT It's easy to live day by day and never really take the time to praise God. Part of this is because we've relegated worship and praise to one hour a week. We've segmented our lives, with spirituality being only a small part. When we do praise, it's often with just an intellectual assent and is not wholehearted. This is not the way God intended our worship to be. Instead, God wants us to praise Him with everything that is inside us. David wrote, "Let all that I am praise the Lord!" This includes our emotions, knowledge, and personality. He wants us to praise Him with our *whole* heart. It is not a half-hearted activity or relationship. God wants our all—everything we are and hope to be. Today, praise God for all that He is. Praise Him for what He has done. Praise Him with everything you have! Praise Him with your whole heart. Truly, God is worthy!

TODAY'S PRAYER Father, I come now to praise Your holy name. I praise You for all that You are. I praise You from my whole heart. I sincerely love You and praise You with everything inside me. Praise You, Lord! Amen.

Rest in Him

TODAY'S VERSE "Then Jesus said, 'Come to me, all of you who are weary and carry heavy burdens, and I will give you rest'" (Matthew 11:28).

TODAY'S THOUGHT How many times have we qualified for this verse of scripture? Difficulties in life can bring us down. Relationships, finances, worries about the future, guilt over the past—there are many contributors to the stress we find ourselves under. Jesus knew what it was to be under duress. He felt the fatigue from endless ministry. He grew exasperated over the religious controversy surrounding His ministry. And yet with all the pressures and temptations, the Bible made it clear that He did not sin. Who better to come to for rest when we are weary? Today, Jesus offers you relief. He knows you are weary and often carry heavy burdens. He says, "Come and I will give you rest."

TODAY'S PRAYER Father, You know how often I am weary and heavy burdened. You promise that if I come to You that You will give me rest. I come, Lord Jesus; I come to You with all my burdens. Please give peace and rest to my soul today. Amen.

Pursuing You

TODAY'S VERSE "Surely your goodness and unfailing love will pursue me all the days of my life" (Psalm 23:6).

TODAY'S THOUGHT Psalm 23 is perhaps the most popular passage in the Bible. Verses like, "Though I walk through the shadow of death I will fear no evil," make it a favorite at funerals. At the end of the chapter, there is a glorious verse that many have memorized: "Surely goodness and mercy shall follow me all the days of my life and I shall dwell in the house of the Lord forever." It sounds so poetic, but do we really understand the meaning? The New Living Translation used above really brings out the true meaning: "Surely your goodness and unfailing love will pursue me all the days of my life." It's not passive *following* or a result of any good we have done. Instead, it says that *God pursues us* with His unfailing love and goodness. Not just temporarily, but all the days of our lives! He pursues you. If you ignore Him, He pursues. If you take Him for granted, He pursues. Even if you turn your back on Him, His unfailing love and goodness pursue you. Today, live in the joy that God is pursuing you with His love.

TODAY'S PRAYER Oh Father, thank You for pursuing me with Your unfailing love and goodness. Today, help me live in the joy of that reality. Amen.

God's Faithfulness

TODAY'S VERSE "The LORD who delivered me from the paw of the lion and the paw of the bear will deliver me from the hand of this Philistine" (1 Samuel 17:37).

TODAY'S THOUGHT If we could remember all the times that God delivered us from trouble, we would enjoy a much more peaceful life. So many times, I start my day as if it was the only day I've ever lived. Now, I don't mind forgetting some of the bad things in my life, but when I begin to live as if God were not alive, then I need to do some memory exercises. God created us with a powerful memory, equipped to grow mentally, socially and spiritually. Throughout the Bible, we are admonished to *remember* the goodness of God. Hope, peace, and faith all come from our remembrance of God's faithfulness in the past. When David went to face Goliath, all he took with him was a sling, five smooth stones and memory of God's deliverance in the past. Listen to what he said when he went to face the giant: "The LORD who delivered me from the paw of the lion and the paw of the bear will deliver me from the hand of this Philistine." What are you facing? What giant is between you and victory? Remember God's faithfulness in the past and trust Him with today.

TODAY'S PRAYER Father, thank You for Your faithfulness in my life. Help me remember all the good things You have done and how You have acted on my behalf. Then when trial and struggles come, help me step out in faith, knowing that You're the same today that You were yesterday. Amen.

September 6
Your Testimony

TODAY'S VERSE "Always be prepared to give an answer to everyone who asks you to give the reason for the hope that you have" (1 Peter 3:15).

TODAY'S THOUGHT There's something about a testimony that touches people deep in their heart. It's a powerful spiritual force. Sure, it is important to share the scriptures. We need to tell the gospel story. But we also need to share with others the reality of Christ in our life. You may think your story is not as dramatic as, "I once was blind, but now I see." Yet God has allowed you to *see* peace in the midst of despair. He's provided the food that you eat. He has given you another day to live. People are looking for a God that is alive and is relevant to everyday issues, like the ones you face. Today, use the love you have to witness to those around you. When you can, let others know how meaningful prayer, scriptures, and God are to the many different facets of your life. Many will come to know Christ better as they see the gospel as it appears in your life.

TODAY'S PRAYER Lord, help me share today with someone who needs to know You. Help me share how You affect my life. Help others see You in the way I live. Help me be ready to give to anyone who asks the hope I have in You. Amen.

Everlasting Love

TODAY'S VERSE "Long ago the Lord said to Israel: 'I have loved you, my people, with an everlasting love. With unfailing love, I have drawn you to myself'" (Jeremiah 31:3).

TODAY'S THOUGHT It can be difficult to accept God's love. We're taught from a young child to do good. If we do well, get good grades and make the sports team, we'll be liked. It sets us up to believe that love is *earned*, not given freely. Worse, some learn that love can be taken away. Is it a wonder that the love of God gets lost in translation? In his book *The Deeper Journey*, author M. Robert Mulholland Jr. writes, "We fear that we might not be valued. If our false self's identity is rooted in our performance, then our value must necessarily be rooted in how well we perform. Consequently, our false self-attempts to perfect our performance, at least in our own estimation." This is where fear and anger rise up in us. We're afraid that someone else's success will rob us of value. Anger can rise up inside us when we find something getting in the way of what we think we must have or do that will cause us to be appreciated and loved. Instead, God told us that He loves us with an everlasting and unfailing love—*everlasting* in that it never ends. God's love is unquenchable, unconditional, and undeserving. It's *unfailing* because nothing will stop it from reaching its objective. We are the object of God's love, and nothing will stand in the way of His expression of that love to us. So today, rejoice in the love that God has for you! Let the joy of His undying love for you cast away all your fear and anger.

TODAY'S PRAYER Father, I thank You that I am valued and loved. Thank You that I do not have to earn it. Today, help me to really understand Your unconditional love for me. Amen.

September 8
Overcoming Fear

TODAY'S VERSE "For God hath not given us the spirit of fear; but of power, and of love, and of a sound mind" (2 Timothy 1:7).

TODAY'S THOUGHT We often think of fear as the reaction to scary events, like screams in a horror movie. But some of our most fearful behavior is often hidden from us. Many people who are daily living in fear aren't even aware of it. In *Surrender to Love*, Dr. Benner writes, "One of the things that block us from gaining freedom from fear is that most fearful people don't think of themselves as afraid. Unless their fears are focused on something external (such as snakes, heights or crowds), in bondage to fear most people fail to recognize the true nature of their inner distress. Although the object of one's fears may seem to be external, the real source of the fear is internal. The danger is within. The enemy is one's own self or at least some aspect of their self." This is what Paul was trying to get across in today's verse. We become so focused on our behavior that we don't see the motivation behind it. Paul called it a *spirit of fear*—an internal, pervasive fear that controls what we do. It's spiritual and emotional. Satan is a liar and accuser, so he fills our heads with fear and our own experience and belief systems do the rest. Most of our fear is based on what others will think or do. But today's verse says that we don't have to live in that kind of fear. Why? Because God has given us something else—power, love and a sound mind. What an alternative to anything we might dread! Anything we fear can be defeated either by God's power, His love or the sound mind He has given us. So today, when you are tempted to act out of fear, remember—there are other options. Give the power, love and the sound mind that God has given you a chance.

TODAY'S PRAYER Father, I thank You for not giving me a spirit of fear. Today, I want to live in Your power, love and the sound mind that You've given me. Amen.

The Journey

TODAY'S VERSE   "Peter asked Jesus, 'What about him, Lord?' Jesus replied, 'If I want him to remain alive until I return, what is that to you? As for you, follow me'" (John 21:21-22).

TODAY'S THOUGHT   Life is a journey with many twists and turns. It's different for each of us. None of us travels the same road. If we're going to live the way He desires, we must be willing to follow Him. In his book *Sacred Companions*, David Benner writes, "It is impossible to specify precisely the route that has to be followed in a soul's journey of transformation. This is because, rather than following a map, in this journey, we follow a person—Jesus. Jesus does not tell us where to go; He simply asks us to follow Him." Jesus compared us to sheep, saying, "My sheep hear my voice, and I know them, and they follow me." When thinking about his future, Peter questioned the Lord about John's fate. Jesus answered, "What is that to you? As for you, follow me." It's the same for us today. We don't need to be concerned with others and what God has for them. We need to get to know God, strive to understand the purpose He has for us and begin to follow Him. Today, obey His command to "follow me" and seek God's direction for your journey.

TODAY'S PRAYER

Father, help me follow You. Give me the wisdom, courage, and understanding I need to participate in the journey You have for me. Amen.

His Presence

TODAY'S VERSE "You have endowed him with eternal blessings and given him the joy of your presence" (Psalm 21:6).

TODAY'S THOUGHT In today's verse, King David writes a psalm about God's blessings in his life. David felt blessed because God gave him the joy of being in His presence. Joy comes from deeply bonded relationships, especially with God. That's why we were created. God desires our fellowship. He has endowed each of us with eternal blessings that come from the joy of His presence. But do we even pay attention to God? Much like a marriage, you can choose to enjoy each other's company, or you can stay busy, ignore each other's companionship and years later wonder why the love is gone. Today, choose to be conscious of the presence of God. Choose to stop and meditate on who He is and the infinite love He has for you. When you do, you will find true joy.

TODAY'S PRAYER Father, make me conscious of Your presence. Help me to experience today the deep joy of knowing You. Fill me with Your Holy Spirit and fill my heart with Your love. Amen.

Freedom

TODAY'S VERSE "And because you belong to him, the power of the life-giving Spirit has freed you from the power of sin that leads to death" (Romans 8:2).

TODAY'S THOUGHT David knew what it was to struggle with moral choices. Doing the right thing is not always easy. We struggle with all kinds of conflicting thoughts, attitudes and emotions. Paul struggled this way, too. In the book of Romans, he wrote, "I have discovered this principle of life—that when I want to do what is right, I inevitably do what is wrong." But Paul knew where to look for help, asking the question, "Who will free me from this life that is dominated by sin and death?" Both David and Paul knew the answer. It's God that can set us free if we let Him. David cried out to God, "Keep your servant from deliberate sins! Don't let them control me." Paul wrote, "The power of the life-giving Spirit has freed you from the power of sin." What a glorious thought! God, through the power of His Holy Spirit, enables you and me to be free from the tyranny of sin with all its guilt and shame. Through the empowerment of the Holy Spirit, the instruction from the word of God and the encouragement of other believers, we can live the life God desires for us. Will we sin? Yes. But sin doesn't have to be our master. Our allegiance is to Christ, and He has set us free!

TODAY'S PRAYER Father, thank You for forgiving me. Thank You for the power of the life-giving Holy Spirit that has freed me from the power of sin, guilt, and shame. Amen.

Maturity

TODAY'S VERSE "Until we all come to such unity in our faith and knowledge of God's Son that we will be mature in the Lord, measuring up to the full and complete standard of Christ" (Ephesians 4:13).

TODAY'S THOUGHT Spiritual maturity is something to be aspired to. It is not an automatic by-product of salvation. Jesus brings us salvation and with that, He brings deliverance and healing. Thank God that this changes our identity, our nature and who we are. We can, however, become a Christian and remain immature. Maturity is a process. This is why Paul says that God has given us, "apostles, the prophets, the evangelists, pastors, and teachers." He writes, "Their responsibility is to equip God's people to do his work and build up the church, the body of Christ." As we subject ourselves to the teaching and authority of those that Christ has given to the church, we will mature in the Lord. Christ has come to give us life and give it more abundantly. This means He's come to help us mature. Where are you in your spiritual maturity? Today, examine your own life. Ask God to show you where you need to mature. Ask Him to guide you and help you to be all that He intends for you to be.

TODAY'S PRAYER Father, point out my immaturities. I want to grow in You. I want to be all that You want me to be. In Jesus' name. Amen.

September 13
Live the Gospel

TODAY'S VERSE "We live in such a way that no one will stumble because of us, and no one will find fault with our ministry. We prove ourselves by our purity, our understanding, our patience, our kindness, by the Holy Spirit within us, and by our sincere love" (2 Corinthians 6:3,6).

TODAY'S THOUGHT Christ commanded us to be His servants in this world. We are representing Him. When people see us, they should see Him. Paul knew this. In today's verse, we see Paul trying to live in such a way that nobody would be able to discredit the Lord because of his ministry. But how did he do this? He did it by the way he lived. He was able to overcome allegations by his pure lifestyle and allowed him to have moral authority. His understanding of God, the scriptures, his ministry and the culture also allowed him to be above reproach. Paul was also patient in his suffering and his kindness caused many to consider believing in the God Paul believed in. Paul believed deeply in the Holy Spirit and allowed Him to move in the hearts of those that opposed Him. It was the Holy Spirit that filled Paul with love, joy, peace, patience and all the other attributes that he needed to be effective in his testimony of Christ's love. Finally, it was Paul's sincere love that enabled him to live among so many different people groups and win people to Christ. Today, let us go into the world that God has called us to minister in. Let's live the same way Paul did and help others come to the saving knowledge of Christ.

TODAY'S PRAYER Father, help me live like Paul. Help me live every day in a way that those around me will see something in me that will lead them to You. Amen.

Love Others

TODAY'S VERSE "While Jesus was having dinner at Matthew's house, many tax collectors and 'sinners' came and ate with him and his disciples" (Matthew 9:10).

TODAY'S THOUGHT So often we forget that God loves all of mankind. Jesus came and exemplified this. We get so caught up in our churches, small groups and Bible studies that we can't remember how to relate to everyday, normal people. Jesus expects us to be good neighbors. He desires that we share His love with those that don't know what it's like. The Pharisees didn't get it and were offended that Jesus ate with sinners. In response to their disdain, Jesus said, "Healthy people don't need a doctor—sick people do." Then he added, "Now go and learn the meaning of this scripture: 'I want you to show mercy, not offer sacrifices.' For I have come to call not those who think they are righteous, but those who know they are sinners." There are people all around us in need—broken hearts, addictions, depressed, lonely, angry, poor, and hungry—needing someone to stop and show mercy and love; someone to invite them in and eat with them; someone to be their friend. God has called you and me to be that someone. Today, let Jesus love someone through you. Look around and ask God who He wants you to befriend.

TODAY'S PRAYER Father, thank You for Your love and mercy in my life. Help me go and give the same to others. In Jesus' name. Amen.

Keep on Keeping On

TODAY'S VERSE "Keep on asking, and you will receive what you ask for. Keep on seeking, and you will find. Keep on knocking, and the door will be opened to you. For everyone who asks, receives. Everyone who seeks, finds. And to everyone who knocks, the door will be opened" (Matthew 7:7-8).

TODAY'S THOUGHT I've probably fought with this passage more than any other portion of scripture. Many times, I've prayed about situations that seemed impossible without God's intervention—overcoming mental anguish, living in poverty, wondering how the bills were going to be paid, facing fatal illnesses, rebuilding a failing relationship, seeking direction when I didn't have a clue what to do. I'm sure you can add your own experiences to this list. And so, you find yourself before God, praying. Nothing happens, so you pray again and again. After a while, you begin to wonder, "God, are You there?" That soon turns to, "God do You care?" There's a saying that goes something like this: "The definition of insanity is to keep doing the same thing over and over again, expecting different results." And sometimes that's how you feel. You start to doubt, and then God brings you back to this passage. You read with tears in your eyes, "Keep on asking...keep on seeking...keep on knocking." So, you must make a choice. Is this insanity or is it faith? There's an enormous difference! The difference is God. When God is in the picture, every time we pray we know that the God who is able to do all that we ask is there. He cares, and He hears our prayers. He knows our situation and has not abandoned us. Because we have prayed, He is moved. And so, we keep on keeping on. We live by faith, we ask by faith and many times we have to wait by faith. But it's faith in the God who is there—the God who knows; the God who cares. So today, let us again hang on to His promise, "Everyone who asks, receives. Everyone who seeks, finds. And to everyone who knocks, the door will be opened."

TODAY'S PRAYER Father, I come to You in faith. I come asking, seeking and knocking. I come in faith, believing. Amen.

September 16
Praise God

TODAY'S VERSE "Praise the Lord! For the Lord our God, the Almighty, reigns. Let us celebrate, let us rejoice, let us give him the glory" (Revelation 19:6-7).

TODAY'S THOUGHT How excited are you about knowing God? You would think we'd be ecstatic, but instead, our joy is minimal. I've seen sports fans get more excited about their team winning a championship than most churches do during worship. This is because most of us only know *about* God. Sure, we've asked Him to be our Savior, but we haven't taken the time to really *know* Him. We know nothing of His power, wisdom or glory. How, then, can we say with John, "The Lord our God, the Almighty reigns"? If we're going to celebrate God, if we're going to rejoice because of Him, then we need to *know* God in a deep and personal way. This will only happen if we spend time in His presence. In His presence, He will reveal Himself to us. In His presence, we will learn of His power, wisdom and His glory. In His presence, we will learn to praise, celebrate and rejoice in Him. So today, stop everything! Stop and become conscious of His presence and consider who He is. Sense that He is the Almighty One. Feel how worthy He is of all our praise. For just a moment, consider how great He is, and then know this—He loves you! The Almighty One loves you, so go ahead—celebrate, rejoice and give Him the glory!

TODAY'S PRAYER Father, forgive me for not appreciating You enough. You are the Almighty One and You reign on high. I rejoice that I know You and come to You with joy and celebration. You are worthy of all my praise and I give You all the glory. Amen.

Friend of God

TODAY'S VERSE "I have called you friends, for everything that I learned from my Father I have made known to you" (John 15:15).

TODAY'S THOUGHT There are many things to aspire to in life. The world holds up its honors, riches, and fame as worthwhile goals. There are many things that we can do, and many roles that we can become, but there's something very special and unique about being a *friend of God*. This is the only relationship that can fully fill the empty spot in our heart. In his book *Surrender to Love*, Dr. David G. Benner explains our need for unique friendship. He writes, "The deepest ache of the soul is the spiritual longing for connection and belonging. We seek bridges from our isolation through people, possessions, and accomplishments. But none of these are ever quite capable of satisfying the restlessness of the human heart. To be human is to have been designed for intimate relationship with the Divine." God has made it clear that we can have friendship with Him. It is the life, death, and resurrection of Christ that has paved the way for you and me to be friends with our Heavenly Father. Today, listen to the words of Christ, "I have called you friend." Let them sink deep into your heart.

TODAY'S PRAYER Father, I desire to know You more. I long for Your intimacy. I yearn to know Your love deep in my heart. Thank You for loving me; thank You for calling me Your friend. Amen.

God Is Love

TODAY'S VERSE "Dear friends, let us continue to love one another, for love comes from God. Anyone who loves is a child of God and knows God. But anyone who does not love does not know God, for God is love. This is real love—not that we loved God, but that he loved us and sent his Son as a sacrifice to take away our sins. Dear friends, since God loved us that much, we surely ought to love each other. No one has ever seen God. But if we love each other, God lives in us, and his love is brought to full expression in us" (1 John 4:7-8, 10-12).

TODAY'S THOUGHT Christianity is rooted in the deep love of God. It was in love that we were created. It is in love that our sins are forgiven. It is in love that we are to live for Jesus. In his book *Surrender to Love*, Dr. David G. Benner writes, "Christianity is the world's great love religion. The Christian God comes to us as love, in love, and for love. The Christian God woos us with love and works our transformation through love. Only love can soften a hard heart. Only love can renew trust after it has been shattered. Only love can inspire acts of genuine self-sacrifice. Only love can free us from the tyrannizing effects of fear. There is nothing more important in life than learning to love and be loved. Jesus elevated love as the goal of spiritual transformation. What about you? Have you surrendered to God's love? Have you accepted His free gift of salvation and His unconditional love? If not, surrender today. Give Christ your heart. Allow His love to wash over your soul and renew you from the inside out. God is love, and He loves you. Live in that love.

TODAY'S PRAYER Father, You indeed are love. It is your essence. Your love is pure and powerful, and You have set Your affection for me. Thank You for Your love. I accept it and want to live every moment in the keen awareness that You love me. Help me to that end. In Jesus' name. Amen.

Living for Jesus

TODAY'S VERSE "I am praying not only for these disciples but also for all who will ever believe in me through their thought. I pray that they will all be one, just as you and I are one—as you are in me, Father, and I am in you. And may they be in us so that the world will believe you sent me" (John 17: 20-21).

TODAY'S THOUGHT This was more than a prayer that Jesus prayed. It was His mission statement. His goal was to spread the *thought* that there is a loving God that has salvation for all people to all ends of the earth. He knew that this would only happen if we worked together. It's through a oneness of purpose and the empowerment of the Holy Spirit that we can spread His thought to all the ends of the earth. In his book *The Deeper Journey*, M. Robert Mulholland Jr. writes, "Union with God results in our being a person through whom God's presence touches the world with forgiving, cleansing, healing, liberating and transforming grace. The world will not believe in Christ because of our sound theology, our correct creed, our well-defined dogma, our rigorous religiosity. The world will believe when it sees Christ-likeness manifested in our life." Today, might we commit ourselves to be a more effective witness for Christ through our unity, faith, and love.

TODAY'S PRAYER Father, help me live for You. Help me join other believers in a deep, loving relationship so together, we will be a witness to Your love, grace, and truth. Amen.

Grace, Truth and Time

TODAY'S VERSE   "The Word became flesh and made his dwelling among us. We have seen his glory, the glory of the One and Only, who came from the Father, full of grace and truth" (John 1:14).

TODAY'S THOUGHT   Jesus came to earth to be our Savior. He came to give us an abundant life. The way He does this is through the very expression of who He is. We see this in today's verse. Jesus, or as John calls Him, the Word, came from the Father, took on a human form and was full of grace and truth. It is *grace* that saves us, sustains us and forgives us. But it is His *truth* that corrects us, directs us and, as Jesus said, "Sets us free." Dr. Henry Cloud talks about this in his book *Changes That Heal*. He explains that it is the combination of God's grace and truth that gives us the balance we need to live an emotionally healthy life. Grace without truth will never lead to true change. Truth without grace will never allow us the space we need to fail and start over. We need both. Dr. Cloud adds one more ingredient. He adds *time*. How wise. When we add time to the grace of God to forgive and the truth of God to guide us, true maturity results. Today, may we rejoice in God's wonderful plan for our spiritual growth.

TODAY'S PRAYER   Father, how I thank You for Your wonderful amazing grace that loves me unconditionally. Thank You for Your truth that has as its aim, my maturity. And Father, thank You for the time and patience that You have given me so that I may mature in You. Amen.

What Spirit Do You Have?

TODAY'S VERSE "For God has not given us a spirit of fear and timidity, but of power, love, and self-discipline" (2 Timothy 1:7).

TODAY'S THOUGHT What attitude are we letting control our life? With the rise in crime and a cyclical economy job market, it's easy to let fear, doubt, and insecurity fill our hearts. When we do, we find ourselves paralyzed—not able to live by faith; not stepping out to trust God. It was the same way in Paul's time. There was poverty, persecution, sickness and government unrest. It would have been easy for the early churches to be gripped by fear, but Paul insisted that they had another choice. Why? Because of God! God makes the difference. It's God that gives us power, love, and self-discipline. What a combination! Is there any combination that is stronger? God gives us His power—an unlimited source of strength for whatever we set out to do. Then He adds to it love—the greatest force in the universe. People armed with love can overcome any odds. Finally, God has given us the ability to be disciplined in doing His will. With our consistent, disciplined use of His power and love, what should we be afraid of? Today, put off fear and timidity. Let God's power and love guide your journey.

TODAY'S PRAYER Father, how I thank You that You have not given me a spirit of fear or timidity. Instead, Lord, You have given me power, love, and self-discipline. Help me use it today. Amen.

Filled with His Love

TODAY'S VERSE "For we know how dearly God loves us because he has given us the Holy Spirit to fill our hearts with his love" (Romans 5:5).

TODAY'S THOUGHT It's possible to have someone love you and not be able to comprehend it. I know. For whatever reason, I was able to love others, tell others about God's love, but when it came to feel that same love, I experienced a major block. A sense of shame, false guilt and emptiness would come over me if I was forced to acknowledge that anyone loved me. I could hear the words, "I love you", but could never get the emotions through my defenses. It was only after the ministry of the Holy Spirit who gently brought me to the place where I could experience God's grace that I felt His unconditional love. But it was not easy. What about you? Do you know that God loves you? If so, do you know it in a deep and personal way? Has the Holy Spirit filled your heart with His love? If not, do not despair; talk to God about it. Ask the Holy Spirit to work in your heart and make you more and more aware of the unconditional love that God has for you.

TODAY'S PRAYER Father, I know You love me, but today I want to know it with my heart. I need Your Holy Spirit to minister to me in ways that help me understand deep in my soul that I am loved. I give You my heart; fill it with Your love. I pray in Jesus' name. Amen.

His Great Power

TODAY'S VERSE "I also pray that you will understand the incredible greatness of God's power for us who believe him" (Ephesians 1:19).

TODAY'S THOUGHT Here's a mystery. How in the world can I have something so great in my possession and totally ignore it? If I was a soldier on a mission, I'd be conscious that I had powerful weapons at my disposal. If I were a rich man going on a vacation, I'd be fully aware of my bank account. Yet day after day, I live my life as if there were no presence of God or any of His power available for my life. How can this be? Is it that I'm simply not conscious of the spiritual battle I'm in, rendering Christ's power as having no relevance in my life? Is it pride or arrogance that allows me to live as if everything depends on me instead of Christ? I thank God that Paul realized this spiritual cancer and set an example for us to follow. Paul wrote that I must ask God to help me understand the incredible power that He has available for my spiritual journey. It is with this understanding that I begin to ask God to do mighty things. What about you? Are you applying the power of God in your life? If not, start today. Ask God to help you begin to understand the incredible greatness of His power available for your life.

TODAY'S PRAYER Father, I pray that You would help me trust You and understand the power you have available for my life. In Jesus' name. Amen.

Light Up the Darkness

TODAY'S VERSE "You light a lamp for me. The Lord, my God, lights up my darkness" (Psalm 18:28).

TODAY'S THOUGHT Life can be unpredictable and messy. Every one of us has drama in our life. We all have a story. We would rather have control over our situation, but so often we are simply left in the dark, wondering what to do. David experienced this. He had his difficulties, but instead of staying in the dark, he turned to God for help. He cried out to God, and God became his light. He wrote, "You light a lamp for me. The Lord, my God, lights up my darkness." Today, if things become unclear, if you are bombarded with problems or if dark clouds start to clutter up your sky, turn to God. He will light your path.

TODAY'S PRAYER Father, thank You for being a light in my life. Whenever I have been left in the dark, Your light has been right there. Thank You for being a lamp for my path, showing me where to go. Guide me today, I pray. Amen.

Who Is Your God?

TODAY'S VERSE "The Lord is my rock, my fortress, and my savior; my God is my rock, in whom I find protection. He is my shield, the power that saves me, and my place of safety" (Psalm 18:2).

TODAY'S THOUGHT What you believe about God makes a difference. Not in God, but in the way you live. Your comprehension of God has everything to do with your faith and hope in this world. Look at what David believed. He saw God as his rock, fortress, savior, protection, shield, power and safety. How do you think this affected his attitude during a crisis? Time and experience had taught David well. All that he went through made him stronger and deepened his beliefs about the God who is there; the God who cares; the God who is able. What is God to you? Is He your rock, fortress, and protection? Do you come to Him when the world gets too tough? Is God your power? Can you trust in Him to supply all that you need for each and every day? David did, and so can we. Today, step out in faith. Ask God to reveal Himself to you and give you a fresh faith like David. When you do, you will find God to be all that you need.

TODAY'S PRAYER Father, please reveal Yourself to me. Help me see what David saw. Help me see You as my rock, fortress, savior, protection, shield, power and safety. Help me step out in faith and trust You today. In Jesus' name. Amen.

Be Honest with God

TODAY'S VERSE "Pay attention to my prayer, because I speak the truth" (Psalm 17:1, *New Century Version*).

TODAY'S THOUGHT You would think being honest with God would be natural, but it isn't. It's not necessarily that we tell God big lies, but we often omit the truth. We pray, "Lord, help me! I need money for my bills." Perhaps a more honest prayer would be, "Lord, please show me how to manage my finances better." We pray that God will help us with a poor relationship when we should be praying for our behavior and attitude toward the other person involved. We ask God to forgive our sins, but not for the wisdom and discipline to change our behavior. Sometimes we would be better off starting our prayers with, "Lord, what do You want me to pray about?" Then wait to see what God challenges us with. This kind of honest, life-changing prayer only comes from a sincere relationship with God. As we spend more time with Him, we'll find it easier to pray in an open, honest and fresh way.

TODAY'S PRAYER Father, help me share with You in an honest and open way. I want nothing between us. I want to serve You with all my heart and pray that honesty will be at the core of our relationship. Amen.

Approaching God

TODAY'S VERSE "Because of Christ and our faith in him, we can now come boldly and confidently into God's presence" (Ephesians 3:12).

TODAY'S THOUGHT How do you approach God? It often depends on your presuppositions of who God really is. Is He some mean, unreasonable disciplinarian that is watching your every move? Is God some detached, non-involved creator that has no desire to relate to you? Perhaps your view of God is like Santa Claus—you give him your wish list and hope to get wonderful things in return. Perhaps worse than any of these is that God is unpredictable—you never know if God will show up, and if He does, what kind of mood He'll be in. What we believe about God has a lot to do with the way we come to Him. In today's verse, Paul writes about his faith in God. He says that because of Christ, we can come boldly and confidently into God's presence. The author of Hebrews says it best. He writes, "So then, since we have a great High Priest who has entered heaven, Jesus the Son of God, let us hold firmly to what we believe. This High Priest of ours understands our weaknesses, for he faced all of the same tests we do, yet did not sin. So, let us come boldly to the throne of our gracious God. There we will receive his mercy, and we will find grace to help us when we need it most." Today, rejoice and join Paul in saying, "Because of Christ and our faith in him, we can now come boldly and confidently into God's presence."

TODAY'S PRAYER Dear Father, thank You for Your love for me. Thank You for the death and resurrection of Jesus Christ that has made it possible for me to come boldly to You. I come into Your presence to receive afresh all Your love and grace. In Jesus' name. Amen.

September 28
Dual Citizenship

TODAY'S VERSE "All praise to God, the Father of our Lord Jesus Christ, who has blessed us with every spiritual blessing in the heavenly realms because we are united with Christ" (Ephesians 1:3).

TODAY'S THOUGHT We live in two worlds. Yes, we are here on earth, but our life in Christ exists in the heavenly realm, as well. This is where our spiritual blessings come from. God decided this destiny for us a long time ago. Paul writes, "Even before he made the world, God loved us and chose us in Christ to be holy and without fault in his eyes. God decided in advance to adopt us into his own family by bringing us to himself through Jesus Christ." We are a product of God's sovereign will and He has chosen to bless us with every spiritual blessing—forgiveness, grace, peace, joy, and other byproducts of the Spirit. These spiritual traits are sent from the very throne of God, given to us to enjoy here and now in this world. We are united with Christ, and this union is the intertwining of both worlds. Therefore, we can say boldly with Paul, "All praise to God, the Father of our Lord Jesus Christ, who has blessed us with every spiritual blessing in the heavenly realms." Today, might the realization of your Heavenly citizenship bring you joy.

TODAY'S PRAYER Thank You, Father, for creating me and blessing me with every spiritual blessing. I know that these are gifts from Your very throne and that You determined to bless me before the world was even made. Thank You for making me part of Your plan. Thank You for Your eternal love. In Jesus' name. Amen.

Joy and Quiet

TODAY'S VERSE "My heart is glad, and I rejoice. My body rests in safety. You will show me the way of life, granting me the joy of your presence and the pleasures of living with you forever" (Psalm 16:9,11).

TODAY'S THOUGHT We were made for rhythms of joy and quiet. David is a perfect example. His heart was full of joy and peaceful rest. What was his secret? Was it his circumstances? Was it his wealth? Was it the adoration of thousands of followers? No, David's joy and peace came from his enjoyment of God's presence. It was in God's presence that David felt love and grace that overwhelmed him with joy and reverent rest. It was the pleasure of living in God's presence that resulted in David's rhythm of joy and rest. You can experience the same. Today, spend time in God's presence. Meditate on His love for you. Let His presence bring you the same joy and quiet that it gave David.

TODAY'S PRAYER Father, I come to You now. I want to experience the joy and peace of Your presence. Amen.

He Is Our Guide

TODAY'S VERSE "I will bless the Lord who guides me; even at night, my heart instructs me" (Psalm 16:7).

TODAY'S THOUGHT I've appreciated a few guides in my day. There is nothing worse than being in a deep forest and not knowing where you are. How thankful I was to have a guide who knew every square inch of the terrain. Most of us have needed a guide. We sometimes get ourselves into deeply complex situations, way in over our heads, and are not sure what to do. When someone familiar with the situation offers their assistance and shows us the way out, we are greatly relieved. How intricate life can be! Every day has new challenges. Just when you think you know the terrain, you turn a corner and...bam! You don't know where you are. Panic, frustration, doubt, and fear start to set in. Then you remember, "Why am I worried? The Lord is my guide!" And He is. David believed this. He knew what it was to depend on God. He knew what it was to be in circumstances where he wasn't sure which way to turn. So, he blessed the Lord, who was his guide. David's God is the same God who will instruct you. Try it today. Let God guide you. Call out to Him for wisdom, instruction, help, and strength for all you do. He will be your guide.

TODAY'S PRAYER Father, be my guide. I need Your wisdom, Your strength, and Your guidance. Thank You, Lord, that You love me and long for me to come to You for help. I come now, Lord Jesus. Amen.

Can or Can't?

TODAY'S VERSE "For I can do everything through Christ, who gives me strength" (Philippians 4:13).

TODAY'S THOUGHT I can or I can't? They are two opposite paths that take you to very different places. *Can't* takes you into the territory of doubt, despair and eventually hopelessness. We can't. They can't. Soon, we're believing that God can't. Paul knew this. That is why he spent his life encouraging unbelievers to follow Christ and believers to increase their trust in Christ and eventually entrust God with their whole life. Paul was the consummate example. He trusted Christ for everything. And everything is what he expected. That is why he proclaimed, "I can do everything through Christ, who gives me strength." Today, decide to join Paul. Make your motto, "Through Christ, I *can*."

TODAY'S PRAYER Father, help me change my *can't* to *can*. Help me trust in Your strength and not in mine. In Jesus' name. Amen.

Live in Peace

TODAY'S VERSE "Live in harmony with each other. Don't be too proud to enjoy the company of ordinary people. And don't think you know it all! Never pay back evil with more evil. Do things in such a way that everyone can see you are honorable. Do all that you can to live in peace with everyone" (Romans 12:16-18).

TODAY'S THOUGHT God wants us to live in peace with others. This is easier said than done. Yet as God's ambassadors, it's imperative that we really try to do so. Ken Sande, the author of *The Peacemaker*, writes, "Something significant happens when you decide to follow God's instructions for relationships, especially His insights on conflict. When you focus on Him and His ways, you do more than cope. When you choose to study and act on God's plan in every area of your existence, you're living for His glory. When you glorify God by doing relationships according to His plan, you're allowing God to reign in your life. You're enjoying a powerful connection that alters your whole life. And it's far more than personal. You're also giving everyone around you a reason to respect and praise God's fame." Conflicts will come, but today, choose God's way of dealing with them. Turn it over to Him. Do as Paul writes: "Live in harmony, don't be proud, don't think you know it all, don't repay evil with evil and do all you can to be at peace with everyone."

TODAY'S PRAYER Father, I need Your help with relationships. I get so frustrated. I need Your Holy Spirit to guide me and help me love others the way You do. Help me, guide me and empower me. I pray in Jesus' name. Amen.

October 3
Don't Be Weary

TODAY'S VERSE "But they that wait upon the LORD shall renew their strength; they shall mount up with wings as eagles; they shall run, and not be weary; and they shall walk, and not faint" (Isaiah 40:31).

TODAY'S THOUGHT Life can get hard. Feelings from inside, forces from outside—it can become overwhelming. David knew this, and he was honest in his writings. While David's writings culminate in praise and a trusting relationship with God, they do not spare his very real, raw human emotion. He challenges God by asking, "O Lord, why do you stand so far away? Why do you hide when I am in trouble?" How many times have we been perplexed by our situation and have wanted to say the same thing? And yet, somewhere deep in our hearts, we know that there must be more. The *more* is in the wait— "Be still and know that I am God." Waiting is part of the process of renewal. Isaiah writes, "But they that wait on the Lord shall renew their strength." He uses three glorious metaphors: 1) a high soaring eagle, 2) a person running without getting weary, and 3) a person on a long, difficult walk without fainting. And how is it we can experience victory even in defeat, peace amidst turmoil, or strength in a long weary journey? The author of Hebrews gives us the answer. He writes, "Let us come boldly to the throne of our gracious God. There we will receive His mercy, and we will find grace to help us when we need it most." Might you, today, experience all the grace of our loving God that you need so you can rise up with the wings of an eagle and not be weary or faint.

TODAY'S PRAYER Father, I need You. I need Your grace. I need Your renewal. Today, I come to Your throne and wait on You. Be my strength, help me run and not be weary and walk and not faint. I ask this in the name of Jesus Christ. Amen.

The Joy of His Presence

TODAY'S VERSE "You have given him the joy of being in your presence" (Psalm 21:6).

TODAY'S THOUGHT What a gift! God has put the capacity to experience His presence in us! An antenna picks up signals, but no antenna in the world can pick up an unsent signal. Like an antenna, the Holy Spirit—put within us by God—picks up God's message of love and enables us to experience God's presence. This verse is more about God than us. It is God that sends His presence out to us. It is God that desires our fellowship. It is His grace that causes Him to seek us out. Does that grab you? Let me say it again: the God of the universe not only allows us an audience with Him, He comes to us and seeks us out! And when we respond, we find out what David knew. There is extreme joy in being in His presence!

TODAY'S PRAYER Father, thank You for seeking me out. Thank You for allowing me to enjoy Your presence. I pray that I may experience the joy of Your presence more and more. Amen.

Get Right with God

TODAY'S VERSE "We are made right with God by placing our faith in Jesus Christ. And this is true for everyone who believes, no matter who we are" (Romans 3:22-23).

TODAY'S THOUGHT Are you right with God? This is a serious question, and yet most of us don't spend much time thinking about it. Somewhere along the line, we have developed our own theory of how to be right with God. It usually involves doing good; at least, more good than bad. But the Bible displays a different plan. It talks about a God that loves us and has made a way that we can be forgiven. It shares how receiving Christ as our personal Savior will bring us into right standing with God. By putting our faith in the sacrifice of God's Son, Jesus, on the cross, we become His child and are born again into His family. This brings us to a whole new relationship with God and we are made right with Him. Today, you can have this relationship. Accept Christ as your own Savior, ask Him to forgive your sins and make you His child. Put your faith in Christ's sacrificial death on the cross for you and you will have a right relationship with God.

TODAY'S PRAYER Father, I accept Christ's death on the cross for me and ask You to forgive all my sins. I accept Christ as my Savior and put my faith in Him. Take my life and help me live it for You. Amen.

What Fruit Are You?

TODAY'S VERSE "By their fruit, you will recognize them" (Matthew 7:20).

TODAY'S THOUGHT Not all things are what they seem. Jesus once cursed a fig tree that gave the impression that it was bearing fruit when, in fact, it was barren. This example of *saying one thing and doing another* really got to Jesus. Perhaps it was the Pharisees that posed as religious zealots but knew nothing of the righteousness God was interested in. It may have been a reference to a false prophet that pretended to know what God wanted to say and led people down the wrong path. Jesus made it clear that He would rather be with a prostitute, a tax collector or lepers—all scorned by society and the religious community—that sincerely repented than those that had the pretense of faith. Jesus simply said it this way. "You can tell a tree by the fruit it produces." A peach tree should produce peaches. An apple tree should produce apples. Christians should demonstrate the fruit of the Spirit, which is love, joy, peace, patience, kindness, goodness, faithfulness, gentleness, and self-control. Today, when people look at your life, what fruit will they see?

TODAY'S PRAYER Father, I pray that the Holy Spirit will bear His fruit in my life, so when people see me, they will glorify You. Amen.

Lord, Lord

TODAY'S VERSE "So why do you keep calling me 'Lord, Lord!' when you don't do what I say?" (Luke 6:46).

TODAY'S THOUGHT It's so easy to speak half-truths. It's easy to say we're committed to a cause and yet not live that way. What exactly is loyalty? Jesus asked this in His day. People were beginning to follow Him just for the miracles or food and not for the new spiritual reality He was teaching. What was worse, people claimed to be His followers but ignored His words. He compared this to a person who was building a house. Jesus insisted that if you're going to build a house, build it on a good foundation. Likewise, if you are going to build a life worth living, it must be built on the good foundation of scriptures. Jesus was right. He said that you can call Him a lot of things, but if you are going to call Him Lord, you have to do what He says.

TODAY'S PRAYER Father, help me follow You. Be the Lord of my life and help me build my life on a solid foundation of Your word. Amen.

October 8
Peace to You

TODAY'S VERSE "In peace, I will lie down and sleep, for you alone, O
Lord, will keep me safe" (Psalm 4:8).

TODAY'S THOUGHT It is God's desire that we live in peace. However,
peace can be a relative term. Some would limit it to a *peaceful situation*.
Yet many people live in a safe and friendly environment and still find
themselves in desperation. The kind of peace that the Bible emphasizes
most is a *state of mind*. It is the inward peace that comes from knowing
that God is sovereign and that we can trust Him. It is the ability to delay
gratification, solutions, answers or understanding and substitute it with
hope, trust, and faith in God's ultimate goodness and love for us. So today,
choose peace. May peace fill your day and take you through the night.

TODAY'S PRAYER Father, I ask for You to flood my heart and my soul
with Your peace. Today, may I sense You love and presence and rest
myself in You. Amen.

My Own Eye

TODAY'S VERSE "And why worry about a speck in your friend's eye when you have a log in your own? How can you think of saying to your friend, 'Let me help you get rid of that speck in your eye,' when you can't see past the log in your own eye? Hypocrite! First get rid of the log in your own eye; then you will see well enough to deal with the speck in your friend's eye" (Matthew 7:3-5).

TODAY'S THOUGHT I don't agree with everything Freud wrote. There is, however, one of his observations that I think has some truth to it. Freud wrote about *projection*—the action of pointing out faults in others that we have ourselves. Have you ever caught yourself criticizing someone and suddenly realize that you exhibit the same behavior? Jesus warned us about pointing out other people's faults and ignoring our own. He said not to point out the little failings in other people while we have huge issues to deal with ourselves. He mastered the use of hyperbole with the comparison of a speck in another person's eye while we have this huge beam in our own. How funny this must have sounded to His audience, yet how true! We so often take offense at other's shortcomings when we have glaring inconsistencies in our own life. Today, let us examine ourselves. Let us come to God and ask Him to point out our own sins and deal with them before we worry about someone else's behavior.

TODAY'S PRAYER Father, forgive me for judging others. Help me to bring myself to You and allow Your Holy Spirit to work on my behavior. Lord, make me more like You. Amen.

October 10
What Do You Want?

TODAY'S VERSE "What do you want me to do for you?" (Mark 10:49-51).

TODAY'S THOUGHT One of the first verses I preached on as a teenager was this one. As a young man tasked with giving a gospel message, I still remember the impact this simple verse had on me. A blind man sitting by the road and hears that Jesus was coming. Nothing could shut him up! He started shouting out to Jesus. The disciples tried to make him quiet down, but Jesus told them to bring the man to Him. I love what happens next. Jesus looked at the blind man and said, "What do you want me to do for you?" The blind man answered simply, "I want to see." What appealed to me then, as a teenager, still appeals to me decades later. It is the sincerity of Jesus and the invitation to tell Him what it is that we want. This is the same Jesus that we pray to. It's the same heart of Christ that bids us come to Him. It is the same power available that asks such an open-ended question. Today, picture Him passing your way. Take the time to sit before Him and answer His question, "What do you want me to do for you?"

TODAY'S PRAYER Jesus, I thank You for coming my way today. I thank You that You care so much about me that You would ask me what I need from You. I come silently before You and share my request. Thank You, Lord, for hearing the desire of my heart. Amen.

Treasures

TODAY'S VERSE "Wherever your treasure is, there the desires of your heart will also be" (Matthew 6:21).

TODAY'S THOUGHT Where are our priorities? What is important to us? We can pretend that we believe certain spiritual truths, but what we really treasure usually gives us away. In this verse, Jesus is warning us that it's easy to get caught up in this life and not really look at the whole picture. We're not just part of this physical world. We're part of a much larger system. We're part of the spiritual realm. We are connected with eternity and, therefore, need to integrate what we believe in this life with a heavenly perspective. The questions that we need to ask ourselves are: "What do we really care about?" "What is really important to us?" "What do we treasure?" When we answer these questions, we will find our heart. Then we need to ask ourselves a difficult question: "Does our heart reflect Christ's values or the world's?" If we're going to follow Christ, if we are going to be His representative in this world, then our heart needs to reflect what is important to Him. Today, might we check our heart's priorities and realign what's important to us to be more in tune with Christ.

TODAY'S PRAYER Father, help me love what You love. Help me live with Your priorities foremost in my thinking. Help me live for You today. Amen.

Perfect Peace

TODAY'S VERSE "You will keep in perfect peace all who trust in you, all whose thoughts are fixed on you" (Isaiah 26:3).

TODAY'S THOUGHT It's easy to fret. We are, after all, a predicting machine—always observing, calculating and predicting the future. The trouble is, much of the time our predictions of doom and gloom are wrong. Often, the worry, fret, and precautions are for naught. Most of what we worry about doesn't happen. Look at all the time wasted! Look at the lost opportunities for joy and peace! Depression looks at the *past*; anxiety looks at the *future*. And we forget to live in the *now*. That's why Isaiah said that we should fix our thoughts on God. If we want to experience God's perfect peace, we need to trust in God. The way we trust in Him is to focus on His love, His strength, and His ability. When we focus on His love and power, our worries will pale in comparison. He will keep us in His peace. Like a person sailing a boat, when the winds come up and the waves toss us back and forth, keep your eyes on the shore and constantly correct your course. You will reach your destination.

TODAY'S PRAYER Father, when I begin to worry, help me correct my thoughts and meditate on Your love and power. Help me fix my eyes on You and put my trust in You. Thank You, Lord, that the result will be Your peace. Amen.

Don't Be Deceived

TODAY'S VERSE "You say, 'I am rich. I have everything I want. I don't need a thing!' And you don't realize that you are wretched and miserable and poor and blind and naked" (Revelation 3:17).

TODAY'S THOUGHT It's so easy to deceive ourselves. Look at the Pharisees. They thought they were doing everything God required of them to be holy, yet Jesus constantly pointed out how far they missed the target of true holiness. It was that way with the church in Laodicea. In Revelation, it says they were rich, had many things and felt they didn't need anything. However, God pointed out to them that they were deceived. They were spiritually wretched, miserable, poor, blind and naked. What about us? How can we avoid becoming deceived? We must spend time with God—open ourselves to hear His voice, read His word and spend time in introspection. We must humble ourselves before God, spend time with Him and listen to His leading. When we do, He will guide us. He will correct us. He will help us discern what we need to change. Today, ask God to make you aware of your spiritual condition. Might we pray what David prayed: "Search me, O God, and know my heart; test me and know my anxious thoughts. See if there is any offensive way in me, and lead me in the way everlasting."

TODAY'S PRAYER Father, help me be honest with myself and with You. Help me see if there is any offensive way in me and then lead me on a more spiritual path. In Jesus' name. Amen.

October 14
Mockery

TODAY'S VERSE "They stripped him and put a scarlet robe on him. They wove thorn branches into a crown and put it on his head, and they placed a reed stick in his right hand as a scepter. Then they knelt before him in mockery and taunted, 'Hail! King of the Jews!' And they spit on him and grabbed the stick and struck him on the head with it. When they were finally tired of mocking him, they took off the robe and put his own clothes on him again. Then they led him away to be crucified" (Matthew 27:28-31).

TODAY'S THOUGHT Who were these guys? Were they regular working guys with families to support? Were they patriotic servants of Rome? Were they just some guys trying to do their job? Whoever they were, they acted according to their beliefs. They weren't followers of Jesus and did not ascribe to His teachings. Instead, they mocked His claims to be King of the Jews. They beat Him, spit on Him and led Him away to be crucified. But we are believers. And yet I can't help but ask, "How do I treat Jesus?" No, I don't spit on Him, but do I follow His commands? I haven't hit Him with a stick, but do I confess my sin and keep a clean conscience with Him? I don't put a crown of thorns on His head, but do I worship Him in daily prayer? I don't mockingly call Him, "King of the Jews," but do I make Him king of my life today? Who hurts Jesus more—the soldiers in this passage or the believer who ignores Him and lives as if Christ never existed at all? Today, remember He died for you. He gladly took all the pain and mocking so you could know Him in a deep and personal way. Today, worship and serve Him.

TODAY'S PRAYER Lord Jesus, forgive me for the times I have mocked You with my life. Forgive me for the times I have spit upon You with my indifference. I confess my apathy and today ask for You to rekindle a fire in my heart. I want to follow You. I want to live for You. Amen.

October 15
God's Power

TODAY'S VERSE "I relied only on the power of the Holy Spirit. I did this so you would trust not in human wisdom but in the power of God" (1 Corinthians 2:4-5).

TODAY'S THOUGHT We like to move toward balance. Homeostasis, a relatively stable state of equilibrium, seems to work in many systems. But sometimes that is not the best move. Balance is good if you want to have normalcy. But many times, if you want to reach worthwhile goals, you must unbalance a few things. Does the professional athlete balance his or her practice time with other activities? No, they are consumed with their sport and devote many hours to that single pursuit. Soon or later, if you're going to excel at something, you must unbalance some things. Paul was sharing Jesus with people groups that had never heard of Christ before. He was starting churches from scratch, and he learned that the spiritual life must not be balanced with worldly wisdom. There needs to be a radical dependence on God to do mighty things if you are going to see His kingdom come. You need to ask for wisdom, but it's spiritual discernment that you should seek. You need to move in faith and hope in the spiritual realm, not logic and theory in the earthly realm. Today, what are you depending on God's power for? What "big hairy audacious goal" are you trusting the Holy Spirit to accomplish in and through you? Paul trusted in the power of God and we should do the same today.

TODAY'S PRAYER Father, I confess that many times conventional wisdom tells me to move in one direction when I know I should trust You for greater things. Lord, I want my life to make a difference. I want to see Your kingdom come as a result of Your Holy Spirit's guidance in my life. Lead me, use me, I pray. Amen.

Blessing

TODAY'S VERSE "Now may our Lord Jesus Christ himself and God our Father, who loved us and by his grace gave us eternal comfort and a wonderful hope, comfort you and strengthen you in every good thing you do and say" (2 Thessalonians 2:16-17).

TODAY'S THOUGHT After a worship service, a pastor usually gives a benediction—a blessing pronounced upon the congregation. A blessing is meant to help people have faith and hope in their Christian experience until they meet again. Of course, a benediction itself has no magical powers. It's not meant to be a magic chant. Rather, it is a pronouncement of God's strength, provision, and ability to guide and protect us during our mission in this world. Paul wrote many wonderful benedictions. Being far from the churches that he loved, he wrote blessings to bring joy and hope in the Lord for all those he loved. In today's verse, Paul is pronouncing a blessing of comfort and strength upon the church—power and strength from God in every good thing that they will do and say. Does this sound like something you would want? Today, let God minister to your heart as you read and apply this benediction to your life.

TODAY'S PRAYER Father, thank You for Your love, grace, comfort, and hope. I pray that today You will comfort and strengthen me in every good thing I do and say. Amen.

Grace

TODAY'S VERSE "From his abundance, we have all received one gracious blessing after another. For the law was given through Moses, but God's unfailing love and faithfulness came through Jesus Christ" (John 1:16-17).

TODAY'S THOUGHT   Every time I visit southern California, I'm overwhelmed by the fact that many of the people that live there seem to be oblivious to the fact that they live in paradise. They are surrounded by mountains, sun, and surf—but they don't see it. All they see is the everyday struggles of life. It's like that with God's grace. We can get so bogged down with life that we don't see all the grace that God has brought into our life. Not so with the Apostle John. Instead, John starts out his gospel with an overwhelming appreciation for the grace that God has for us. He writes that we have all received grace from God manifested in "one gracious blessing after another." He introduces this manifesto of grace in contrast to the Law that was given through Moses. Moses gave us the Law, but Jesus gave us God's grace. This grace was manifested in God's unfailing love and faithfulness toward us through the death and resurrection of Christ. What about you? How is your life? Are you experiencing God's unfailing love? Are you aware of His many blessings? Do you appreciate His faithfulness toward you? Or have you been like the person walking a few miles from the beach, totally unaware of all its beauty and serenity? Today, stop and take the time to be conscious of the many blessings God has given to you. Rejoice in His wonderful grace and faithfulness.

TODAY'S PRAYER   Father, forgive me for taking Your love and faithfulness for granted. Thank You for Your unfailing love and grace for me. Amen.

Mercy

TODAY'S VERSE "I cry out to the Lord; I plead for the Lord's mercy. I pour out my complaints before him and tell him all my troubles. When I am overwhelmed, you alone know the way I should turn" (Psalm 142:1-3).

TODAY'S THOUGHT Have you ever felt overwhelmed? I talk to people every day that feel that way. Divorce, hunger, disease, addictions, homelessness, debt, trauma—people come to our church every day for help. And it should be that way. The church is God's representative on earth. We should be telling everyone that God deeply cares about their personal affairs. David knew this. He was overwhelmed with life and all the challenges it had for him, yet he knew he could turn to the Lord. He cried out to God and plead for mercy. And God listened. Jeremiah attests to this. In Lamentations 3:22-24, Jeremiah writes, "The faithful love of the Lord never ends! His mercies never cease. Great is his faithfulness; his mercies begin afresh each morning." What an overwhelming truth! God's faithful love *never* ends, and His mercies *never* cease. I can't even begin to get my brain wrapped around that. And the beauty is that every morning when I wake up, God is there, with all His love and mercy, waiting for me. Today, when you need to, cry out to God. Pour out your complaints to Him. Tell Him all about your troubles. He has a brand new day's worth of mercy and love waiting for you.

TODAY'S PRAYER Father, I am so glad I can come before You and share all my burdens. I am so grateful for Your mercy and faithfulness. Thank You that they never cease but are new every morning. Praise You, Lord. Amen.

Offering

TODAY'S VERSE "Accept my prayer as incense offered to you, and my upraised hands as an evening offering" (Psalm 141:2).

TODAY'S THOUGHT There are many things you can do with your life. You have skills, knowledge, and experiences that afford you many different and unique occupational opportunities. However, there is one vocation that God has put in the heart of all who follow Him. It does not require skill, special knowledge, certain aptitudes or a pedigree. It only requires a heart that loves God. He has called you to be a priest. You have been given the sacred privilege to come before God in humble adoration. Dressed in a robe, cleansed by the blood of Jesus Himself, you stand before God, forgiven and accepted as His child. There, you are before God, your prayers received by Him as an incense offering, bringing Him extreme pleasure. As you praise Him, your hands reach up to Him in a holy embrace, received as an offering of love and praise. There is nothing God desires more. No offering has ever been so precious to God as your adoration, praise, and prayers. Come today as God's priest and offer Him your love. Come into His presence, love Him, talk to Him, and adore Him. It is your sacred privilege.

TODAY'S PRAYER Father, I come before You now with a humble heart. Hear my prayers. Receive them as a sacred offering. I lift up my hands to You in love and adoration. Please accept my praise as a holy sacrifice to You in all Your majesty. I worship You today as my Lord and my God. Amen.

Overcomer

TODAY'S VERSE "You, dear children, are from God and have overcome them because the one who is in you is greater than the one who is in the world" (1 John 4:4).

TODAY'S THOUGHT The early church was persecuted for their faith. Many were ostracized from society, living in poverty and starvation. Others were imprisoned, and many martyred for their faith. But ironically, this persecution caused the church to flourish. It forced them to band together and have a bond of love that the world has never seen again. It was an infectious witness to those around them. As the church rose to the spiritual challenge, Satan battled for their minds. It was an all-out assault on the truth of the gospel. During the time this verse was written, there many people challenging the core of Christianity. There were some who said that the death of Jesus was not enough; that we still had to obey the Jewish law. Others said that Christ was not the real Messiah or that He was not the real Son of God. Today, it's the same story. Neil Anderson, in his book *Bondage Breaker,* reminds us that our battle with Satan is not a power struggle but a truth encounter. Satan comes to us as the father of lies. We are assaulted by one lie after another. Doubts and half-truths constantly attack our minds. But we need not despair. Why? Because John wrote that we are from God and have overcome all these falsehoods and lies of Satan. How is that so? Because Christ in you is greater than Satan and his spirits of deception that are in the world. Today, when lies, doubts, and half-truths come your way, resist them. Tell them to flee from your mind and focus on the greater thing—the truth of Christ and His love for you.

TODAY'S PRAYER Thank You, Lord, for Your strength and power. Thank You for protecting me. But also, Lord, thank You for Your truth and the fact that You are greater than Satan and his lies. Lord, fill me with Your truth. Amen.

October 21
God's Thinking of You

TODAY'S VERSE "How precious are your thoughts about me, O God. They cannot be numbered! I can't even count them; they outnumber the grains of sand! And when I wake up, you are still with me" (Psalm 139:17-18).

TODAY'S THOUGHT What a mood David was in! You can hear the enthusiasm in his words. He is full of appreciation and amazement. Could he get any more excited about God? He got it! He understood that the Almighty God of the universe was aware of him. More than aware, God was constantly thinking about him. More than just thinking, David said that God's thoughts about him were precious! Have you come to that same awareness? Have you stopped to consider how much God thinks about you? Today, meditate on the fact that God is keenly aware of you. You are precious to Him. In fact, if you tried to add up all the thoughts God has about you, you would never be able to do it! And here is the amazing part—every day you wake up, God is still with you and is still having precious thoughts about you. Today, live joyfully in this awareness.

TODAY'S PRAYER Father, I thank You for all Your precious thoughts about me. I thank You for caring and being there for me. Thank You for Your love. In Jesus' name. Amen.

Purpose

TODAY'S VERSE "I cry out to God Most High, to God who will fulfill his purpose for me" (Psalm 57:2).

TODAY'S THOUGHT I can understand God's purpose for Michael the Archangel. I understand when God chooses a Moses, Abraham, or David to do His will. I can comprehend Jesus picking twelve disciples to follow Him and God choosing Paul to be a great missionary. What completely mystifies me, however, is that God has a purpose for me! Not only does God have a purpose for me, His purpose is to fulfill that purpose. Now you try. Read today's verse and put yourself in the picture. God will fulfill His purpose for you! Do you get a sense of what that means? Perhaps you're thinking, "I'm nobody special." Sorry, but God thinks you are! Maybe you don't think you have exceptional skills, but you have exactly what God wants you to have. You may say, "I have done too many wrong things." God's grace is greater than all your wrongdoing. Do you think you can't do anything out of the ordinary? All God asks you to do is show up and be willing to live for Him—He will do the rest. Stop and hear God saying to you, "I am so glad I created you! I am so excited about you living out your purpose." Today, surrender yourself to Him. Purpose in your heart to live out the purpose He has for you.

TODAY'S PRAYER Father, I surrender my life to You. Use me; live through me. Guide me and help me fulfill Your purpose for my life. Amen.

A Clear Conscience

TODAY'S VERSE "Cling to your faith in Christ, and keep your conscience clear. For some people have deliberately violated their consciences; as a result, their faith has been shipwrecked" (1 Timothy 1:19).

TODAY'S THOUGHT If we want to live a joyful Christian life, we need to keep our conscience clear. We have a large propensity toward rationalizing away our attitudes and behavior. We'll do anything to keep from feeling guilty about something we've done. We bury negative emotions, and before you know it, our conscience has been seared. But the truth is, we end up paying a toll for our lack of repentance. Like the person in today's verse, our faith becomes shipwrecked. This isn't what God intended. He wants us to enjoy His grace. Christ is the perfect sacrifice for our sins, and His blood shed on Calvary has made it possible to have our conscience clear for all of eternity. All He asks is that we repent, confess our sins to Him and accept His forgiveness and unconditional love. What is it that has alienated you from God? Today, bring it to God. Confess it and ask His forgiveness. For your own sake, keep your conscience clear.

TODAY'S PRAYER Father, help me keep my conscience clear with You. Convict me of sin, and by Your grace, lead me to repentance. Thank You, that when I confess my sins, You are faithful and willing to forgive me for every transgression. Amen.

Renewed

TODAY'S VERSE "Put on your new nature, and be renewed as you learn to know your Creator and become like him" (Colossians 3:10).

TODAY'S THOUGHT Paul starts this verse by writing, "But now is the time to get rid of anger, rage, malicious behavior, slander, and dirty language. Don't lie to each other, for you have stripped off your old sinful nature and all its wicked deeds." What a list! And how many times have we tried to do this? The only way we can successfully get rid of these negative characteristics is by getting rid of our old sinful nature. However, the best way to *put off* our old nature is to focus on *putting on* the new! But how? By getting to know our creator God and becoming more like Jesus. God put in us the capacity to know Him. His Holy Spirit guides us, and as we attune ourselves with Him, the renewing of our minds takes place. Today, spend time with God. Get to know Him. Experience His presence and His immense love for you. Let Him speak to your heart. As you do, you will experience yourself becoming renewed.

TODAY'S PRAYER Father, I want to know You more. I want to experience Your presence more. I want to be renewed more and more so I can be like You. Amen.

Grace, Love, and Fellowship

TODAY'S VERSE "May the grace of the Lord Jesus Christ, the love of God, and the fellowship of the Holy Spirit be with you all" (2 Corinthians 13:13).

TODAY'S THOUGHT What a wonderful God we have! He could have set creation in motion and ignored the human race. He could have given up on mankind with all the rebellion and rejection we have given Him. Instead, God has made us the object of His affection; the crown jewels of His creation. And as a triune God, He has purposely given us everything we need to have a relationship with Him. As God the Son, He has given us grace through the life, death, and resurrection of Jesus Christ. As God the Father, He is love, so He shares His own nature with us. As God the Spirit, He fellowships with us in a way that is compatible with the way we think and feel. Grace, love, and fellowship. Today, spend time with God and get to know Him and what He has for you.

TODAY'S PRAYER Dear Lord, I thank You that You have manifested Yourself in ways that I can understand. Thank You for Your love, grace, and fellowship through Father, Son, and Spirit. Amen.

Comfort

TODAY'S VERSE "Praise be to the God and Father of our Lord Jesus Christ, the Father of compassion and the God of all comfort, who comforts us in all our troubles, so that we can comfort those in any trouble with the comfort we ourselves have received from God" (2 Corinthians 1:3-4).

TODAY'S THOUGHT We all live with stress. There's pressure from all sides—relationships, finances, health. How do we get any relief? Where can we go to get help? Paul knew. He wrote, "Praise be to the God and Father of our Lord Jesus Christ, the Father of compassion and the God of all comfort, who comforts us in all our troubles." Paul knew about God's compassion. He also knew God's comfort. Often it is hard to find comfort in difficult situations. Will God answer our prayer? Will we find the answer we seek? Will He act supernaturally on our behalf? We don't know all the variables, have a limited grasp of the situation and we can't always explain the way things turn out. But we can count on one thing—God will comfort us! He will, in His great compassion, visit us and bring supernatural comfort to our hearts. More than that, God will orchestrate other believers to comfort us, as well. That's His plan. When we're comforted by His grace and mercy, God wants us to go and comfort others that He brings our way. We are to comfort others in the same way we were helped. I fear that sometimes that we have forgotten this. Somehow, the church has traded our role as a hospital, shelter, and place of sanctuary for a country club. We have all sorts of programs for ourselves, but we fail to bring comfort to the world. We've lost the witness of God's comfort. God has commanded us to take His love to the streets. That's what Jesus did. Today, bring your own burdens to the Lord. Let Him comfort you. And when He does, go with the same compassion He had and comfort someone else.

TODAY'S PRAYER Father, I pray that You, in all Your compassion, will comfort me in my struggles. And as You do, I ask that You bring people into my life that I can comfort in return. In Jesus' name. Amen.

Forgiveness

TODAY'S VERSE "Finally, I confessed all my sins to you and stopped trying to hide my guilt. I said to myself, 'I will confess my rebellion to the Lord.' And you forgave me! All my guilt is gone" (Psalm 32:5).

TODAY'S THOUGHT Hope is found when we decide to stop doing something that is wrong. Peace is ours when we set out to make right those wrongs that we have committed. We experience joy when we unburden ourselves from the things that have held us prisoner in the dungeon of guilt. David paints a picture of the inner turmoil and anguish we bring upon ourselves when we store the toxic emotions of a guilty conscience. He writes, "When I refused to confess my sin, my body wasted away, and I groaned all day long." But later, David writes, "Oh, what joy for those whose disobedience is forgiven, whose sin is put out of sight! Yes, what joy for those whose record the Lord has cleared of guilt, whose lives are lived in complete honesty!" Where there is pain, there can be joy. Where there is guilt, there can be forgiveness. Today, come to God with anything that is bothering your conscience. Don't go another day without experiencing the joy that comes from a heart forgiven.

TODAY'S PRAYER Father, thank You for the substitutional death of Christ for my sins. I know I can bring any of my wrongdoings to You for Your complete forgiveness. Lord, hear my prayers of repentance and restore joy deep into my soul. Amen.

Joy and Quiet

TODAY'S VERSE "I have stilled and quieted myself, just as a small child is quiet with its mother. Yes, like a small child is my soul within me" (Psalm 131:2).

TODAY'S THOUGHT Have you ever seen the behavior of a mother and her infant? They go through a rhythm of joy and quiet. The mother is happy to be with the baby and the baby is joyful in return. Laughter and a lot of love are exchanged. Next, the baby quiets itself and just wants to rest. This is especially true after nursing. The joy bond between the mother and child is followed by quiet. A deep, serene trust is built. This is the way God prepares us for life. He knows that in this world, we need joy and quiet. David knew this too. David purposely stilled himself; he entered into to a place of quietness where he could enjoy and be nourished by the fellowship of God. He knew that peace, hope, courage, and strength all came from the love bond he had with his Heavenly Father. This love bond was the result of times of joy and quiet he spent with God. We need to do the same. God offers us peace that passes all understanding. He gives rest to those that He loves. He asks us to be still, so we can know that He is God. Today, put aside some time and quiet yourself before God. Be at peace, resting in His love for you.

TODAY'S PRAYER Father, I come to You today and desire a sacred time of quietness before You. I need Your peace. I need to be assured of Your love. I desire to experience Your quiet presence. As I come before You, like a child resting in their mother's love, I ask You to please quiet my heart and fill me with your joy, love, and peace. In Jesus' name. Amen.

October 29
Really Knowing God

TODAY'S VERSE "I know the greatness of the Lord" (Psalm 135:5).

TODAY'S THOUGHT Have you ever tried to describe the Grand Canyon to someone who hasn't been there? Pictures help. Your descriptions can get them excited. However, nothing can compare to actually being there. Until they stand on the rim and look across the vast expanse for themselves, they will not know its majesty. It is the same way with today's verse. David writes, "I know the greatness of the Lord." This was first-hand, *observational* knowledge—he knew the greatness of the Lord because He had seen the Lord in action. This was *experiential* knowledge—he knew the greatness of the Lord because he spent quiet time with Him. This was *relational* knowledge—he knew the greatness of the Lord! Because of this, David stepped out in faith trusting God for all his needs. Today, don't just settle for head knowledge about God. Stop and know the greatness of the Lord!

TODAY'S PRAYER Father, help me to know You. Help me know Your greatness. Might Your Holy Spirit lead me to a deeper knowledge of You. Amen.

Comfort and Strength

TODAY'S VERSE "Now may our Lord Jesus Christ himself and God our Father, who loved us and by his grace gave us eternal comfort and a wonderful hope, comfort you and strengthen you in every good thing you do and say" (Thessalonians 2:16-17).

TODAY'S THOUGHT God knows exactly what we need to make it in this life. He offers to us two indispensable tools for getting us through any of life's situation. He gives us comfort and strength. Comfort calms us. Comfort gives us hope and encourages our faith. Comfort gives us the ability to trust God for the strength to press on. Strength helps us overcome obstacles and is needed for everyday life. Today, may God comfort your heart and mind and give you all the strength you need.

TODAY'S PRAYER Father, I pray that You will give me all the comfort and strength I need for this day. In Jesus' name. Amen.

Direction

TODAY'S VERSE "Show me the right path, O Lord; point out the road for me to follow. Lead me by your truth and teach me, for you are the God who saves me. All day long I put my hope in you" (Psalm 25:4-5).

TODAY'S THOUGHT There are so many paths to choose from. Wouldn't it be nice if we had just one turn to make and never had to ask for directions again? But that isn't going to happen. Life has many variables, and we were given free will and are destined to make choices. The good news is, we're not alone! We don't have to make decisions on our own. As a mighty warrior, and later as king of the nation, David had to make many decisions. Although he had the right to choose what he wanted to do, David knew that having God's guidance was the only way to make good decisions. He prayed that God would show him the right path. He asked God to be specific and point out the way that he should go. He trusted God to guide Him by teaching him His truth. As David meditated on God's word and character, he put more and more trust in God. This trust resulted in hope and direction. Today, you have many different directions you could take. Stop and commit your journey to Him. Ask God to guide you and direct you in all that you do and say.

TODAY'S PRAYER Father, I commit this day to You. You know all the decisions ahead of me. Grant me wisdom and show me the paths I should take. I put my hope and trust in You. Amen.

Forgiveness

TODAY'S VERSE "Lord, if you kept a record of our sins, who, O Lord, could ever survive? But you offer forgiveness" (Psalm 130:3-4).

TODAY'S THOUGHT It's easy to keep a record of sins. How many times have we found ourselves caught up in bitterness over someone's repeated offenses against us? How many times should we continue to forgive? Jesus addressed that very question when Peter asked Him how many times we should forgive someone. In a magnanimous gesture, Peter suggests seven times, but Jesus replied, "Seven times seventy," meaning we should forgive continuously. The truth is, God's love is greater than we can imagine. David was trying to make that point in this passage. He was amazed at the fact that God was totally justified in keeping a record of all our wrongs but chooses not to. Instead, what does God do? He offers forgiveness. Forgiveness is a powerful healer. Is there something weighing heavy on your heart? Is there a secret sin or something from the past you need to repent of? Today, bring it to God. He does not keep a ledger of your wrongdoings but instead offers complete forgiveness.

TODAY'S PRAYER Father, thank You for not keeping a record of my wrongs. Instead, I bring my sins to You and ask You to forgive me and set me free. In Jesus' name. Amen.

Help the Poor

TODAY'S VERSE "There should be no poor among you—do not be hard-hearted or tightfisted toward them. Instead, be generous and lend them whatever they need. Give generously to the poor, not grudgingly, for the Lord your God will bless you in everything you do" (Deuteronomy 15:4, 7, 8, 11).

TODAY'S THOUGHT The Lord cares about those that are poor. It's true that Jesus said we will always have the poor with us, but He never said to leave them that way. God knew there would be circumstances that would make some poor and destitute, so He created a system that would provide support during life's struggles and troubles. He told those that have plenty not to be hard-hearted toward those that are poor, but rather to loan them money so they can provide for their family. How often have we been hard-hearted toward those that are homeless or destitute? Have we been quick to judge and say that it's their fault that they are poor and not deserving of our assistance? Do we turn our backs and hang on to our wallets? This is not God's desire. Instead, God told His people, "Give generously to the poor, not grudgingly, for the Lord your God will bless you in everything you do." We are to be salt and light to a lost and dying world. This includes helping those around us who are poor to find their way out of poverty. Today, ask God to help you be more generous to those in need.

TODAY'S PRAYER Father, help me to see those that are poor around me through Your eyes of compassion. I pray that You will guide and direct me to be more generous to those in need. Amen.

Strength

TODAY'S VERSE "The Lord gives his people strength" (Psalm 28:8).

TODAY'S THOUGHT Strength is a mighty gift from God. With strength, you have many options—strength to make it through a tough time; strength to accomplish a difficult task; strength to overcome overwhelming circumstances; strength when all else has failed; strength to be patient and wait on the Lord; strength to tear down strongholds; strength to get through another day; strength to outlast a temptation; strength to give it another try; strength to accept grace; strength to face your deepest fears; strength to start over; strength to admit when your wrong; strength to accept your weakness; strength to trust in God. Today, God has all the strength you need. It's yours for the asking.

TODAY'S PRAYER Father, how I thank You that You give Your people strength. You know my needs. You know where I am weak and where I need Your strength. Give me all the strength I need for today. In Jesus' name. Amen.

Complete Joy

TODAY'S VERSE "I have told you this so that my joy may be in you and that your joy may be complete" (John 15:11).

TODAY'S THOUGHT God created us for joy! And where does joy come from? Jesus said, "I have told you this so that my joy may be in you." What was it that He told us? The answer lies in the preceding verse. It says, "As the Father has loved me, so have I loved you. Now remain in my love." Jesus said that His joy would be in us and that our joy would be complete as a direct result of the love He and our Heavenly Father have for us. Our joy comes from knowing this love in a personal way. It comes from the fact that God is very, very glad to be with us. As the Psalmist suggests, we can come into God's presence with thanksgiving, and into His courts with praise! Why? Because He loves us unconditionally and has bonded with us in a way that gives us true, deep down joy. Today, don't accept mediocre joy. Instead, meditate on the love that God has for you and let it deeply move your soul. Today, ask God to fill you with joy.

TODAY'S PRAYER Father, thank You for creating me for joy. Help me to know the extent of Your love and how happy You are to call me Your own so that my joy will be full. Amen.

Change Your Spots

TODAY'S VERSE "Therefore, we do not lose heart. Though outwardly we are wasting away, yet inwardly we are being renewed day by day" (2 Corinthians 4:16).

TODAY'S THOUGHT You've heard the saying, "A leopard cannot change its spots." Well, today's verse begs to differ. God is the God of change. When we become His child, He begins a process of making us more and more into His likeness. How? Paul writes about this process of transformation. He says that we're transformed by the renewing of our mind. By his own testimony, Paul shares that he was inwardly changed and renewed, day by day. The good news? Our God, the Great Creator, is also the Re-creator. Today, we can present our whole self to God and ask Him to renew our mind and personality, day by day.

TODAY'S PRAYER Father, I am so thankful that You do not give up on me. Instead, You believe in me and have a wonderful plan for my life. I come and commit myself to You and ask that You will renew me, day by day, and make me more like You. Amen.

November 6
Follow God

TODAY'S VERSE "Oh, that you would choose life so that you and your descendants might live! You can make this choice by loving the Lord your God, obeying him, and committing yourself firmly to him. This is the key to your life" (Deuteronomy 30:19-20).

TODAY'S THOUGHT Choices can make all the difference in the world! We are constantly taking in data, predicting and making decisions. There are so many choices to make each day we can't keep count. Some choices are, of course, more important than others. Vanilla or chocolate ice cream may not affect your world one little bit. But decisions about moral or legal issues can alter your entire life. The friends you choose and the things you choose to do can steer the direction of your life. Who you marry, decisions about college and career choices are life-altering milestones. But the one choice that guides all others is your choice to follow God or not. Moses calls it *choosing life*. And like many major choices, they are only as good as the thousands of little choices you make to support your decision. You can decide to cross an ocean in a sailboat, but it's the daily choices you make in correcting the course that gets you to the other shore. In a marriage ceremony, we ask the groom, "Will you love her, comfort her, honor and keep her, in sickness and in health, and forsaking every other, keep to her only, for as long as you both shall live?" He can say, "I do" but that momentary decision is only as good as him getting up every day and saying, "I will!" Moses said that you can choose life by making a choice to love God, obeying Him and committing yourself firmly to Him. Today, choose to follow God in all you do because choosing to follow God is the key to your life.

TODAY'S PRAYER Father, today I choose You. I choose to live for You. I choose to follow You in all that I do. Guide me, direct me. Give me the strength to do this, in Jesus' name. Amen.

Kindness

TODAY'S VERSE "But the fruit of the Spirit is – kindness" (Galatians 5:22).

TODAY'S THOUGHT Kindness is not an option. It's not something we can decide to do only when it's convenient. Kindness is evidence of the Holy Spirit alive in our life. Jesus instructed us to behave toward others in the same way we want them to behave toward us. When have we ever turned away kindness? Paul admonishes us to esteem others better than our self. Kindness is love in action. I have seen family members *say* they love each other, but don't *act* kindly toward each other. I have seen churches where kindness to each other is a rarity. You can be kind to someone without loving them, but you can't love someone and continually refuse to be kind to them. Today, purpose in your heart to be kind to those around you.

TODAY'S PRAYER Father, kindness can make such a difference in someone's life. Help me today to be Your ambassador of kindness to all those I come in contact with. Amen.

Forgiveness

TODAY'S VERSE "Forgive us our sins, as we forgive those who sin against us" (Matthew 6:12).

TODAY'S THOUGHT Forgiveness is crucial to our mental health. More than that, it's imperative for a right relationship with God. God puts a premium on grace and forgiveness. Forgiveness is love in action. It's an act of grace that is inspired by Jesus Himself. In fact, Christ taught us to pray when He said, "Forgive us our sins, as we have forgiven those who sin against us." There are two key elements in this verse. First, we see that God wants us to confess our own sins and ask for His forgiveness. He didn't say, "Put on a mask and pretend you did no wrong." Jesus didn't say to rationalize away our attitudes of pride, anger, and bitterness. Instead, He admonishes each of us to focus on our own sinful situation and remember how He forgave us. When we do, God will bless our heart and give us the capacity to participate in the second part—that is, to forgive others. God wants us to be ambassadors of His grace. Today, as we have been forgiven, let us go and forgive others.

TODAY'S PRAYER Father, thank You for Your grace and forgiveness. Thank you for not giving up on me. I pray that I might express the same kind of forgiveness to others. Amen.

Patience

TODAY'S VERSE "Being strengthened with all power according to his glorious might so that you may have great endurance and patience" (Colossians 1:11).

TODAY'S THOUGHT In his letter to the Colossians, Paul admonishes the Christians to "live a life worthy of the Lord and please him in every way." He then tells them how to live a worthy life. He says to exercise "great endurance and patience." Endurance and patience please God. This is a lot easier when there is hope. When things seem to be going our way, it's easy to endure. It's in demanding situations, where all seems lost, where hope is nowhere to be found, that we must trust God and be strengthened in a way that only His power can accomplish. We come to Him, with all His glorious might, and choose to deliberately be patient and endure. It is an act of faith, one that is pleasing to Him. Today, trust God and His power. Put your situation into His hands and choose to be patient and endure.

TODAY'S PRAYER Dear Father, help me trust in Your power and might and exhibit patience and endurance today in all I do. Amen.

Inner Strength

TODAY'S VERSE "I pray that from his glorious, unlimited resources He will empower you with inner strength through his Spirit. And may you have the power to understand, as all God's people should, how wide, how long, how high, and how deep his love is. Then you will be made complete with all the fullness of life and power that comes from God" (Ephesians 3:16, 18-19).

TODAY'S THOUGHT How many times a day could you use strength? Pulled in every direction, we live with a lot of stress. Life can be difficult, and so many times we feel too weak to do anything about it. Paul knew what weakness was. He knew what struggles and trial were like. And so out of this great empathy, he prayed for the church in Ephesus to have the same thing that got him through each day. He prayed that God would empower each one with inner strength. Not just any inner strength. Not false hope built on a trendy slogan or routine steps to follow. Paul was encouraging you and me to build our inner strength on knowing "how wide, how long, how high, and how deep God's love is." It's experiencing this great love that makes us complete. It's knowing God's love in a deep and personal way that gives us all the fullness of life and power that He has available for us. Today, come to God. Ask Him to reveal to you how truly great His love for you really is. As He does, you will experience all the inner strength you need.

TODAY'S PRAYER Father, give me the inner strength that comes from understanding Your great love. Help me draw upon all the power that You have available for me this day. I pray this in Jesus' name. Amen.

Working with God

TODAY'S VERSE "Unless the Lord builds a house, the work of the builders is wasted. Unless the Lord protects a city, guarding it with sentries will do no good" (Psalm 127:1).

TODAY'S THOUGHT God created us to work in harmony with Him. We're at our best when we allow God to guide us and be Lord of whatever we do. Paul wrote, "For we are God's workmanship, created in Christ Jesus to do good works, which God prepared in advance for us to do." The Psalmist suggests that making plans and working toward goals without God is foolishness. It is wasted! Instead, seeking God's guidance, blessing and partnership on everything we do is the wise and prudent thing to do. How much of our lives will never reach their full potential because we do not let God work with us? Today, seek God's guidance, wisdom, and partnership in all you do.

TODAY'S PRAYER Father, lead me, guide me and direct me in all I do today. Help me join You in Your work so what I do today will not be in vain, but for Your glory. Amen.

Trust and Obey

TODAY'S VERSE "Be on guard. Stand firm in the faith. Be courageous. Be strong. And do everything with love" (1 Corinthians 16:13-14).

TODAY'S THOUGHT What a to-do list! Do you need something to do today? Try today's verse. Such an important list for our spiritual vitality! I am encouraged that God will not ask us to do something that He will not help us with. This is within our grasp. All we need to do is focus, ask God for His help, and be as diligent as possible. He will guide us. He will give us the strength and power to do what He has asked of us. Today, be on guard against spiritual apathy, attacks, and adversaries. While you are on guard, stand firm on His word and your faith in what He has said and who He is. When trouble comes, remember who God is and what He has asked us to do and be courageous in your attempt to be strong. Finally, if all else fails, allow Him to work through you and do everything today with love! God is good, and He will help you do what He has asked you to do. Simply trust and obey.

TODAY'S PRAYER Father, thank You that You will provide all the help and strength I need. Help me to be on my guard and stand firm in my faith. I need Your help to be courageous and strong. Lord, please help me do everything I do today with love. I ask this in the name of Jesus. Amen.

Know Him

TODAY'S VERSE "May God give you more and more grace and peace as you grow in your knowledge of God and Jesus our Lord" (2 Peter 1:2).

TODAY'S THOUGHT Are you growing in your knowledge of Jesus Christ? Have you been spending time reading the Bible to know what He wants you to do? Have you examined His life so you can follow His example? Do you know how He feels about you? Do you see life, with all its people and situations, with the eyes of Christ? God's design was that you have more than a superficial knowledge of Christ. It is His desire that you grow in what you know and experience of Christ; that you will understand more and more about the unending grace that He has for you. As you do, you will have more peace in your life. Today, spend time and get to know Christ better. Learn about Him as you learn from Him.

TODAY'S PRAYER Dear Jesus, help me to know You better. Help me to learn more about Your desires and passions. Help me to know Your love, grace, and peace. Teach me, guide me and instruct me, I pray. Help me grow more and more in You. Amen.

Talk with God

TODAY'S VERSE "My heart has heard you say, 'Come and talk with me.' And my heart responds, 'Lord, I am coming" (Psalm 27:8).

TODAY'S THOUGHT What a glorious invitation! There are two elements to an invitation that can make it special: who is inviting you and what you are invited to do. In both cases, this invitation is extraordinary! First, it is God who is doing the inviting. David said that his heart heard God's invitation. Have you? Have you sensed the call of the Holy Spirit to come and fellowship with God? He bids you come to Him. God desires your fellowship, but you must come. Second, we see that God has invited you to talk with Him! So many times, we talk *to* God, not *with* Him. What kind of friendship would you have with someone if you did all the talking? That's not fellowship; it's not a relationship. God Almighty has asked you to talk with Him. You can share your innermost thoughts and then wait and listen to what He has to say. God wants to commune with your heart if you will let Him. Today, God has invited you to come talk with Him. Stop now and start a conversation. Talk with Him, listen and begin a lifelong dialog.

TODAY'S PRAYER Father, thank You for Your invitation to come and talk with You. Today I come to share my own thoughts and situations and to listen. Talk to me, God. I want to hear from You. In Jesus' name, I pray. Amen.

November 15
Hungry?

TODAY'S VERSE "Then Jesus declared, 'I am the bread of life. He who comes to me will never go hungry" (John 6:35).

TODAY'S THOUGHT Have you ever been hungry? Have you ever had a craving for a certain kind of food? Hunger is a forceful human drive. Jesus said that He is "the bread of life" and if we believe in Him, we won't be hungry again. But He wasn't talking about alleviating our physical hunger. Instead, Jesus is talking about another kind of hunger—a hunger that is just as real. It's spiritual hunger—hunger of the soul. Just like a physical hunger, you can have many soulful cravings. These cravings come from the needs of our heart. You may have a taste for love. Many people have a hunger for inner peace, joy, and happiness. But there is also a hunger that is born out of unfulfilled needs like a hunger for recognition, fame or glory. There are also unspiritual appetites like lust, greed, and materialism. The good news is that Jesus knows what will satisfy our deepest needs. Today, hear the words of Jesus, "I am the bread of life. He who comes to me will never go hungry." Come to Jesus. Feed on His teachings and the personal relationship that He offers to you. He is the only one that can truly satisfy your hunger.

TODAY'S PRAYER Father, thank You for giving me a spiritual appetite. I really need You to feed my soul. I need Your bread of life to feed and nourish the deepest parts of me. I come to You now, dear Jesus. Feed me, I pray. Amen.

November 16
What Do You Really Need?

TODAY'S VERSE "And God is able to make all grace abound to you, so that in all things at all times, having all that you need, you will abound in every good work" (2 Corinthians 9:8)

TODAY'S THOUGHT Need. That is certainly a relative word. We've taken the word *need* and have turned it into everything from a wish list to a whim. Larry Crabb addresses this in his book, *The Pressure's Off*. He writes about what we really need. He writes, "Nothing wrong with desiring safe airplane flights and warm marriages and a decent income. But none of these things, none of our hopes for a 'better life of blessings,' represents God's priority agenda. We need only to be safe from any power that opposes God's agenda for our lives." And what is that agenda that we need? Dr. Crabb shares three needs that God wants for us—radical forgiveness, supernatural love, and spiritual might. The good news is that God can grant you these needs! Through His grace, God provides all of the forgiveness, love and might you will need in order to be involved in His good work. Today, lay aside those other needs that you think are so important, and ask God to meet your real needs for forgiveness, love and spiritual might.

TODAY'S PRAYER Father, I need You and Your spiritual provisions of forgiveness, love and spiritual might more than anything else in the world. Help meet my real needs today. In Jesus' name. Amen.

The Lord's Face

TODAY'S VERSE "The LORD bless you and keep you; the LORD make his face shine upon you and be gracious to you; the LORD turn his face toward you and give you peace" (Numbers 6:24-26).

TODAY'S THOUGHT At first, this just seems like a benediction that you hear after church on Sunday; a platitude to give you hope throughout the coming week. But when you stop to really read this passage, it's a tremendous reality that you need to really consider. Why? Because believing this passage can change your life! It starts out stating that God wants to bless and keep you. What a wonderful reality! You can come to God knowing that it's His full intent to bless you. But then the author adds a very personal twist, saying that God wants to make His face shine upon you. This means that God Almighty is fully aware of you and is turning His face deliberately toward you so you can make full contact with Him. What an invitation! Today, right now, God has turned His face toward you. His goal is to be gracious toward you and give you peace. He is looking. Will you look back? Stop now and experience the presence of the Lord.

TODAY'S PRAYER Father, thank You that You have taken such a personal interest in me. I want to know You better. Please be gracious toward me, help me experience Your face shining upon me, and give me peace. Amen.

Blessing or the Blesser?

TODAY'S VERSE "Jesus asked, 'Were not all ten cleansed? Where are the other nine? Was no one found to return and give praise to God except this foreigner?' Then he said to him, 'Rise and go; your faith has made you well'" (Luke 17:17-19).

TODAY'S THOUGHT It's so easy to seek the blessing more than the blesser. The story that precedes this verse tells of ten lepers with the same putrefying disease, all with the same hopeless situation. Unless. Unless the Jesus that they heard about could really do miracles. Unless this Jesus was as compassionate as everyone said that He was. They came to seek a blessing, and as Jesus came down the road, a blessing they received. All ten were healed! But only one gave thanks to the blesser. He was the one that was touched in his body and his soul. He was the one that stopped to worship and give thanks. Nine came to *get* a blessing; the tenth *met* the blesser. How different are we? Is it possible that we've gotten so used to our faith that we're running on auto-pilot? We get our daily dose of blessing and go down the road as if nothing significant has happened. But let something go wrong! Then what do we scramble for? We cry out again, like the leper, for a blessing. But, it's not a blessing that we need. It's the blesser. It's Jesus, who loves us, that we need to seek. We need to come to Him, let Him know our situation, commune with Him and let Him guide us. He is what our soul requires. Today, let us commit our situation to God and come to Him, seeking the Blesser, not the blessing. He *is* the blessing.

TODAY'S PRAYER Father, forgive me for being more worried about blessings than worship. Forgive me for taking You for granted. You are what my life needs. You are the blessing. Today, I choose to seek Your fellowship more than anything else. In Jesus' name. Amen.

His Will

TODAY'S VERSE "But seek first His kingdom and His righteousness, and all these things will be added to you" (Matthew 6:33).

TODAY'S THOUGHT It's easy for us to assume what God's will is instead of asking Him for it. The truth is that God's ways are not always our ways. Life has so many variables. If we're going to know His will, we must seek His face. Jesus said to seek His kingdom and righteousness before anything else. If we want to live out God's will in our life, then we must seek God. A quarterback has the same goal as his coach—they both want to win the game. But the coach is better versed in the game, with more experience and a comprehensive view of the whole game. If the quarterback is going to do his best, he needs to work in harmony with the coach. How much more should we align our behavior and attitudes with God Almighty? A hurtful situation, a wayward son, a sudden illness, a loss of a job—life has many twists and turns. When they come, stop and seek God. Let Him know your thoughts, your apprehensions, your fears, and frustrations. Come to Him, seek Him first and He will direct your path.

TODAY'S PRAYER Father, I confess that I do my own thing so many times. I don't take the time to know Your will. I just assume that what I am doing is the right thing. Forgive me. Help me to stop when I am tempted to run in a certain direction. Help me to seek You first. Amen.

Made for Joy

TODAY'S VERSE "Be glad in the LORD, you righteous ones, and give thanks to His holy name" (Psalm 97:12).

TODAY'S THOUGHT The Christian life was meant to be a life of joy. God created us for joy. That doesn't mean that there won't be pain or suffering. There will be. But like a child who cries when it hurts itself soon returns to joy in the loving and compassionate understanding of its mother, we find joy in the loving arms of our Father God. It is this relationship with our Creator, this love bond that He puts in our hearts through the presence of the Holy Spirit, that returns us again and again to joy. That is why David could say, "Be glad in the Lord." It is knowing that God is glad to be with us, that we are loved beyond measure, that allows us to come to His altar singing a song of thanksgiving. It is this relationship of complete forgiveness and unconditional love and acceptance by God that has us telling others of His wonders. So today, know that you have a God that loves you more than you will ever know. Bask in the warmth of this realization so that later, when your way gets difficult and you experience deep pain, you will be able to experience God's loving presence and return to the joy you were created for.

TODAY'S PRAYER Father, thank You for creating me for joy. Thank You for Your unconditional love that fills my heart and causes me, no matter what, to return to joy over and over again. Amen.

Holy Spirit

TODAY'S VERSE "So, I say, let the Holy Spirit guide your lives. Then you won't be doing what your sinful nature craves. The sinful nature wants to do evil, which is just the opposite of what the Spirit wants. And the Spirit gives us desires that are the opposite of what the sinful nature desires" (Galatians 5:16-17).

TODAY'S THOUGHT The fight between good and evil can really get old. This is especially true when we're talking about our own behavior. Which of us has not experienced the struggle between the Holy Spirit inside us and what Paul calls our *sinful nature*? Paul points out the difference in outcomes between both. He writes, "When you follow the desires of your sinful nature, the results are very clear: sexual immorality, impurity, lustful pleasures, idolatry, sorcery, hostility, quarreling, jealousy, outbursts of anger, selfish ambition, dissension, division, envy, drunkenness, wild parties, and other sins like these. But the Holy Spirit produces this kind of fruit in our lives: love, joy, peace, patience, kindness, goodness, faithfulness, gentleness, and self-control." The point is clear. Paul says that we need to let the Holy Spirit guide our lives if we want to see the spiritual results that our heart really desires. Today, yield to the guidance and direction of the Holy Spirit. Ask Him to assist you in everything you do. Focus on the fruit of the Holy Spirit and watch it grow.

TODAY'S PRAYER Father, thank You for the gift of the Holy Spirit that is alive in my heart. I confess my struggle with my sinful nature and ask that the fruit that comes from fellowship with the Holy Spirit will grow in my life. Amen.

Compassion

TODAY'S VERSE "He made heaven and earth, the sea, and everything in them. He keeps every promise forever. He gives justice to the oppressed and food to the hungry. The Lord frees the prisoners. The Lord opens the eyes of the blind. The Lord lifts up those who are weighed down. The Lord loves the godly. The Lord protects the foreigners among us. He cares for the orphans and widows, but he frustrates the plans of the wicked" (Psalm 146:6-9).

TODAY'S THOUGHT How the Church has distorted the purpose of God in this world! We've made it all about us. Our worship, the discipleship of our own, care of our people, buildings, and programs that take top priority. Obviously, we are to worship Him. Certainly, God inhabits the praise of His people. And we must disciple those who have come to faith in Christ. Christ Himself told us to go and make disciples of all nations. Finally, we must take care of the resources God has given us to use. But we have an incomplete picture of God's purpose if we never consider the compassion He has toward those that are needy. We are woefully short of God's purpose for the church if we do not love those that are outside our four walls. The question is, will we join God in His work? God has called you and me to follow Him. Let us follow Him by helping those around us that so desperately need our help.

TODAY'S PRAYER Father, help me see the needs of others the way You do. Help me to respond in a way that honors you. In Jesus' name. Amen.

More Than a High Priest

TODAY'S VERSE "This High Priest of ours understands our weaknesses, for he faced all of the same testings we do, yet he did not sin. So, let us come boldly to the throne of our gracious God. There we will receive his mercy, and we will find grace to help us when we need it most" (Hebrews 4:15,16).

TODAY'S THOUGHT The author of Hebrews is using the High Priest as a model for Christ. It was the High Priest who represented the Israelites to God, confessed their sins, and gave an offering for their offenses. To do this, he would first have to confess his own sins and make a sacrifice for his own failings. Only after his own cleansing could he represent the people. You see, there was the limit to what the High Priest could do. He couldn't help the people stop their sin. He could not meet the individual needs of the people. Today, God has created a better way. He came to be our High Priest. God, in the person of Jesus Christ, came once and for all time, sacrificing Himself so we could be forgiven. More than that, Christ is on the right hand of the Father, interceding for our every need. He knows our weaknesses and gives us complete access to His love, power, mercy, and grace. He is our *personal* Savior. When Christ became our High Priest, He made it personal. Today, come to God's very throne. Come to the One who loves you and has everything you need.

TODAY'S PRAYER Father, I thank You for the sacrifice of Your Son, my savior, Jesus Christ. I thank You that You know who I am; You know my weaknesses and still love me. I especially thank You for promising to take care of my every need with Your mercy and grace. In Jesus' name. Amen.

New Reality

TODAY'S VERSE "Christ made us right with God; he made us pure and holy, and he freed us from sin" (1 Corinthians 1:30).

TODAY'S THOUGHT It's easy to miss the reality of what Christ has done for us. We get so caught up in our everyday living. Our habits, thoughts, and emotions constantly remind us of our humanness. However, Paul shares another reality. There is a *new* you! It was created when you were born again; born again as in a *new creature*. So, what is this new creature? It's royalty; a new child of God. Not made with flesh and blood like you were in your mother's womb, but born again in the spiritual realm. God took you, with your own self-will and sinfulness, and made you right with Him. He created you this time, pure, holy, and most of all freed from the power of sin. It's hard to believe, but you don't have to strive to be right with God. You don't have to earn God's love. When Christ died on the cross, you received His free gift of salvation. He freed you from sin at that very moment. He made you over again, pure and holy. He canceled all records of your wrongdoing and made you right with Him. Today, live in this freedom. Look into the mirror of God's love and see what He sees.

TODAY'S PRAYER Father, thank You for Your love and forgiveness. Thank You for freeing me from sin. Thank You for Your salvation and making me pure and holy in Your sight. Amen.

Realization

TODAY'S VERSE "On that day you will realize that I am in my Father, and you are in me, and I am in you" (John 14:20).

TODAY'S THOUGHT A realization is different than assuming something. You can *know* how difficult something may be and later explain, "I never realized how much work it was really going to be!" Knowing can be academic or theoretical, whereas realization is *experiential* knowledge. True realization is an awakening. It is an aha moment. We can *know* all about Christ, but *realizing* His presence is something totally different. Jesus explained that because He rose again from the dead, we should realize that He is equal with God the Father. Jesus is also saying that because we believe He has a special relationship with God the Father, that we should likewise realize that He has a special relationship with us. As God the Father is *in* Jesus, Jesus is *in* us. This is the crux of the matter. When are we going to start living as if the Almighty God of the Universe is living *in* us? When are we going to realize all that is ours in Christ? It is not too late. Today, meditate on God's love for you and His desire to live in and through you. Ask Him to help you realize what that should mean to you and the way you live.

TODAY'S PRAYER Father, thank you for your presence in my life. Thank You for making me Your child. I pray that today I may come to a full realization of what it means to have You alive in me. Amen.

November 26
God's Provision

TODAY'S VERSE "And this same God who takes care of me will supply all your needs from his glorious riches, which have been given to us in Christ Jesus" (Philippians 4:19).

TODAY'S THOUGHT Self-reliance. Isn't that the modern-day dream? Actually, it's been the dream of man since the beginning of time. And faith seems to go right along with it. We have all kinds of faith when things are going well. But is it faith in God or self-reliance? The answer comes when money, health, or relational situations start to falter. When things fall apart, does our faith go downhill? Does fretting, worry, and fear start to occupy our minds? If so, listen to what Paul is saying. "And this same God who takes care of me will supply all your needs from his glorious riches, which have been given to us in Christ Jesus." We have a God who loves to provide all our needs! He wants to lavish us with His loving provision. So today, when we feel threatened, when we consider bad news, when something comes up that goes straight to the pit of our stomach, let us stop and consider what Paul wrote, "God will supply all your needs from His glorious riches."

TODAY'S PRAYER Father, forgive me when I become self-reliant, forgetting that it is You that provides everything I need. I need You Lord and I thank You that You will supply all of my needs today from Your glorious riches. Amen.

No Revenge

TODAY'S VERSE "Dear friends, never take revenge. Leave that to the righteous anger of God" (Romans 12:19).

TODAY'S THOUGHT Revenge. What a toxic emotion. What a deceptive motive. It's so easy to slip into this deadly trap. It starts with a wound; perhaps a deep hurt, humiliation, or betrayal. Life isn't fair, but this is just too much! Soon our wound festers, and anger becomes an obsession. But what makes revenge so deceptive is that we feel justified in slandering the person, shunning them, campaigning against something they are doing, or a million other ways of getting nasty. We want to get even, give them what they deserve or settle the score. But this is revenge. Sometimes, it's difficult to not go there. What then can we do? Paul shares the only thing we can do—let go. Give it to God. Let Him take over your case. The author of Hebrews was serious when he wrote, "Watch out that no poisonous root of bitterness grows up to trouble you, corrupting many." Today, follow that advice. Let God search your heart and pull out any bitter root that has taken ground in your emotions. Don't let a wound fester into something worse.

TODAY'S PRAYER Father, search my heart. Show me any toxic bitterness I may have. Show me any attitude or behavior of revenge. Forgive me and help me change my attitude. In Jesus' name. Amen.

Eyes Open

TODAY'S VERSE "My help comes from the Lord, who made heaven and earth! He will not let you stumble; the one who watches over you will not slumber. The Lord keeps you from all harm and watches over your life. The Lord keeps watch over you as you come and go, both now and forever" (Psalm 121:2, 3, 7, 8).

TODAY'S THOUGHT I once saw a little boy crying hysterically, afraid that he had been abandoned by his father in a large crowd of people. I remember thinking it seemed odd because his father was standing right next to him. Something had frightened the son, and in his despair, he closed his eyes. As he cried, with his eyes shut tight, he was not aware of his father's presence. It was not until the father picked the child up that he opened his eyes and returned to joy. How often are we like that little child? Something frightens us—it could be a confrontation, an anxious thought, or dread of things to come. When our mind is in that state, faith seems to go out the window. It's as if we've stepped out of the presence of God when what we really did was shut our eyes. The Psalmist decided to go into his day with his eyes wide open. He writes, "My help comes from the Lord, who made heaven and earth! He will not let you stumble!" He then affirms his faith by believing, "The Lord keeps watch over you as you come and go, both now and forever." Today, open your eyes. Wipe away your tears. Look up—the Lord is here! He will watch over you and keep you from harm. Put your trust in Him.

TODAY'S PRAYER Father, make me conscious of Your presence so I will put my faith in Your precious promise. You promise to watch over me and protect me. You promise to keep me from harm. Help me today to open my eyes to Your power and love. Amen.

Discernment

TODAY'S VERSE "O Lord, listen to my cry; give me the discerning mind you promised" (Psalm 119:169).

TODAY'S THOUGHT There are many things that we need in life, but perhaps one of the most important is discernment. Things are seldom the way they appear making it very important to know the mind of God when we're in various situations. Solomon told us in Proverbs that we need to seek wisdom. We need to go after it like we would a golden treasure. James writes that if we lack wisdom, all we need to do is ask God for it. What a gift! What love, that God would not leave us here clueless! The Psalmist asks God to "give me the discerning mind you promised." God promised. Are you asking? Today, stop and seek the wisdom of God. Ask Him for discernment in all that you do.

TODAY'S PRAYER Father, how I need Your wisdom. How I need Your understanding. I desire Your discernment to see me through this day. Thank You that You will give me the discerning mind you promised. Amen.

Bear Each Other's Burdens

TODAY'S VERSE "Bear one another's burdens, and thereby fulfill the law of Christ" (Galatians 6:2, *New American Standard Bible*).

TODAY'S THOUGHT If you asked me to describe Christianity using only one word, I would choose the word *love*. John tells us that God *is* love. It is His love that makes mercy and grace possible. It's no wonder, then, that if we're really going to fulfill what Christ wants us to do, we must bear each other's burdens. Bearing a burden means to take a burden as your own. We're called to help the wounded, love the hurting, and to do whatever it takes to help those that are overburdened. If we don't, who will? Who else is called to do this? It's this love of Christ, lived out by us in community together, that is the mark of true Christianity. And if community is going to work, then each of us must prefer the needs of others to our own. We must put the needs of others above ourselves. Jesus set the example. His whole life exemplified sacrificial love. So must ours. Today, ask God to help you sense when someone needs help. Ask Him to help you bear their burden.

TODAY'S PRAYER Father, I am so grateful that You have borne every one of my burdens. Give me a heart like Yours and the filling of Your Spirit so I might love others in the way You have loved me. Amen.

Be a Blessing

TODAY'S VERSE "Do not let any unwholesome talk come out of your mouths, but only what is helpful for building others up according to their needs, that it may benefit those who listen" (Ephesians 4:29).

TODAY'S THOUGHT What would you do if you were given two potions, one that could cure cancer the other that would make people deathly sick? It's obvious that you would give every cancer victim you could find the cure and little doubt that you would do away with the poison. Yet what do we do with our words? Each sentence carries the potential to cure or destroy. We can use our tongue to heal those that are hurting, bring joy to a broken heart, or hope to those that are suffering. We could also choose to use unwholesome words that tear down, wound, and destroy those that get in our way. James writes, "Sometimes it (the tongue) praises our Lord and Father, and sometimes it curses those who have been made in the image of God. And so, blessing and cursing come pouring out of the same mouth. Surely, my brothers and sisters, this is not right!" Today, be careful with what you say to others. Use the wonderful gift of language as a blessing to others, not a curse.

TODAY'S PRAYER Father, help me use my tongue as a blessing. Direct my mouth with Your power and help me use my words to share love and peace with others. Amen.

December 2
The Beauty of the Lord

TODAY'S VERSE "One thing I have asked from the LORD, that I shall seek: That I may dwell in the house of the LORD all the days of my life, to behold the beauty of the LORD And to meditate in His temple" (Psalm 27:4, *New American Standard Bible*).

TODAY'S THOUGHT It's so easy to get wrapped up in life and not catch all the beauty. Can you imagine being on a business trip to Hawaii and never stopping to gaze at the magnificent ocean or the incredible sunsets? Yet how different is that from going through day after day, week after week, and never meditating on God's goodness and unfailing kindness? David knew the treasure he had in his relationship with God and decided to appreciate it. He made it his priority. He said that the ability to be in God's presence and behold His beauty was the most important request he made of God. I love the imagery. "Beholding the beauty of the Lord." Have you ever beheld true beauty? It takes your breath away. It saturates your senses. It changes you. Oh, that we would behold God in the same way. Today, take time and behold the beauty of God.

TODAY'S PRAYER Father, forgive me for letting so much time go by and not appreciating Your presence. Forgive me for taking You for granted. You are God and Your love, kindness, grace, and forgiveness are beyond description. Today, help me behold Your true beauty. Amen.

December 3
His Love

TODAY'S VERSE "And we pray this in order that you may live a life worthy of the Lord and may please him in every way" (Colossians 1:10, *New International Version*).

TODAY'S THOUGHT There's a fine line between doing good to earn someone's affection and doing good because you already have it. Take God. He created us out of love. He redeemed us out of love. We don't need to earn His favor—it's through our acceptance of His finished work on the cross that we become His child. From then on, it's love and gratitude that should motivate us. But some of us have a hard time receiving that kind of unconditional love. What kind of marriage would it be if we had to constantly earn our spouse's love? Wouldn't it be a shame to have a spouse who loves you so much and yet, because you couldn't receive that love, you constantly feel as if you must earn it? It's the same way with God. Paul asks us to "live a life worthy of the Lord" and to "live in a way that pleases God." But nowhere does it intimate that we should live this way to *earn* His love. Instead, the Apostle John wrote that we should love God because He first loved us. Today, rejoice in the love that the Father has for you. Love God because His love for you is secure.

TODAY'S PRAYER Father, thank You for Your love. Thank You that I don't need to earn it. I don't have to live in fear and condemnation but can simply enjoy Your favor. Help me to truly receive Your kindness and Your abiding love. Amen.

Abide in His Love

TODAY'S VERSE "As the Father has loved me, I also have loved you: abide in my love" (John 15:9, *Darby*).

TODAY'S THOUGHT   Where do you abide? According to Merriam-Webster, *abide* means "to continue in a place, to sojourn." In this situation, Jesus is referring to continuing in a certain state of mind. This gives us a lot of choices. It's not uncommon to find ourselves having painful emotions like fear, anger, disgust, bitterness, or doubt. But do we have to stay there? Are we choosing to abide in that emotional state? Instead, as Jesus abided in the love of the Heavenly Father, He invites us to do the same with His love. He offers His own life as an example. What a picture! You can feel the love bond that God the Father has with His Son. And as you read about Jesus, you can sense that Jesus has the same kind of love for us. Is there a better place to abide? Is there a better place to call home than the loving arms of Jesus? Today, find your rest in Him. Find the peace that passes all understanding. Abide in Jesus and the incredible love He has for you.

TODAY'S PRAYER Father, thank You for Your love. Thank You that I can abide in Your love, experiencing all the peace, joy, and faith that comes with it. Help me abide there today. Amen.

Choices

TODAY'S VERSE "Choose for yourselves this day whom you will serve" (Joshua 24:15, *New International Version*).

TODAY'S THOUGHT Choices can make all the difference in the world. Of course, not all choices are equal. It probably won't matter much if you had meatloaf or fish for dinner. However, what you choose to commit your life to does. Jesus constantly challenged us about our commitments. He said that we can measure our commitments by looking at what we consider to be important. "Where our treasures are, there will our heart be also." So, what choices will we make today? Will you choose things that matter? Will serving God permeate the choices you make? Given other options, will you choose God's peace, joy, and love? Make choices based on the things that God values. Today, choose whom you will serve.

TODAY'S PRAYER Father, You know that I don't always make good choices. But today, I choose You. I choose to follow You. I pray that You will help me make the right choices. Amen.

His Power

TODAY'S VERSE "Finally, be strong in the Lord and in His mighty power" (Ephesians 6:10, *New International Version*).

TODAY'S THOUGHT   There is no doubt that in this life we need to be strong! How many times are we gripped with uncertainty, fear, and doubt? How often are we attacked by rouge thoughts that try to take us captive and leave our souls barren? It seems that no matter how weak we get, we still have more room for weakness. But today's verse says, "Finally, be strong." And we try! But our strength just doesn't seem to be enough. That's why I rejoice in the rest of the passage. When we read on, we see that we're not alone in this spiritual battle. "Finally, be strong in the Lord and in His mighty power." What a difference a few words can make. We are to be strong, but not in our own power. We are to lean upon the generosity of our Lord Jesus Christ and His mighty power. Today, take a few moments and meditate on what *His power* really means. Consider what it can do; think about your life and how different it would be if God unleashed His power in it. This is what He offers. He says, "Come today and use my power. Don't try to do it on your own. Lean on me. I will give you my power to use. Come, be strong in me!"

TODAY'S PRAYER   Father, today teach me about Your power. Show me how strong You are. Open my eyes to the possibilities before me as I choose to trust You and Your mighty power. Amen.

God's Grace

TODAY'S VERSE "Answer this question: Does the God who lavishly provides you with his own presence, his Holy Spirit, working things in your lives you could never do for yourselves, does he do these things because of your strenuous moral striving or because you trust him to do them in you?" (Galatians 3:5, *The Thought*).

TODAY'S THOUGHT How is it we come humbly to Christ for the forgiveness of our sins and then later think that we must earn His favor? Paul reminds us that Christ has lavishly provided us with His own presence and works things out in our lives that we could never do by ourselves. And He does it because He wants to! We live within the grace of God. We live because He has given us everything we need for the godliness He requires. God has already changed us into His likeness. His Holy Spirit has given us His spiritual DNA. All we need to do is grow in Him. Today, accept the fact that when you received Christ as your Savior, He became alive in your heart, and there is nothing else to do to make that a reality. It already *is*! All you need to do now is to love and trust Him. Accept His deep love for you and completely trust the fact that you are His child and He is pleased with you.

TODAY'S PRAYER Father, thank You for the reality of Your love. Thank You that I can live with the full knowledge that there isn't anything I need to do or could do to get You to love me any more than You do right now. I pray this in Jesus' name. Amen.

Mercy

TODAY'S VERSE "He who conceals his sins does not prosper, but whoever confesses and renounces them finds mercy" (Proverbs 28:13, *New International Version*).

TODAY'S THOUGHT Confession is good for the soul. If done correctly, it's a tremendous spiritual discipline. As a counselor and pastor, I've heard many confessions in the form of remorse, sadness, guilt, and fear. As a person struggling with my own sinful nature, I've had the blessing of confessing my own sins that so easily beset me. There's something about cleansing our heart that gives life. The Apostle John shares, "If we confess our sins, he is faithful and just and will forgive us our sins and purify us from all unrighteousness." Jesus listens with never-ending love and forgives with matchless grace. And yet, even with His forgiveness only seconds away, many of us end up with a false suspicion that we are unlovable, condemned, and damaged goods. So, we work harder and put on our Christian *mask* in our efforts to *make the mark*. Where does that come from? From God? No. This false condemnation, this poor sense of God's love, comes from our own heart. Today, let go of that nagging doubt and self-condemnation. God loves you! Period. He completely forgives you! It is finished. You've found mercy! Don't give it back. Keep it. Treasure it. Believe it. Hear Jesus say, "Go. Your sins are forgiven. Be whole!"

TODAY'S PRAYER Father, You know my sins. I confess them to You. You know my struggles, my fears, the masks that I put on. Help me believe you so I can put down this heavy burden of shame and condemnation and live in the freedom of your mercy. In Jesus' name. Amen.

Today

TODAY'S VERSE "Therefore, do not worry about tomorrow, for tomorrow will worry about itself. Each day has enough trouble of its own" (Matthew 6:34).

TODAY'S THOUGHT Have you ever noticed how much time we spend on tomorrow? You know, all those worries, fears, and apprehensions. So, we plan, connive, and obsess about things that will probably never even happen. God, however, emphasizes that we should live for today. In the Lord's Prayer, Jesus told us to thank God for our *daily* bread. He also said not to worry about tomorrow, but to put our focus on today. It was that way with God's children in the wilderness. God gave them enough food for one day at a time. He told His people, "I will rain down bread from heaven for you. The people are to go out each day and gather enough for that day." God provided what they needed for that day, and then they would have to trust Him for the next. God wants us to focus on today and He will focus on tomorrow. He wants us to experience Him and all His love for us today. So, live as if this is the day that the Lord has made. He has, you know. He's made this day just for you, so rejoice and be glad in it!

TODAY'S PRAYER Father, thank You for this day. I pray that I may live it to its fullness. Help me to discern Your will for this day and to be obedient to do it. I pray this in Jesus' name. Amen.

Remember

TODAY'S VERSE "Think back on those early days when you first learned about Christ" (Hebrews 10:32).

TODAY'S THOUGHT It's easy to lose our confident trust in God. We get so wound up in our present situations that we forget God has been faithful over and over again. This is why the author of Hebrews warns us to remember what God has done in the past. He says, "Think back on those early days when you first learned about Christ." Remember how you were full of joy over your salvation? Think back to the early years when you took God at His Word and trusted Him for mighty things. What has changed? Has God? No! Perhaps you've become more cynical. Perhaps you've chalked off your early years as idealism, and today you're more realistic about God's involvement in your affairs. But beware! The author of Hebrews also wrote, "Do not throw away this confident trust in the Lord." God is as alive today as He was when you first met Him. It's our cynicism that has changed. Instead, have patience and endurance. Put your faith in the God who is faithful to you. Trust Him today and continue to do His will.

TODAY'S PRAYER Father, help me to remember all that You have done for me. Help me to remember Your faithfulness. Help me trust You more today. Amen.

Forgiveness

TODAY'S VERSE "But when you are praying, first forgive anyone you are holding a grudge against, so that your Father in heaven will forgive your sins, too" (Mark 11:25).

TODAY'S THOUGHT Forgiveness can be difficult. It's hard to forgive some of the offenses against us. But we must remember that forgiveness is a very important part of our spirituality. We go to church, we pray, and we read the scriptures. This is all good. But Jesus makes it clear—the true test of Christianity is to forgive others. That's because all of Christianity is built on forgiveness. Where would we be without the forgiveness of Christ? In *Steps to Freedom In Christ*, Neil Anderson shares the following six important elements of forgiveness.

1. Forgiveness is not forgetting; rather, forgetting is a long-term by-product of forgiveness.
2. Forgiveness is a choice, a decision of the will.
3. Forgiveness is agreeing to live with the consequences of another person's sin.
4. We forgive from our heart, not our head.
5. Forgiveness is choosing not to hold someone's sin against them anymore.
6. Finally, do not wait until you feel like forgiving. If you do, you will never get there. Instead, make a hard choice to forgive those that you are bitter toward.

Let go of all the unforgiveness that is eating you up inside. Today, let God help you forgive.

TODAY'S PRAYER Lord Jesus, You know the pain I harbor in my heart. Forgiveness seems so far from my grasp, yet I know that You have commanded me to forgive. Help me to forgive those who have offended me like You have so graciously forgiven me. In Jesus' name. Amen.

December 12
Trust in God's Love

TODAY'S VERSE "We know how much God loves us, and we have put our trust in his love" (1 John 4:16).

TODAY'S THOUGHT Trust is a beautiful word. According to Merriam-Webster, it means the assured reliance on the character, ability, strength, or truth of someone or something. Now put the word *trust* with the word *love* and you really have a concept. John did just that. He wrote, "We have put our trust in his love." When is the last time you put your assured reliance on the character, ability, strength, or truth of God's love? John could have suggested putting trust in God's strength or His power. How about His wisdom? The truth is, when we get God's love, we get everything else. We get all of God, wrapped in His amazing unconditional love. So today, when you are tempted to go to no ends to try to solve everything your own way, when you are slipping into anxious thinking or fearful apprehension, stop and trust in His love. Simply trust in all that He is, loving all that you are.

TODAY'S PRAYER Father, help me today to really put my trust in Your love. Amen.

Love One Another

TODAY'S VERSE "Dear friends, let us continue to love one another, for love comes from God. Anyone who loves is a child of God and knows God. But anyone who does not love does not know God, for God is love" (1 John 4:7-8).

TODAY'S THOUGHT How can we miss it? How could God make it any clearer? There's one central theme throughout the Bible and, yet, we don't seem to get it. When asked what the greatest commandment is, Jesus said that it consisted of one thing—love. It's not optional. It's not a suggestion. We are to love God with *everything* we have and to love our neighbor in the same way. John, the disciple who Jesus loved, says the same thing. He says that if we know God, we *will* love because God *is* love. God, Himself set the example by giving the extreme example of love. He gave the life of His Son as a sacrifice for our sins. How then can we argue with John's conclusion? Might this be the theme for today: "Since God loved us that much, we surely ought to love each other."

TODAY'S PRAYER Father, I need Your strength. I need Your power, I need Your heart, in order to love in the way You love. Help me to love all those that come my way today. Help me make love a priority in my life. In Jesus' name. Amen.

It's All About Grace

TODAY'S VERSE "God saved you by his grace when you believed. And you can't take credit for this; it is a gift from God. Salvation is not a reward for the good things we have done, so none of us can boast about it" (Ephesians 2:8-9).

TODAY'S THOUGHT What happens? When we first become a Christian, we revel in His forgiveness, knowing that only by His grace could we ever be forgiven from our past sins. And yet, as time goes by, we get sucked into believing we somehow earned His forgiveness. We live as if God's love was conditional and we're actually good enough to earn it. Then we begin to feel the pressure to keep ourselves in this earned salvation position. So, we begin to play a game of hiding our sins and pretending to be perfect instead of perfectly forgiven. The authors of the book *TrueFaced* write, "As we try to hide the sins we can't control, we are unwittingly inviting blame, shame, denial, fear, and anger to become our constant companions. A theology of 'more-right, less-wrong behavior' creates an environment that gives people permission to wear dozens of disguises and masks. It triggers and complicates the chain reaction of unresolved sin, causing us to lose hope." This thinking leads to us trying to please God by trying to be something we aren't. We play a role of *perfect, pleasing Christian* instead of being grateful and trusting God for our full forgiveness. It's our trust in His sacrifice and forgiveness that pleases God, not the sanctimonious pretense of being righteous. It's our trust that God is working with us in His process of changing us more and more into His likeness. Today, quit performing and trust the love that God has for you. Rejoice that your name is written in the Lamb's Book of Life.

TODAY'S PRAYER Father, if You were to judge me according to my sins, I would never be able to sit here, praying in Your presence. Instead, You've lavished Your unconditional love upon me. I am forgiven! I am a new creature. I am loved. Thank You for Your grace. Thank You for my new identity in You. In Jesus' name. Amen.

Renew Me

TODAY'S VERSE "They tell the seers, 'Stop seeing visions!' They tell the prophets, 'Don't tell us what is right. Tell us nice things. Tell us lies. Forget all this gloom. Get off your narrow path. Stop telling us about your Holy One of Israel'" (Isaiah 30:10-11).

TODAY'S THOUGHT Have you ever been at the place where the last thing you want to hear is a word from God? Nothing like a twinge of conscience to ruin a good time, right? Who needs a sermon that meddles in our affairs? That's what the children of Israel felt like. They wanted to abolish visions and prophetic words from God. Instead, they wanted the prophets to tell them *nice* lies. They didn't want gloom and doom. They didn't want to live the narrow way. Sadly, we can become this way, too. It starts slowly, like a frog in boiling water. If we knew the attitude we were cultivating was going to reach the boiling point, we'd never allow it to grow, but apathy never starts out that strong. It's subtle. It's an insidious process. We become too busy for spiritual discipline. We begin to fill our minds with television and internet and other distractions. Work and other affairs begin to distance us from church and fellowship with other Christians. Our conscience slowly loses its conviction. We find it easier and easier to ignore that still, small voice. Where are you? Do you feel far from God? Who moved? God is always there and His love for you is unconditional. Turn to Him today while there is time. Before your heart gets hardened, tell God how sorry you are. Repent. Come back to God and you will find Him there. He is ready to forgive you and restore you to a real and relevant fellowship with Himself.

TODAY'S PRAYER Father, You know how far I have wandered from You. Forgive me. I desire today to renew my fellowship with You. Restore my heart. I want to hear Your voice. I desire to do Your will. Hear me, dear Lord, guide and direct me I pray, in Jesus' name. Amen.

Covenant

TODAY'S VERSE "But this is the new covenant I will make with the people of Israel on that day, says the Lord: "I will put my laws in their minds, and I will write them on their hearts. I will be their God, and they will be my people. And I will forgive their wickedness, and I will never again remember their sins" (Hebrews 8:10, 12).

TODAY'S THOUGHT We get married and say, "For better or for worse." We buy a house and sign a loan agreement. We get bids on a job and award a contract. We accept a job for an agreed-upon salary. We live much of our life with promises, contracts, pledges, and covenants. How difficult is it when one of them is broken? Doesn't it wreak havoc with our life? That's why I find it fascinating that God has actually made a covenant with us. Who are we that God would make us a promise? And yet what a promise He has made! And God does not break His promises. In today's verses, God is saying that He is making a covenant with us. He promises to make us His people by working in our heart and mind. He promises to be our God. And then He takes away the one hindrance toward the fulfillment of the covenant—our sins. Yes, our personal sins would have breached our relationship contract. It's our sins that separate us from God, but by His mercy and grace, He even takes care of that! He promises to forgive all of our sins! He makes a covenant with you and me to absolutely forgive our wickedness and to never, never—not ever—remember any of our sins. How great is that! How awesome! Only God could make a promise like that! Only God can keep it. Today, take God at His Word and confess all your sins to Him. Let Him love you; let Him totally forgive You.

TODAY'S PRAYER Father, thank You for Your precious promises. Thank You for promising to never remember any of my sins. I come to You today for total forgiveness and freedom. Amen.

Doing His Will

TODAY'S VERSE "Now may the God of peace—may he equip you with all you need for doing his will. May He produce in you, through the power of Jesus Christ, every good thing that is pleasing to him. All glory to him forever and ever! Amen." (Hebrews 13:20-21).

TODAY'S THOUGHT Isn't it exciting to know that God is more interested in you doing good than you are? In fact, He is so invested in your success that He has equipped you with everything you need to do what He wants you to do. In fact, the author of Hebrews says that God is going to produce in you every good thing that is pleasing to Him, through the power of Jesus Christ! No wonder the author could finish this passage by saying, "All glory to Him forever and ever! Amen." Today, you can bring glory to God by living the way He has called you to. Ask Him to help you do His will. Ask Him to provide all the power you will need to do every good thing that pleases Him today.

TODAY'S PRAYER Father, thank You for equipping me with everything I need to do Your will. Thank You for Your power that You make available to me, so I can do every good thing that is pleasing to You. Give me the strength to live for You this day. Give me the wisdom to know what to do, the courage to follow through, and the faith to trust You with the outcome. Amen.

The Holy Spirit

TODAY'S VERSE "We prove ourselves by our purity, our understanding, our patience, our kindness, by the Holy Spirit within us, and by our sincere love" (2 Corinthians 6:6).

TODAY'S THOUGHT In this verse, Paul was talking about the hardship and suffering that he and the church were experiencing. Even though the times were rough, he writes that the Holy Spirit still produced the attributes that God desired in their lives. Attributes like purity, understanding, patience, kindness, and love were able to get them through the hardest of times. In another verse, Paul writes, "The Holy Spirit produces this kind of fruit in our lives: love, joy, peace, patience, kindness, goodness, faithfulness, gentleness, and self-control." How is this done? Paul answers, "Let us follow the Spirit's leading in every part of our lives." Today, commit your way to Him. Ask for the leading, direction, and influence of the Holy Spirit in all that you do, think and say. When you do, He will produce the desired effects in your life.

TODAY'S PRAYER Holy Spirit, lead me today. I desire Your fruit to be evident in my life. Guide me, direct me, influence everything I do. Amen.

Full Understanding

TODAY'S VERSE "May the Lord lead your hearts into a full understanding and expression of the love of God and the patient endurance that comes from Christ" (2 Thessalonians 3:5).

TODAY'S THOUGHT Do you understand your daily situations the way God does? Do you see through His eyes? In today's verse, Paul wrote about an understanding that expresses itself in God's love and patience: "May the Lord lead your hearts into a full understanding of the love of God." What an amazing treasure to be able to see the situations you're in through Christ's eyes; having Him lead you to His loving ways. This results in patient endurance. Today, let the Lord lead your heart. Try to see the world you live and work in through His eyes. Let God's vision and love permeate everything you do.

TODAY'S PRAYER Father, give me a spiritual vision. Help me see what You see today. Lead my heart to a full understanding and expression of Your love and patience so I can apply it to my life and those around me. In Jesus' name. Amen.

Living Love

TODAY'S VERSE "Live a life filled with love, following the example of Christ" (Ephesians 5:2).

TODAY'S THOUGHT We spend so much of our life looking for a cause to believe in; something that we can excel in by using our gifts and passions; something that will give our lives significance. And yet, as we search for that certain mission, the answer lays right before us. Paul writes, "Live a life filled with love, following the example of Christ." What better cause is there? What could give us so many options and allow us to use our own giftedness and passion? What could possibly give more significance to our lives than loving the way Christ did? There are so many people that need love. There are so many people for whom your presence in their life would make all the difference in the world. Paul said it this way in I Corinthians 13: "Three things will last forever—faith, hope, and love—and the greatest of these is love." Today, ask God to help you love those that He leads you to.

TODAY'S PRAYER Father, help me live a life filled with love. Thank You for Jesus, who loves me so much. Might I follow His example of loving others. Amen.

Core Beliefs

TODAY'S VERSE "And this same God who takes care of me will supply all your needs from his glorious riches, which have been given to us in Christ Jesus" (Philippians 4:19).

TODAY'S THOUGHT Does it seem hard to believe some of the scriptures? Reading today's verse, if we listen closely, we can hear an inner dialog arise within us to deny this promise. It may be, "Why should God help me?" "God didn't help me last time." It could be a muffled sound from a deeper level, saying, "I don't deserve His help." "It will never work out." These are lies that keep us from believing the truth of God's love for us. I wish I could simply say, "Hey, stop believing a lie and believe the truth" to make everything work out. But it isn't that easy. Lies often serve a purpose, and until the need for the lie is taken care of, we'll keep lying to ourselves. If I'm hurting because of a trauma I experienced, then simply pointing out the lies will not change anything. I need Jesus to tell me the truth about the trauma; more specifically, about *me* during the trauma. He needs to help me hear the truth. Only then will I be free to destroy the lie. When we feel doubts and pain, we need to ask, "What happened that makes me feel this way?" We need to let our mind go to those moments when we first experienced the pain and ask ourselves, "What lies did I believe when it happened?" Then we can bring those lies to God and ask Him for the truth. The truth will set you free ... free to believe!

TODAY'S PRAYER Father, I am often hampered by lies I choose to believe instead of believing Your word. I have wounds, hurts, and scars that have left me believing the wrong things. I need You to heal me. Lord, come visit my pain. Speak truth to my heart. Heal me. Set me free to believe the truth of Your love for me. I pray in Jesus' name. Amen.

Unity

TODAY'S VERSE "I in them and you in me. May they be brought to complete unity to let the world know that you sent me and have loved them even as you have loved me" (John 17:23).

TODAY'S THOUGHT Unity is supposed to be the trademark of the Church. It's our community, love, and fellowship for all believers that should draw people to Christ. This was Jesus' desire. He prayed that we would be one like He and His Father are One. He said, "May they (the Church) be brought to complete unity to let the world know that you sent me and have loved them even as you have loved me." What changes could we make in our own corner of the world if each church would work together to meet the needs of those around us? We have so much in common. We have the Bible, God the Father, Jesus His Son, and the Holy Spirit. We have similar thoughts, feelings, and objectives, too, but we are seldom intentional about reaching out. Instead, we create country club churches where similarity, status, and exclusiveness are our trademarks. How many churches never wander beyond their own denominational boundaries? We need to work together with other Christians and make a bigger impact. This would send a tremendous message to the world. And the Church needs this kind of diverse yet unified message if we're going to reach the world. Today, may Jesus' prayer be ours: "May they be brought to complete unity to let the world know that you sent me and have loved them even as you have loved me."

TODAY'S PRAYER Father, I confess that I have not reached out to other churches in love. I have not fellowshipped with other believers. I have not been active in pursuing relationships with those from different backgrounds as mine. Forgive me for not seeking unity. Help me to strive to bring Your message of love to the world through a unified church. Amen.

Pleasing or Trusting God?

TODAY'S VERSE "For it is by grace you have been saved, through faith—and this not from yourselves, it is the gift of God— not by works, so that no one can boast" (Ephesians 2:8-9, *New International Version*).

TODAY'S THOUGHT I want to please God more than anything. I want to bring Him joy and thank Him for everything He does. Or at least that's where my mind starts. In truth, what is "pleasing God" about? Is it about *God* and how much I want to thank Him by pleasing Him, or is it about *me* and how I want to make sure God is happy with my behavior? Is it about my own insecurity and inability to receive His unconditional love? Instead, I need to trust God. Why? Because with the death and resurrection of Jesus Christ, I already please God. Paul reminds us that we are saved by God's grace, not by any of our own works. No behavior on my part could ever please God. God loves us, and we don't need to earn it by pleasing Him. Instead, when we really realize what grace is all about, we will trust Him fully. When that happens, it will be our praise and adoration that pleases Him, not our vain efforts to gain His love.

TODAY'S PRAYER Father, it's so hard for me to understand that I don't have to earn Your love to please You. Instead, You already love me. You're already pleased with me. Thank You, Father, for all the grace You have given me. Help me trust Your love and grace. Amen.

Love the Giver More Than the Gifts

TODAY'S VERSE "Jesus replied, 'I tell you the truth, you want to be with me because I fed you, not because you understood the miraculous signs.' At this point, many of his disciples turned away and deserted him. Then Jesus turned to the Twelve and asked, 'Are you also going to leave?'" (John 6:26, 66-67).

TODAY'S THOUGHT Sometimes we don't get it. Our priorities get all mixed up and, like many of Jesus' disciples, we follow Him for His blessings. We have the offer of a deep relationship with God, but instead, we seek the blessings. But what happens when blessings don't come? What happens when the job we wanted doesn't pan out, when sickness interrupts our plans, and our children don't act the way we think they should? When our eyes are on our circumstances and not our Creator, it's easy to get discouraged. We can lose hope and become bitter. Why? Because we've worshipped the gifts and not the Giver; the blessings and not the Blesser. Today, we need to renew our love for God. Knowing Him is the real blessing. We need to love God, who alone is the source of our joy. No matter what circumstances come our way, as we develop a relationship with God and truly love Him, we will find true peace and joy in life.

TODAY'S PRAYER Father, help me love You today more than ever. Help me seek *You* more than Your blessings. Help me understand Your love for me and the incredible joy that is mine as I follow You. Amen.

Your Spiritual Gifts

TODAY'S VERSE "In his grace, God has given us different gifts for doing certain things well. So, if God has given you the ability to prophesy, speak out with as much faith as God has given you. If your gift is serving others, serve them well. If you are a teacher, teach well. If your gift is to encourage others, be encouraging. If it is giving, give generously. If God has given you leadership ability, take the responsibility seriously. And if you have a gift for showing kindness to others, do it gladly" (Romans 12:6-8).

TODAY'S THOUGHT Are you aware that God has given you certain passions and abilities to use for His glory? God has given every believer at least one spiritual gift for doing His will in this world. And His Holy Spirit nudges you to use this gift through a strong desire to serve Him in a way that seems to make sense for you. Paul gives examples of serving, teaching, giving and leadership. Individuals see needs differently. For example, when it comes to helping the homeless in your community, God could motivate one to serve food at a shelter, another to teach at a job readiness class or give of their income to provide for the needed shelter, and yet another to lead a church to get involved. Each person would react to the same problem in the way God motivated them, using the gifts he blessed them with. Today, ask God to reveal to you the different ways you can serve Him. He has given you spiritual gifts and will show you when and where to use them.

TODAY'S PRAYER Father, thank You that You have given me spiritual gifts. Help me learn everything I can about them and help me use them for your glory. Amen.

Surrender

TODAY'S VERSE "Do not let sin control the way you live; do not give in to sinful desires. Do not let any part of your body become an instrument of evil to serve sin. Instead, give yourselves completely to God" (Romans 6:12-13).

TODAY'S THOUGHT Sometimes we emphasize the wrong thing. We try to stop the darkness instead of turning on the light. We punish negative behavior and never reward what is done right. We save our money so tightly that we don't spend money on great opportunities that come our way. Paul writes, "Do not let sin control the way you live; do not give in to sinful desires. Do not let any part of your body become an instrument of evil to serve sin." How difficult is that? How joyful will that experience be? Don't get me wrong, Paul is completely right! We must watch sin in our life. We dare not get loose with our lives and live out sinful whims. But there is a better way. Paul finishes his thoughts by saying, "Instead, give yourselves completely to God." How much better is that? There's real wisdom here; real balance. If we give ourselves completely to God, He will help us our sins. The Holy Spirit will guide us and direct us toward a righteous life. It's like the old saying, "Love God and do as you please." If we truly love God, we will *only* do what honors Him. So today, let's combat sin in our lives in a different way. Let's resist sin by giving ourselves and everything we do and think completely to God.

TODAY'S PRAYER Father, I come to You today and completely surrender to Your control. Guide me, direct me, help me live the way You want me to. I give myself completely to You. Amen.

Experience the Love of God

TODAY'S VERSE "Were not our hearts burning within us while he talked with us on the road and opened the Scriptures to us?" (Luke 24:32, *New International Version*).

TODAY'S THOUGHT When was the last time you really experienced the presence of God? I mean more than just head knowledge; a time you really *felt* His presence? We were meant to *know* God, not just know *about* Him. Isn't that the way it should be with someone you love? Real love is more than head knowledge. Love was meant to be experienced, not just studied. It's the same with God. Stop and close your eyes and focus on a time you really felt the presence of God. When you get that image, relive it again in your mind. Do you remember what it was like? Did your heart burn within you? Paul writes, "And I pray that you, being rooted and established in love, may have power, together with all the saints, to grasp how wide and long and high and deep is the love of Christ, and to know this love that surpasses knowledge—that you may be filled to the measure of all the fullness of God." He says that knowing God's love surpasses knowledge. If that doesn't warm you up, what will? We were meant to experience God, or, as Paul says, "be filled to the measure of all the fullness of God." I pray that today, you will be conscious of His presence and have a deep and meaningful relationship with Him.

TODAY'S PRAYER Father, I long to know You in a deep and intimate way. Guide me to Your presence. Reveal more of Yourself to me. I pray that I may really grasp all the love You have for me. In Jesus' name. Amen.

You Have a Purpose

TODAY'S VERSE "I cry out to God Most High, to God who will fulfill his purpose for me. He will send help from heaven to rescue me" (Psalm 57:2-3).

TODAY'S THOUGHT Have you ever asked yourself, "Do I have a purpose? Is my life significant?" You see the vastness of the universe and wonder, "Can I really matter that much?" The answer to these questions is a resounding, "Yes!" You *do* matter! You have a purpose and you are significant. Like the Psalmist, when we feel overwhelmed, when we doubt whether we matter or not, we can cry out to God, the same God who said that He will fulfill His purpose for you. Did you get that? God has a purpose for you and He will fulfill it! And God is committed to doing whatever it takes to fulfill that purpose, even if it means sending help from Heaven itself to help you. So today, rejoice in your significance. God loves you. He will fulfill His purpose for you.

TODAY'S PRAYER Father, thank You for creating me for a purpose. I pray that You will give me the wisdom to know that purpose and the courage to live it out. In Jesus' name. Amen.

I Am a Loved Child of God

TODAY'S VERSE "How great is the love the Father has lavished on us, that we should be called children of God! And that is what we are" (1 John 3:1, *New International Version*).

TODAY'S THOUGHT It's very difficult to get our minds around certain concepts, such as infinity, predestination, and omnipresence. There are things about God that will take all of eternity for us to understand. Why is it so difficult to believe that we are the loved children of God? John emphatically tells us that God's love for us is proven in the fact that He calls us His children. John even punctuates the fact with the phrase, "And that is what we are!" Paul knew how hard it would be and challenged us. He wrote, "And may you have the power to understand, as all God's people should, how wide, how long, how high, and how deep his love is. May you experience the love of Christ, though it is too great to understand fully." Can you imagine what our life would be like if we really knew and experienced His love? How different would we approach the challenges that come our way? Most of us wrestle with the concept of being loved as God's child and have no clue how it should affect our lives. Today, this can change. Ask God to help you understand the depths of the love He has lavished on you. It will change your life.

TODAY'S PRAYER Father, I pray that my life will be a living testimony of the fact that You have lavished Your love on me by making me Your child. Might everything I think, say, and do today be shaped by this glorious fact. In Jesus' name. Amen.

Telling Others

TODAY'S VERSE "I will tell everyone about your righteousness. All day long I will proclaim your saving power, though I am not skilled with words. I will praise your mighty deeds, O Sovereign Lord. I will tell everyone that you alone are just. O God, you have taught me from my earliest childhood, and I constantly tell others about the wonderful things you do" (Psalm 71:15-18).

TODAY'S THOUGHT It's hard to keep quiet about something you really love! Imagine not telling anyone about your favorite food, sports team or hobby. If you were offered a prestigious job or were asked to spend time with a famous celebrity, everyone would soon find out about it! Isn't it strange that we find ourselves going day after day, week after week, and month after month never talking about God? He is the God of the universe, our Father, who has forgiven all our sins through the death and resurrection of Jesus Christ. We have the Holy Spirit living in us. Perhaps we need to examine our faith to see if it's real? Maybe we need to examine where God is on our list of priorities? Could it be that we need to spend more time getting to know God more fully? The Psalmist is telling everyone about God—all day long he proclaims God's love and power and the wonderful things He does. Today, pray and ask God to give you the same joy and zeal in your heart.

TODAY'S PRAYER Father, I am so easily distracted by everything in this world that I often forget all that You mean to me. Forgive me. Thank You for all that You have done in my life. Thank You for Your salvation and Your abundant provisions. I praise You, Lord, and will tell others of all Your goodness. Amen.

Serve God

TODAY'S VERSE "Acknowledge the God of your father, and serve him with wholehearted devotion and with a willing mind, for the LORD searches every heart and understands every motive behind the thoughts" (1 Chronicles 28:9).

TODAY'S THOUGHT It's easy to say that we are a Christian. There isn't much of a demand being placed on that confession. As far as the world knows, saying that you're a Christian doesn't mean much. Unfortunately, in many cases, the lives of Christians don't differ much from their secular counterparts. But that's not the way God intended it to be. We've been called to follow Christ in the way we think, feel, and behave. David knew the seriousness of following God. When he commissioned his son, Solomon, to build the Temple, he challenged Solomon to live in a godly way. He told him to acknowledge God as the Lord of everything and serve Him with wholehearted devotion and a willing mind. God doesn't want pretense; He wants sincerity and authenticity. That's why He searches our heart and motives. Today, dedicate your life to His service. Decide to serve Him wholeheartedly.

TODAY'S PRAYER Father, thank You for the opportunity to serve You. Help me to be true to You and to serve You with wholehearted devotion and a willing mind. In Jesus' Name. Amen.

Do you want to
know about your
spiritual gifts but
aren't sure where
to begin?

GIFTED
Understanding My Spiritual Gifts

Not sure what your spiritual gifts are or how to use them? Tired of surveys that leave you hanging? *Gifted* dispels the mystery around this vital topic. **Close to a million people have used these materials to research spiritual gifts.** Many have come to learn their gifts and how to put them into action. Now you can discover yours!

With a fail-safe duo-discovery method combining an online survey and individual descriptive pages on each gift, you will better understand how God has equipped you and what to do about it. Each gift description includes definition, benefits, pitfalls, ministry opportunities, and recommended further training.

Ron Ovitt, *Gifted*

GILGAL
PUBLISHING

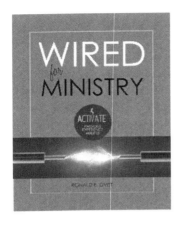

Tired of how-to information that doesn't help you actually begin to minister?

WIRED FOR MINISTRY
Activate Your Passion, Experience, and Skills

Now there is a tool that will help you understand how you are wired for ministry! *Wired for Ministry* holds **the secret to activating your ministry potential by discovering your spiritual gifts, ministry preferences, ministry skills, and unique ministry drive.**

This workbook culminates with a development of a *Personal Ministry Profile*, your unique "ministry resume." Presenting this to church or non-profit leaders will help them identify ministry opportunities that match your unique strengths and passions.

Used annually at Moody Bible Institute for all incoming students, this workbook can also help you learn more about your ministry potential. Activate the ministry God has inside of you!

Ron Ovitt, *Wired for Ministry*

GILGAL
PUBLISHING

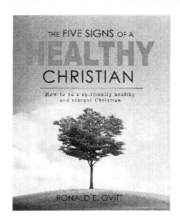

Health is on everyone's mind. Are you a healthy Christian?

THE FIVE SIGNS OF A HEALTHY CHRISTIAN
How to Be a Spiritually Healthy and Vibrant Christian

Our personal health, the health of our nation, the health of our economy—all with good reason. When things are unhealthy, bad things start to happen. But what about the health of our Christian experience? *The Five Signs of a Healthy Christian* will lead you to investigate your own spiritual health and encourage you to make adjustments where necessary.

There are five signs that are general indicators that we are spiritually alive. **If you keep focused on these factors, praying over them and taking baby steps toward improving where needed, you will find yourself living a healthy Christian life!**

This book will help motivate and encourage you in maintaining a deep and meaningful spiritual life.

Ron Ovitt, *The Five Signs of a Healthy Christian*

GILGAL
PUBLISHING

13635980R00241

Made in the USA
Lexington, KY
02 November 2018